Dungeons and Dragons and Philosophy

Popular Culture and Philosophy® Series Editor: George A. Reisch

For full details of all Popular Culture and Philosophy® books, visit www.opencourtbooks.com.

Popular Culture and Philosophy®

Dungeons and Dragons and Philosophy

Raiding the Temple of Wisdom

Edited by
JON COGBURN and MARK SILCOX

OPEN COURT
Chicago and LaSalle, Illinois

Volume 70 in the series, Popular Culture and Philosophy ®, edited by George A. Reisch

To order books from Open Court, call toll-free 1-800-815-2280, or visit our website at www.opencourtbooks.com.

Open Court Publishing Company is a division of Carus Publishing Company.

Cover photo: Brandi Miller

Printed and bound in the United States of America.

Library of Congress Cataloging-in-Publication Data

Dungeons and dragons and philosophy / edited by Jon Cogburn and Mark Silcox.
    p. cm. — (Popular culture and philosophy ; v. 70)
    Includes bibliographical references and index.
    ISBN 978-0-8126-9796-4 (trade paper : alk. paper)
    1. Dungeons and Dragons (Game) 2. Philosophy. I. Cogburn, Jon. II. Silcox, Mark.
    GV1469.62.D84D388 2012
    794.8—dc23

                              2012025161

Contents

Rolling a Wisdom Check

There are two quite different ways to tell the story of how *Dungeons and Dragons* (D&D) came to be. According to the more widely-known version of the story the two original creators of D&D, Gary Gygax and Dave Arneson, were big fans of the writings of J.R.R. Tolkien, and wanted to be able to fight elaborate pretend battles in a fantasy setting similar to the world described in *The Lord of the Rings*. But they also wanted their invention to resemble the types of tabletop wargames such as *Tactics*, *Centurion*, *Luftwaffe*, and *Starship Troopers* that were fashionable during the 1970s—complicated, highly strategic games involving miniatures, toy soldiers, or decorated cardboard playing pieces. The full, unwieldy subtitle of the original 1974 edition of D&D itself was "Rules for Fantastic Medieval Wargames Campaigns Playable with Paper and Pencil and Miniature Figures."

The second version of the story begins earlier, and is much less widely-known. Gygax tells it in a preface he contributed to the relatively little-played "live action" espionage role-playing game *Agent X*. Apparently, when he was about ten years old, his friend Jim Rausch developed an illness that kept him confined at home. Because the group of young boys he spent time with couldn't play with him outside, young Jim would make up elaborate fictional games for them—usually spy thrillers or murder mysteries—using play money, toy weapons, and even hand-made car and airplane dashboards as props. Rausch also performed the roles of all the other kids' fictional enemies and allies (NPCs, to use the contemporary term), and if you got "killed," you had to leave his house right away without finding out how the day's story ended! "As you play this game 'live'," Gygax remarks, "remember that you are actually carrying on an RPG tradition that outdates the oldest published form. I know because I played one and wrote the other" (*Agent X*, p. vii).

So what kind of a game—if "game" is even the right word—was D&D originally conceived to be? A traditional wargame with a few fantastical elements tacked on? Or a set of loose constraints on improvisational, fantasy make-believe storytelling?

Philosophers love these kinds of puzzles about origins, and they show up in all sorts of places throughout the literature. What (if anything) was the universe like before the Big Bang? Could something as complicated and mysterious as the human mind be built from scratch out of silicon chips and other non-organic materials? Did human society begin when a bunch of people decided to form a co-operative, mutually beneficial commonwealth, or did one big thug just start telling everyone what to do? What sort of person first propagated the strange and subversive idea that we should all try to be nice to one another?

Whatever eccentric muse should be given credit for inspiring D&D's original inventors, we think that this much at least is clear: the game's swift ascent to worldwide popularity in the 1970s and 1980s represents the most exciting event in modern mass culture since the invention of the motion picture. Decried as godless by the pious, dismissed as frivolous by the powerful, and ignored for decades by the arbiters of artistic value, the game appears destined to remain a cultural landmark, and has recently been enjoying a resurgence in popularity. By 2004 consumers had spent over one billion dollars on D&D products, and pundits at Wizards of the Coast estimate that three million people play it each month in the United States alone. The release of a Fifth Edition in 2013 is a testament both to the game's continuing popularity and to the continued willingness of its authors and fans to embrace new styles of gameplay and imaginative new additions to the fantasy worlds they have grown to love.

Perhaps the difficulty that we experience when trying to understand D&D in terms of its early history arises from a broader philosophical problem about the very possibility of defining words like "game" or "play." Ludwig Wittgenstein famously contends in *Philosophical Investigations* that the word "game" simply covers too diverse a range of activities to ever be satisfactorily definable. And Johan Huizinga, author of the seminal anthropological study of games *Homo Ludens*, remarks that

> The more we try to mark off the form we call "play" from other forms apparently related to it, the more the absolute independence of the play-concept stands out. . . . Play lies outside the antithesis of wisdom and folly, and equally outside those of truth and falsehood, good and evil. (*Homo Ludens*, p. 6)

Huizinga's remarks might seem a little melodramatic. Surely, after all, human beings have managed to invent many dull or dangerous games that would be sheer folly to play. And there are many others games and game-like activities that can lead us to the recognition of important truths and falsehoods that might otherwise have eluded our grasp. But what he says here will nonetheless almost certainly resonate with anyone who has ever gotten truly "lost" in a session of D&D. Whether it's the type of semi-hypnosis induced by the game's complex and multi-faceted rule system, or the deep level of immersion that one can feel in the pursuit of its utterly fictitious quests and battles, playing *Dungeons and Dragons* certainly can make a person *feel* as though she has stepped into a realm where the normal standards for judging and classifying human actions simply no longer apply.

In this book, however, we take a half-step back away from this feeling of complete immersion, and get just enough detachment from the absorbing, exciting, and intellectually challenging sensation of gameplay to ask ourselves just exactly what D&D's millions of resolute fans are *really up to*. At its most fundamental level, is all of this wildly otherworldly role-playing really just a form of escapism, or can it be a proving-ground for our ideas about the so-called "real" world? When players are left to themselves in quiet basements, dining rooms, and game stores, working hard at pretending to be Dwarves, Elves, Worforged, and Eladrin, do they slip the bonds of ordinary conscience, or are they inventing brave, new moralities for strange new worlds? How well do they really understand the hidden laws and forces that govern the bizarre alternate universes, otherworldly planes, and magical landscapes that they speak about together with such confidence? And what arcane standards of quality, enjoyment, and hedonic value are being invoked when they look at one another after the snacks are all eaten and the dice have been collected, and speak the mystic incantation that all devoted dungeon-crawlers hope to hear: *"Good game!"*

Do these questions sound unlike the sorts of issues you expect to find discussed when cracking open a college philosophy textbook, or a volume of the works of Aristotle, David Hume, Friedrich Nietzsche, or Bertrand Russell? The authors of this volume will convince you otherwise. Several chapters of this book have been placed side-by-side precisely in order to demonstrate the sort of constructively adversarial back-and-forth style of disputation that philosophers often find themselves conducting. This style of conversation can be just as demanding (and just as rewarding) as any midnight intrusion into a twelfth-level subterranean Dragon's lair stacked with piles of gold and poison traps. Perhaps, though, part of the true value of a revolutionary invention like D&D, and of the utterly novel, seemingly inexhaustible art form that Gygax and Arneson brought into existence, is the very fact that it provokes us to ask questions which are at the same time both absolutely fundamental and entirely new.

I

Heroic Tier

The Ethical Dungeon Crawler

1

Aristotle's Dungeon

Greg Littmann

I've slain a lot of orcs in my time. I started playing *Dungeons and Dragons* so long ago that we only had seven classes, and Elf, Dwarf, and Halfling were *classes.* I was swinging longswords and lobbing fireballs back when a first-level magic-user with three hit-points thought he was *lucky*, back when elves were elves and eladrin was something you found in Appendix J of the *Dungeon Master's Guide*, "HERBS, SPICES, AND MEDICINAL VEGETABLES."

I've seen D&D go through a lot of changes in my time, but it has always held a unique place in geek culture as by far the most popular and influential of the "paper and pencil" role-playing games. A template for most of the online "role-playing games," like *World of Warcraft*, which now addict millions across the world, *Dungeons and Dragons* remains the number one game in which intelligent, mature human beings actually gather together in a room, face to face, to pretend that they are things that they are not—strange things like elves and wizards, halflings and paladins.

A lot of people devote a lot of time to *Dungeons and Dragons*, killing imaginary ogres, saving non-existent villages, and perhaps even arguing over which player can pretend to own the imaginary magic sword that the party just found in the lich's hoard. Like any hobby to which a significant amount of time is devoted, *Dungeons and Dragons* has been accused of being a waste of time. Some folk have just never seen the point to all that *pretending*, to paying so much attention to dealing with imaginary problems in a world that doesn't exist.

Is D&D really a waste of time? To ask how we should spend our time is just another way of asking how we are to live—and the question of how human beings should live has been central to philosophy for as long as philosophy has been around. While D&D itself has only existed since its first publication in 1974 by Gary Gygax and Dave Arneson, the godfathers of hack, the work of even the ancient philosophers is directly relevant to the issue of spending time playing D&D.

The ancient Greek philosopher Aristotle, arguably the most influential art theorist in history, never had the opportunity to know the joy of carving his way through a horde of baying gnolls to see if they'd stolen any good loot lately, but his views on life and art provide a framework for the appreciation of playing *Dungeons and Dragons*. No really—hear me out.

Just for starters, Aristotle had the sense to recognize that pleasure is a good thing as an end in itself. An activity doesn't need any more justification than that people enjoy it. In reference to listening to music for pleasure, he wrote in his *Politics* "For the end is not desirable for the sake of any future good, nor do the pleasures which we have described exist for the sake of any future good but of the past, that is to say, they are the alleviation of past toils and pains. And we may infer this to be the reason why men seek happiness from these pleasures" (Book VIII, lines 1339b35-40). Yet according to Aristotle's way of thinking, D&D is more significant than a mere harmless diversion. Pastimes such as playing D&D are particularly suited to human beings because of the very sort of creatures we are.

What Kind of Monster Are You?

Aristotle believed that every living thing has a natural function, particular to the kind of living thing that it is. We can determine the natural function of a living thing by identifying what it does best compared to other living things. It is the function of fish to swim, since fish are so excellent at swimming compared to other animals, while it is the function of a bird to fly, because birds fly so much better than other animals.

If Aristotle were allowed to observe the manticore, he would conclude that the function of a manticore is to live as a carnivorous predator, since killing and eating other animals is a task that the manticore is so good at. Similarly, he would judge the function of a mind flayer to be flaying minds, since rending your brain with psychic power is exactly what a mind flayer does best. The best life for something, according to Aristotle, is a life in which it performs its function well. The best life for a manticore would be one in which it gets to tear animals to bits and wolf them down, while the best life for a mind flayer would be one in which it uses its psychic abilities to blast victims into submission.

It would be hard to tell what humans in the worlds of D&D are best suited for, when you consider all of the competition they have in the various monster manuals and players' handbooks. Here on planet Earth, though, there is one thing that we human beings excel at beyond all other creatures. We are the best at *thinking*. Not having to compete with cunning yuan-ti and ancient, learned dragons, we stand unchallenged as Earth's intellectual champions, with powers of reasoning surpassing those of any other animal. So according to Aristotle, the function of a human is to think well and the best life for a human being is a life of intellectual activity.

Aristotle wrote in his *Nicomachean Ethics* :

> . . . that which is proper to each thing is by nature best and most pleasant for each thing; for man, therefore, the life according to intellect is best and pleasantest, since intellect more than anything else *is* man. (Book X, lines 1178a5–8)

The most important intellectual activities are those that give us a greater understanding about the universe and our place within it, activities like studying philosophy, politics, and the natural world. However, Aristotle specifically acknowledges that intellectual pleasures undertaken just for fun are a particularly appropriate and important part of a human life lived well. In *Politics* he wrote:

> . . . there are branches of learning and education which we must study merely with a view to leisure spent in intellectual activity, and these are to be valued for their own sake. (Book VIII, lines 1338a9–12)

Dungeons and Dragons is clearly intellectual activity even when played in the simplest and most straightforward possible way, as a vehicle for rules-based combat. This "hack and slash" approach to gaming has its roots in the earliest history of the game. D&D grew out of tabletop war-gaming, a hobby in which players devote tremendous attention to calculating their way to victory in imaginary battles fought against one another. Like a war-game, *D&D* has always maintained an emphasis on providing comprehensive rules that allow fights to be resolved mechanically by rolling dice and consulting tables. Taken in isolation of any story or role-playing elements, *Dungeons and Dragons* combat is a strategy game in which each player controls one piece and the DM controls the rest. A strategy game, in turn, is nothing but a logic puzzle, one that models hypothetical situations according to formal rules. As such, it is an exercise in reason, no less so than a game of chess.

In Fourth Edition combat, a character with a defender role, like a fighter or paladin, must get between the monsters and the "squishy" PCs, attracting attention to themselves and protecting their team. A character with the controller role, like the wizard, should hang back from the melee and rain death on multiple foes at once with their magic. Similarly, strikers like the rogue or ranger, and leaders like the cleric or warlord must carefully position themselves and select the best abilities to use to support their party. The very act of designing a character is an exercise in logic, as class, race, abilities, feats, and powers are selected in combinations calculated to provide solid support for the party.

Attack of the Munchkins

The intellectual character of D&D playing is apparent even in the case of the dreaded "munchkin", a "munchkin" being a player who designs and plays their character with the sole intention of that character being as powerful as it can possibly be. The munchkin treats playing D&D *exclusively* as a game in logic. The munchkin's goal is power for their character and the means to that power are the rules of D&D. Any concern not directly relevant to this, like being true to their character, or even making sure that they support the party, is irrelevant. The munchkin *must* play the combination of race and class that provides the best numerical bonuses in combat, *must* have the most "pluses" on their longsword, and *must* take the best mix of feats and attack powers to maximize their bonuses.

A munchkin would never think of playing a Halfling Fighter. The Halfling bonuses to Acrobatics and Thievery aren't well suited to a character who wears heavy armor most of the time. If the munchkin wants to play a fighter, the munchkin will study the rules carefully to find the racial bonuses that work best with the Fighter class. On the one hand, the dragonborn have +2 Strength and Dragonborn Fury, so useful for hacking, on the other, dwarves get +2 Constitution and Unencumbered Speed, so good for staying alive . . .

Different people enjoy playing *Dungeons and Dragons* in different ways, and while munchkins are undeniably useful around the dungeon, the label "munchkin" is not a flattering one, suggesting, as it does, the childlike midgets who sang and danced for Dorothy in their tiny village in *The Wizard of Oz*. The idea is that the "munchkin" is being small-minded about the possibilities offered by role-playing games beyond the quest for "the most pluses," that there might be some fun to be had in playing a role or building a story, or just trying out some non-optional combinations for fun.

Munchkins are common butts of satire in role-playing game culture, as in the comic *Knights of the Dinner Table* and the card game *Munchkin*. Even so, there's no denying the intellectual nature of what the munchkin *does*. Munchkins play D&D the way that other people play chess, as a clinical study of the best strategies for "winning" the game within the rules, where "winning" in *Dungeons and Dragons* is constituted by the ever-illusive goal of being as powerful as you can be.

Art and the Half-Orc Barbarian

While Aristotle could surely approve of people playing logic games, *Dungeons and Dragons* offers so much more than logic games alone. When playing D&D, people role-play, adopting new personas, creating stories, even inventing entire new worlds. The characterization isn't always perfect, the stories don't always make sense, and worlds that DMs build aren't always triumphs of plausibility and originality, but what *Dungeons and Dragons* players are doing is clearly a form of *art*. Role-playing is a combination of story-telling and improvisational theater. It obviously has roots in the pretending games that children play; but then, so does acting itself.

Recognizing and valuing D&D playing as art does not require us to treat the hobby with reverence, to idealize and elevate our kitchen-table adventures or to equate the local D&D game with the work of Shakespeare or Jane Austen. D&D isn't Shakespeare. If *Hamlet* had been a D&D game, the climactic dual scene would have consisted in Hamlet using *brute strike* with his greatsword to kill Laertes, while Ophelia "stealths up" behind Hamlet's evil uncle King Claudius and strikes him down with a *sneak attack* with *backstabber* on it— after which Hamlet's father, the rightful king, would be raised from the dead and Hamlet and Ophelia would divide Claudius's treasure between them. But art doesn't have to match the heights of Shakespeare or Austen to be worthwhile. The world has room for many forms of art.

Aristotle thought that experiencing art was a vital element of a human life lived well. He wrote extensively on literature, poetry and theatre, and their importance for our intellectual and moral development. While much of Aristotle's writings on art have long been lost, it seems that he saw art as having two legitimate functions beyond merely providing enjoyment. Firstly, he believed that art could improve us morally by purging us of our negative emotions as we experience those emotions through sympathy for imaginary people, a process that Aristotle called "catharsis." For instance, by watching one of the tragic plays so beloved by Aristotle and other ancient Athenians, one could purge the fear and pity from one's system by feeling them for the poor saps suffering on stage. Similarly, a D&D player might get the aggression out of their system by repeatedly smacking an imaginary ogre over the head with an imaginary warhammer, or pretending to cast *meteor-swarm* over a shrieking army of orcs. A player might perhaps even purge their pent-up fears by watching their character stand firm against hordes of the undead, facing terrible odds to try to save the rest of the party. If catharsis functions as Aristotle believed it functions in the case of a spectator enjoying tragic theater, then it seems arbitrary to suppose that people cannot purge a variety of emotions in a variety of means.

Secondly, Aristotle believed that good fiction can improve our understanding of humanity by giving us the opportunity to imagine alternatives to the way things presently are. He wrote in his *Poetics* that the difference between history and poetry is that the one describes the thing that has been, and the other a kind of thing that might be. Hence poetry is something more philosophical and of graver import than history. (lines 1451b3–6)

In other words, through fiction we examine hypothetical situations and by examining what *could* be, we learn more about humanity than if we just examined how things actually *have* been.

There are clearly limits to the degree to which a D&D game can model the world as it "could" be. In the real world, I can't learn to cast *Mordenkainen's Mansion* as an alternative to paying rent, no matter how badly I want to. I will never be able to land a job as a warlock or own so many magic rings that I have to worry about which two to wear. However, Aristotle didn't believe that fiction needs to mirror reality closely to be useful. He acknowledged that the author of a fine good work of fiction might include magic and monsters, along with other amazing and unrealistic elements, provided that they make the story more interesting. He wrote:

Any impossibilities there are in his descriptions of things are faults. But from another point of view they are justifiable, if they serve the end of poetry—if . . . they make the effect of . . . the work . . . more astounding. (*Poetics*, lines 1460b24–26)

We can still usefully explore hypotheticals in amazing stories because these stories still revolve around *people*, and to think about how people are likely to react in various circumstances is to reflect on the nature of humanity. To consider the dwarf chieftain's likely behavior when he learns that his son has been disintegrated by a wandering monster is to consider what a parent might feel to lose a child. To consider how much danger you are required to place yourself in to save the party thief, who has just fallen from the ceiling and into a nest of storm-claw scorpions, is to consider the questions of what a friend owes to a friend, and what any person owes to any other.

Dungeons and Dragons is not reality, but some play reflects aspects of reality through a distorted lens. At base, the stories told through *Dungeons and Dragons* play are stories of people facing stress and danger together in pursuit of their goals. We can relate to these characters precisely because of what we have in common with them. We may not have faced a family of flesh-eating ghouls, but we know what it is to be afraid. We have never prized open an old chest to find it filled with gold coins, but we know what it is to want money.

Aristotle's Guide to Playing D&D

One of Aristotle's requirements for good tragedy was that the unfolding of the plot had to make *internal sense*. Even if the work is based on wild and fantastic premises, "There should be nothing improbable among the actual incidents" of the play (line 1454b6). It seems likely, then, that a good DM from Aristotle's point of view would be one whose setting details and plot development hang together in accordance with the game's internal logic. So for instance, if the DM designs a world, it is important that the lush, lizardfolk-infested Jungles of Xoax do not abut the waterless, efreet-haunted Deserts of Zarr, not unless these is some good in-game reason for high waterfall terrain to be right next to water-starved terrain, perhaps one involving a high-level druid and a wager. Similarly, if the Free City of Melinor is located on the River Chuulwater on Monday, then the DM had better make sure that the city is located on the River Chuulwater on Tuesday, while the poor but peaceful halflings of Oatvalley must not transform overnight into high level rogues with a stash of magic weapons and a passion for chaotic evil. D&D is a game about amazing things happening, but the above events are implausible even in the internal logic of the game.

What goes for the game-world in general goes for the dungeon. A good DM, following Aristotle, will have events unfold in accordance with reason and probability. In the absence of magical interference, the layout of a dungeon must be compatible with the rules of mathematics and geometry—if the party travels in a circle, they have to get back to where they started, while a corridor that is thirty feet long when walking north to south must be no longer or shorter when walking back south to north. Similarly, a poison trap must not go off if a rogue has already disarmed it, a medusa must not turn a character to stone with its petrifying gaze if the character was facing in the other direction, and armies of chain devils and succubi should not be led by a priestess of Pelor the compassionate. Such things cannot occur even in the wild worlds of D&D; they violate the DMs job of telling a story that makes sense within the game.

Sometimes it's debatable whether a method of DMing should count as a violation of reason to be eliminated or a genre trope to be embraced. I have long had a passion for stuffing dungeons with whatever weird monsters strike my fancy, regardless of whether it really makes sense for these creatures to live in close proximity. I don't mind having an enormous carrion crawler living in a room right down the corridor from where a gibbering abomination nests, even though realistically, if two such violent creatures were inhabiting the same area, one of them would have obliterated the other by now. I tend to regard such placing as simply a part of the game, as acceptable as allowing that all of the predators from the Monster Manuals survive together in the same world in the first place, or that magic spells can bring people back from the dead.

Now, I'm not saying that I'm *against* tying dungeons together in accordance with a painstaking internal logic. A carefully designed dungeon, intended to make sense, can be a fascinating thing to hack your way through. However, I also don't see it as indicative of *bad DMing* if, say, a cave with a red dragon in it is arbitrarily included in a given cavern environment, away from all reasonable sources of food and living in close proximity to other large and insanely dangerous animals. Rather, I see this as just a D&D *convention* and an element of the art form.

However, there are DMs who disagree passionately and who would criticize this approach to playing D&D on grounds that are quite Aristotelean. They would insist that the more internal sense the world of a game makes, the better the game. They believe that the good DM must try to ensure that, as far as possible within the rules and underlying assumptions of the game, events unfold in a realistic manner—treants can't be growing downstream of an azer encampment, because the treants would have noticed and attacked the azer for starting fires.

Good players, like good DMs, would be required by the Aristotelean approach to keep their characters' actions as realistic as possible. He wrote "The right thing . . . is in the characters just as in the incidents of the play to seek after the necessary or the probable; so that whenever such-and-such a personage says or does such-and-such a thing, it shall be the necessary or probable outcome of his character" (*Poetics,* lines 1454a32–36). For example, your Bahamut-worshipping, lawful good paladin should never ride by a peasant being attacked by bandits. He must stop and defend the peasant, even if he has nothing personally to gain from it since the bandits are poor and of low xp value. Likewise, if the defining feature of your elven ranger's personality is her lifelong hatred for orcs, she must not give up an opportunity to go orc slaying just because an NPC is offering her better pay to go hack *bears.* Such behavior isn't a natural outgrowth of the character's personality and circumstances. The behavior makes no "in-character" sense.

This is not to say that the player is automatically playing well just because they play to character. That a player was "just playing my character" has been the excuse for all sorts of mean and unsporting behavior throughout the history of role-playing. I recall one adventuring party meeting for the first time at the inn. All the PCs agreed to explore the local ruins together, and then the assassin promptly murdered the magic-user and took his money. The magic-user's player was upset at this, but the assassin's player could see nothing wrong with his character's actions. "I am a chaotic evil assassin," he explained, pointing to the words on his character-sheet.

The problem with the assassin's reply is not that it fails to make a valid point about art, but that it fails to address the bigger problem with assassinating a fellow PC, which is that it shows a selfish disregard for the fun being had by another player. Nobody would like having their character killed by another PC before the party even makes it to the dungeon door. Likewise, Aristotle did not think that the value of art ever gives us grounds to stop displaying the moral virtues that should govern our behavior towards other people. Just because your character is in a position to exploit a fellow player whose character is in need of rescue from a pit trap, or liberation from orc prison, or raising from the dead, that doesn't make it ok to demand all their magic items in return for help, regardless of how well doing so fits your PC's personality.

In fact, it is arguable that Aristotle would condemn *any* wrongdoing by the PCs at all. In the context of tragedy, he wrote "In the characters there are four points to aim at. First and foremost, that they shall be good" (*Poetics,* lines 1454a16–17). Perhaps Aristotle would insist that all PCs should be lawful good, fine upstanding individuals devoted to doing what is right. Gone is the tenacious rogue just out to make it in the world, gone the evil wizard on a mad quest for power, gone the mercenary fighter with a tragic past. We must play clerics of Moradin, paladins of Bahamut, and other such worthy heroes.

On the other hand, Aristotle *might* judge that the rules for tragedy don't apply to D&D in this case because D&D is a different form of art. Aristotle didn't believe that the high standards demanded of the hero of a tragedy apply to all forms of story-telling. Regarding comedy, he wrote "This difference it is that distinguishes Tragedy and Comedy . . . the one would make its personages worse, and the other better, than the men of the present day" (lines 1448a16–17). If comedy can accommodate wicked characters, then why not D&D? Perhaps I'm attributing too much *DM-sense* to someone born two and a half thousand years before Gary Gygax cast his first *magic missile*, but I like to think that Aristotle would have the imagination to see that with the right group of people, a game with unaligned or even evil characters could be a perfectly appropriate way to play.

What Do You Do?

The DM's eternal call of "What do you do?" is a challenge to the player's intellect and creativity. The player is given an agency in *Dungeons and Dragons* that few forms of art provide. As art, playing *Dungeons and Dragons* is unusual in that it is entirely *participatory*. There is no division between the performers and the audience. You can't just sit there and watch the game from outside—if you're going to hang out, you must throw a rogue together and start checking for traps. Naturally, art critics wouldn't *want* to watch you play role-playing games, and rightly so. Watching other people play games can be boring, especially if you don't understand what's going on, or if someone insists on telling you *all* about their half-elf ranger. But D&D is not a spectator sport—the game exists entirely for the benefit of the gaming group itself.

The participatory nature of playing D&D gives it special artistic significance. If exposure to art really is good for us as human beings, it's natural to suppose that producing art is likewise good for us. The agency of D&D players is particularly relevant to the charge that playing D&D can't be *good* enough as art to have artistic significance. The fact that the players are themselves producing the art that they enjoy is itself significant. They are engaging with art in ways that someone who only observes art never does. Playing D&D is not a substitute for reading great books and attending great plays, and it is not intended to be, but it offers an opportunity for the player to be actively artistic.

The participatory nature of playing D&D is *even more* important if Aristotle is right about the ways that art benefits us. If we purge ourselves of negative emotions through catharsis by sympathizing with imaginary people, then this process should be particularly effective when we control the characters, because we identify with characters we control. They are an avatar of *us* in the world of the game—we say "*I* check for traps", "*I* grab the ring", "*I* hack the troll". If art improves us by allowing us to consider people in hypothetical situations, then this process should be particularly effective when we must actually face those hypothetical situations by controlling a character who must decide what to do. This doesn't mean that Aristotle would want you to spend your life playing D&D. The life he recommended was one of moderation and a lot of intellectual work, not slacking off and painting miniatures all day. However, Aristotle is a position to recognize that time spent playing D&D can be time well-spent, that it can be a worthwhile activity.

To Hack or Not to Hack?

That's my take on what Aristotle would say, but is any of it actually *right*? Just because Aristotle said or would have said something doesn't make it true. For instance, I believe that Aristotle was wrong that human beings have a natural function. We humans exist as we are not because we have a role to fulfill, but because our evolutionary ancestors were successful at surviving and reproducing. So, the fact that we are superior thinkers to other animals cannot indicate that a life of thinking well is the "best and most pleasant life" for a human being. All the same, it *is* a good thing to be able to think well, and logical calculation, like that involved in playing a game of strategy like D&D combat, is mental exercise. And Aristotle was right that pleasure is of value as an end to itself—you don't need any more justification for playing D&D than that you enjoy it.

That playing D&D is *cathartic* is obvious to anyone who has ever carved up a goblin with a longsword or fried a troll with a *lightning bolt*. The thing I remember most clearly about playing my first ever D&D character, the cleric Brother Silverwolf, is neither the miracle of being able to cast spells nor the gravity of being the gods' appointed, but rather the sheer joy of using my mace to smack goblins (*crunch!*) and huge spiders (*splat!*). Sometimes, it can be a blessed relief from the stresses of real life to storm your bloody way from one end of a castle to the other, solving your problems with an ease and finality that real life will never offer. If you don't feel better after chopping a twenty-foot giant into one-foot slices, you're not doing it right.

As to whether the hypothetical situations your party faces help you to learn more about humanity, I'll have to leave that up to you, although if your game ever forces you to *think* about what the moral course of action would be, or even how people are likely to act in the face of danger or temptation, then you're reflecting on fundamental questions about human life.

Role-playing games can be used to explore these issues just like any other kind of fiction, with the advantage that in *role-playing games*, everyone is given a character with agency to control, giving them a voice in the story and forcing them to make judgments in another's place. As has always been the case with *Dungeons and Dragons*, the game is what you make of it.

2

Does *Dungeons and Dragons* Refute Aristotle?

David Merli

Sometimes role-playing games put us in morally tricky situations. One of my characters was once faced with a choice between killing a surrendering enemy or taking him prisoner.

Killing would have made his life easier, of course, because it's quick and easy, while keeping prisoners from spoiling your plans takes a lot of effort. But I had always imagined this character as a fundamentally decent guy, rough around the edges but guided by a firm sense of fairness and honor.

He's a bruiser with a heart of gold, or at least silver, and he's the kind of person who would never stick his sword through a disarmed man pleading for mercy. Some of his friends would, and they gave him grief for sticking to his scruples, but he saw the killing of a prisoner as wrong, and, for him, that settled things.

Choices like these are sometimes described as "moral dilemmas," but the hard part of these situations isn't knowing what's right. It's following through when morality asks us to do something difficult. A more interesting kind of moral dilemma comes up when we're genuinely not sure what to do. Maybe killing this particular enemy, or torturing the bad guy's mother, or doing some other ugly deed would save innocent lives or prevent even greater evil. When we ourselves face situations like this (supposing we're good people) we wonder about what action is morally best. We think about right and wrong.

When our role-playing characters face situations like this, we do something more interesting. We ask what *our characters* would make of the situation: How would *they* think about right and wrong? How would they think about how to act? Our characters, with their own values and perspectives on the (fantasy) world, see things differently, and we try, as best we can, to understand their points of view and to make them act accordingly.

It turns out we do this pretty well. This is an important observation because it makes us think about what abilities are required for seeing the difference between right and wrong. In particular, thinking about the way role-playing works will help us see what's wrong with virtue ethics, a popular and interesting theory of morality that starts with the idea of a virtuous agent and then uses that to set standards of right and wrong. The fact that we can role-play well means that virtue ethicists are in trouble.

How Good Characters Make Hard Choices

In *Dungeons and Dragons*, a character's moral personality is represented by alignment. A character's alignment isn't the whole story of her personality, but it gives us a rough idea of how the character sees the world and her place in it. In the original D&D, characters were lawful, neutral, or chaotic. Advanced D&D added suffixes of good, neutral, or evil, giving us nine possibilities (lawful evil, chaotic good, and so on). In the Fourth Edition, alignment has been simplified a bit, and characters can occupy one of five points along a spectrum from lawful good, good, unaligned, evil, and chaotic evil.

Alignment gives us a simple way of identifying a character's values, so it provides some guide to what actions a character will choose. It isn't the end of the story, because many different personalities are compatible with a single alignment. (Characters who share an alignment can still disagree about what to do, just as people can be committed to doing the right thing but disagree about what that really is.) But sharing an alignment will involve sharing broad ethical sensibilities and values.

One of the things that makes role-playing so fun is that we can play characters with alignments (and with values) totally different from our own. Characters can be morally better or worse than the players who control them. Playing these characters well is a challenge, and it makes the game more enjoyable. Players who take the game seriously make real efforts to "get the character right"—to play the character in a coherent way, so that the character's actions, alignment, and personality all fit together.

We've all seen what happens when players fail at this. ("Uh, how come your lawful good fighter keeps running people through whenever he needs more armor?") In practice, though, good players take it seriously. They think hard about what a particular character would do and about the fit between alignment and action. What's more, these players succeed in playing both good and evil well—that is, they do a convincing job of getting it right.

When Bad Characters Happen to Good People

Some players do a good job of playing all sorts of characters convincingly. The most vivid examples (and, let's admit, maybe the most fun) involve skilled players portraying villains. Seeing this sort of thing happen can be striking. It's eye-opening to learn that a really nice guy turns out to be great at playing a vicious, treacherous thief. The player would never hurt a fly, but the character would slit your throat for looking at him wrong, then frame someone else for the killing.

Characters like this thief look *genuinely evil*. They aren't the kind of cartoonish evil personalities found in bad novels or summer blockbusters. They don't cackle maniacally while announcing their wicked plans. They act like actual evil people do, by scheming, dissembling, and betraying, all while thinking, or at least saying, that their actions are justified or defensible. True, there are a lot of bumbling portrayals of evil, but this regrettable fact does not undermine the basic point that good role-players are skilled at seeing what evil characters would do.

You might object to this because you think morally decent people can't be good at role-playing evil. If so, you might support your view by appealing to ways that an ostensibly evil character might go wrong (or less wrong) by falling short of the ideally evil personality. Once you identify those ways, you are thereby imagining a role-player doing a better job by directing his character in a more convincing way. To the extent that we have the tools of dramatic criticism needed to point out the flaws of a not-so-successful portrayal of evil, we also have the tools to construct a more plausible, more lifelike simulacrum of evil. Just imagine making corrections to the performance or the role-play, and you have generated an even better example of portraying wickedness.

I have a few reasons for looking at evil characters first. It's more vivid, and perhaps evil characters are more common simply because they're so fascinating. But the example of good people playing evil characters shows that we don't need to share the values of a character in order to see how that character would act. You might have thought that we know how so-and-so would act only because we're not so different, after all. But few people consider themselves to be morally evil.

Playing Nice

We can make a parallel argument about morally virtuous characters. Players can play virtuous characters with great insight and skill. Even though I'm a moral mediocrity in my own life, my heroic paladin is genuinely and convincingly good, rather than "cartoonishly" good. If you don't believe this, the same critical exercise is available to you. Consider the ways in which the paladin might fall short of true virtue. Perhaps he's too rule-bound or insufficiently sensitive to certain values; he means well but he just doesn't see that he's patronizing rather than helpful . . . and so on. This list of criticisms forms a guide to making my role-playing more successful. And it seems immensely plausible to say that the skill of making these sorts of criticisms is not found only in those of surpassingly excellent character. If so, the keen observer can see what to do without having the full cluster of traits that characterize the virtuous agent.

Two quick arguments for this point about good observers come to mind. First, the most insightful critics of human nature and action are not always the morally best people. Second, this might not be by accident: the sort of skilled observation I have in mind requires a degree of skepticism and willingness to consider uncharitable interpretations that might be ruled out by the morally ideal character. Nuanced observation and criticism might well be incompatible with a virtuous agent's character simply because it requires something like a mean streak.

The Best Rules Sometimes Let Us Down

These observations about how morally good or bad people can portray good or evil characters will show why some of Aristotle's famous claims about ethics are wrong.

Here's a reason to be suspicious of moral rules and principles: they always seem to give bad advice in at least some situations. "Don't lie" is a pretty good rule to live by, but little white lies seem all right, and lying to Nazis searching for Anne Frank seems not only acceptable but required. It's hard to give general principles that don't run into these kinds of problems. Even if they apply to most cases, there will be times when it's better to break the rule than to follow it.

Aristotle and his philosophical descendants seem to buy into this line of thinking. So how else are we supposed to know what to do, if rules won't do the job? Their answer is to start with the agent, not the action. If we knew more about the traits, emotions, and thoughts of the ideal moral agent, this exemplar would give us a standard of right action. The virtuous agent, the one who exemplifies this ideal, gives us our best insight into what to do. The idea of character (in the sense of personality) is fundamental, while right actions are simply the ones that the virtuous person would choose. (This approach is called "virtue ethics" because of its focus on character in general and virtue in particular.)

The appeal of this idea is that while rules will botch morally nuanced situations, the virtuous person has the wisdom and insight to get them right. The virtuous agent will tell us to avoid lies most of the time but not always, for example, because sometimes lying is necessary to protect innocents from evil. The virtuous person—and *only* the virtuous person—has the skill of acting wisely in all of these diverse situations.

We Learn to Feel

Aristotelians like to talk about being virtuous as a kind of skill, comparable to the abilities of a master craftsman. It's not just knowledge of a list of facts. Think of some of the skills our characters develop through experience and practice: a ranger might recognize that an apparently peaceful glen hides a carefully concealed cave entrance, but he doesn't do it by consulting his ranger checklist. His skill of seeing what's amiss is developed by practice and experience, not by memorization. The development of skills like this is represented, in gameplay, by the way experienced characters have an easier time doing things successfully— you need lower rolls for making saving throws or connecting with your weaponry. This is a way of solving the problem that it's the character, not the player, who possesses the skills.

John McDowell claims that we know what to do "by being a certain kind of person: one who sees situations in a certain distinctive way" (p. 73). The development of character is like honing the skill of acting appropriately.

What's more, developing virtue involves training one's emotions and instinctive responses. As Dan Jacobson describes it, "moral knowledge issues from a distinctive sensibility which allows a virtuous person to see what to do, in part through his properly trained emotional responses" (p. 388). Learning to have the right sorts of feelings is part of becoming truly virtuous. (Imagine a fighter who learns, over time, that some situations that look dangerous really aren't, and thus stops being afraid in contexts where novice fighters will feel fear and struggle to resist it.)

Learning to feel the appropriate emotions is, in fact, *required* for the proper perception of what to do, according to a lot of virtue ethicists. Rosalind Hursthouse makes this point in a vivid way:

> . . . the whole idea that a human agent *could* do what she should, in every particular instance, while her emotions are way out of line, is a complete fantasy. Our understanding of what will hurt, offend, damage, undermine, distress, or assure, help, succour, support, or please our fellow human beings is at least as much emotional as it is theoretical. (*On Virtue Ethics*, p. 118)

Hursthouse thinks that we can't act morally without having habituated and trained our emotional responses. Thus, for her, as well as for other Aristotelians, knowing what to do depends on carefully developed skills, *and* those skills include (or require) the right emotional responses.

D&D versus Virtue Ethics

Once we recognize that skilled role-players can play good or evil characters convincingly, it's easy to see what's wrong with the Aristotelian claims about virtue and right action. Just as a perfectly nice and decent person can convincingly play an evil character, a morally so-so person can play good characters, and he can so do with genuine insight into what his morally superior character would do. Hence, some non-virtuous personalities can see what the virtuous person (or character) would do. That means they can judge correctly about what should be done.

The problem is simple. If a non-virtuous player can convincingly direct a virtuous character, that player is seeing what ought to be done in a particular situation (the character's fictional situation, that is). But this means that being fully virtuous is not necessary for making good judgments about the morally best action. Of course, there is, or may well be, a skill involved here. The player is displaying a kind of skill in judging what another sort of personality (the personality of his character) would do in various situations. The player presumably isn't consulting a system of rules or an algorithm. Simply guiding your character by following "how to be lawful good in ten easy steps" is a sure-fire way to get things wrong.

The point is that this skill can exist without the emotional capacities required by the Aristotelians. First, the skill can be used "off-line"—it does not require genuine emotional engagement. (I don't need to feel the fear or disgust that my character feels in order to guide his actions well.) Second, and more important, the argument from role-playing shows that the relevant emotional sensitivities and motivational states are not necessary for good judgment about what to do.

Role-playing provides evidence that some players—not all, not many, but some—are able to play the role of virtuous or morally exemplary characters in a convincing way. This is evidence that these players are "getting it right" playing the alignment of their characters, and since some of these character are morally excellent, we should conclude that these players "see what to do" with respect to virtuous action. The ability to do this is different from full-blown virtue, not only in principle, but in practice as well. In fact, the skill of seeing what a virtuous agent would do seems to be distinct from the motivation to act in morally upstanding ways. The lesson to be learned from skilled role-players is that the ability to judge correctly about what virtue or moral excellence requires is one thing, and truly *being* virtuous is another. The latter requires the former, but not vice-versa.

There are other problems for the Aristotelian. Aristotle thinks that the virtues can be acquired only by habituation and training—that is, by "practicing how to act." Furthermore, he thinks that the skill has to be developed alongside the training of our motivational states, the psychological forces that push us into action. These two ideas have to be modified if what we see in role-playing is correct. It looks as if the skill of judging correctly about action can be developed *without actually acting*, because players can develop it through play. And because taking part in role-playing games does not involve the same desires and emotions that *characters* would experience, the skill can be developed independent of these actual motivational states.

There is also an interesting upshot for moral education, since, if role-playing can serve as part of habituation and training, we can use it to develop the sorts of personalities we want to encourage.

My argument here is related to some clever problems for Aristotelians developed by Robert Johnson. The virtue ethicist starts with the virtuous agent and says that right actions are the ones virtuous agent would perform. Johnson points out that what you ought to do sometimes depends on how good a person you are. Sometimes an agent's *lack* of virtue changes his moral obligations. If I have a flawed character, for example, I might have an obligation to improve myself or to resist situations where I'm exposed to temptation. Virtuous agents don't have these obligations.

In response, the Aristotelian might move to an "advice" model: the right action is the one a virtuous agent would recommend *for me* (with all of my flaws), not the one she would choose for herself. But the advice model creates a gap between the skill of choosing actions for oneself and giving good advice to others. Why should we expect these to go together, when we see that morally flawed people are sometimes the most incisive?

My argument here is based on a similar observation. The skill required for good advice is much like the skill required to play virtuous characters convincingly. Both require the agent to step into another's shoes, to see from another perspective, to choose actions from within a different sensibility. It would be surprising if these skills went hand in hand with all of the traits that are involved in virtue. And there are reasons to think that these skills are distinct from full-blown virtue.

An Objection—and Why It Matters

What does the virtue ethicist say in response? She might reject the premise of my argument. "It *seems* like Joe's paladin is acting the way a paladin should act," she might say, "but that's just not true. Joe's not really playing the paladin right, and you would see this if you were a virtuous person yourself." This objection just rejects the idea that non-virtuous players can accurately direct their virtuous characters.

This is a serious objection, but I don't think it's right. We really do think that some people do a great job at role-playing, even though they're not (morally) the best people. In order to get the objection to work, the virtue ethicist has to say that *real* right actions are so hard to identify that we get it wrong a lot, without even knowing that we get it wrong. The problem is that once she says this, she makes it harder to show that the virtuous agent, the expert, is really "getting it right" instead of "making bogus claims." Making this objection will leave the whole virtue ethics idea on shaky ground.

Suppose , for the sake of illustration, we're taking a break from role-playing and I say I can tell what kind of dice you're holding in your fist. You naturally think this is ridiculous, so you test me. I shock you by getting it right most of the time: when I say you've got a twenty-sided die, you do, and when I say it's eight-sided, lo, there's an eight-sided die in your palm. Suppose that after we do this for a while, you close your eyes when you grab some dice, so you don't know what you're holding. "It's a d4 and a d12," I say.

Believing me makes perfect sense, even though you don't know just how I manage to do it. Maybe I have psionic powers, maybe I've got a way of cheating, but if I get it right often enough, you have to admit that I really do have this ability. Convincing you requires that you understand how to test me, and that you see that I succeed at making predictions.

Now suppose I claim to see what color your aura is. You have no way of verifying this, because you can't see auras and you don't know anyone who can. In this situation, you wouldn't say I have a really amazing ability, you'd say I'm a fraud. My claim to have some special talent for seeing auras looks bogus because no one can verify that I'm getting it right. No one can check.

When I claim to be able to see something that you don't, I've got to back it up with results. If I can't, you're going to be skeptical, and rightly so. As Dan Jacobson points out, all this talk of "seeing what to do" has to be confirmed with recognizable success. In the case of virtue, that means getting it right in action, or acting better as a result of seeing things correctly.

Now suppose I tell you that I can "see what to do" as a result of my careful study and training. Maybe you quiz me about some everyday moral situations and I give answers that make sense to you. Okay, you think, maybe this guy is on to something. When you hit me with harder moral quandaries, I say compelling things that track your own reasoning moderately well, even if you haven't come to a firm conclusion on the question. These responses would convince you that I'm on to something, not merely making stuff up. On the other hand, if I reply in ways that don't match your views at all, you'll think I'm a fraud.

The reply we're discussing—that maybe skilled role-players aren't getting virtuous characters right after all—is in danger of making the virtuous agent's claims to see what to do look fraudulent. If we can't recognize virtuous action when we see it, at least some or most of the time, we have no way of checking that the so-called virtuous agent is really getting it right instead of making things up. Making virtue unverifiable makes it more like the aura example and less like the dice example. In short, making the objection (or denying the basic premise of my argument) leaves the virtue ethicist on very shaky ground.

That's how thinking about what good role-playing is like shows us that Aristotle is (partly!) wrong about ethics. Aristotelians can't account for successfully "playing" at virtue. I suspect that this problem has gone unnoticed for a simple but revealing reason. Discussions of the morally beneficial effects of fiction tend to be somewhat high-minded: we're reminded that reading Jane Austen or George Eliot can hone our ethical sensitivities, for example. But literary fiction doesn't require making choices on behalf of characters. It can show us how a character's mind works, but it doesn't call on *us* to deliberate from that character's point of view. We're passively receiving what the author has portrayed. Role-playing requires creative and active engagement with a fictional world. It requires players to choose actions, not merely reflect on them. Because it demands this of its participants, it reveals a range of abilities that are philosophically more interesting than those involved in traditionally "highbrow" pursuits.

3
Beyond Chaotic Good and Lawful Evil?

JON COGBURN

If you were a literate, nerdy kid in the 1970s and 1980s, then the moral psychology implicit in the *Dungeons and Dragons* alignment system might have been a great influence on your development, as important as when you first began to doubt the central tenets of your religious upbringing.

For many of us the two experiences were actually deeply connected. But now we have all been shocked to learn that, after thirty years and with no explanation whatsoever, the Fourth Edition *Player's Handbook* has radically changed our beloved system.

The original D&D alignments can be broken down as shown on the next page. All quotes are from Edition 3.5's *Player's Handbook*.

Up until 2008, players could chose any of the nine alignments for their characters, and explore moral psychology through such role-playing. But in Fourth Edition, we get the following:

> If you chose an alignment for your character, you should pick either good or lawful good. Unless your DM is running a campaign in which all the characters are evil or chaotic evil, playing an evil or chaotic evil character disrupts an adventuring party and, frankly makes all the other players angry at you. (Heinsoo, p. 19)

This sentiment is in line with the redesign of the game so that player characters are heroes surrounded by a world of darkness, more like fantasy novel main characters. This still makes

	Lawful	Neutral	Chaotic
Good	Lawful Good: "Crusader. . . Combines honor and compassion."	Neutral Good: "Benefactor. . . True good. Doing what is good without bias toward or against order."	Chaotic Good: "Rebel. . . Combines a good heart with a free spirit."
Neutral	Lawful Neutral: "Judge. . . True lawful. Reliable and honorable without being a zealot."	Neutral Neutral: "Undecided. . True neutral. Act naturally, without prejudice or compulsion."	Chaotic Neutral: "Free Spirit. . True Chaotic. True freedom from both society's restrictions and from a do-gooder's zeal."
Evil	Lawful Evil: "Dominator. . . Methodical, intentional, and frequently successful evil."	Neutral Evil: "Malefactor. . . True evil. Pure evil without honor and without variation."	Chaotic Evil: "Destroyer. . . Represents the Destruction not only of beauty and life but on the order on which beauty and life depend."

room for exploration of moral psychology through role-playing, but it is quite different from what we grew up with.

Alignment does not just characterize player characters; every sapient creature in the *Dungeons and Dragons* universe has an alignment. Therefore, not only the heroes and heroines are affected, but also the evil thieves and neutral shopkeepers. In this manner, any change to the alignment system changes the moral landscape of the entire D&D world. And, thus, much more extreme than the advice to play good characters is the Fourth Edition contraction of the nine alignments sketched above into these five: good, lawful good, evil, chaotic evil,

	Lawful	Neutral	Chaotic
Good	Lawful Good: "An ordered society protects us from evil."	Neutral Good: "Protecting the weak from those who would dominate or kill them is just the right thing to do."	Chaotic Good:
Neutral	.	Unaligned: "Just let me go about my business."	
Evil		Evil: "It is my right to claim what others possess."	Chaotic Evil: "I don't care what I have to do to get what I want."

unaligned. Since neutral alignments are traditionally labeled "true" versions of the other axis (so "true good" equals "neutral good"), the new system can be shown as above.

The change represents a staggering metaphysical and psychological shift. Lawful Neutral, Lawful Evil, Chaotic Good, and Chaotic Neutral have been removed as archetypes for all of the denizens in the *Dungeons and Dragons* universe.

Though the design team never justifies their decision, we can gather from the new descriptions why they excised the others. For example, "When leaders exploit their authority for personal gain, when laws grant privileged status to some citizens and reduce others to slavery or untouchable status, law has given in to evil and just authority becomes tyranny" (Heinsoo, p. 20). Clearly "law" is being thought of in such a way that tyranny does not count as "law." So "law" in Fourth Edition can't be identified with the law of a society, but must be identified with a higher moral law that a society can fail to instantiate. From this perspective, if you're Lawful, then you endorses and follow morally justified laws (as opposed to the laws of the land). So you can't fail to be Good if you're Lawful.

Evil is characterized in terms of people who are sociopathic in their selfishness, but who "don't necessarily go out of their ways to hurt people." So again it's impossible to see how you could be Evil and be Lawful in the new sense. Somebody who completely disregards the desires of others would not sacrifice to bring about and support morally justifiable laws.

Merely Evil people usually go along with a society's rules for large stretches of their lives because they regard it as being in their self interest. Though their behavior is incredibly wicked when nobody is in a position to stop them, their public personas can make them seem to be of the highest virtue. In contrast, Chaotic Evil creatures are so psychologically disorganized that they are not able to refrain from acting on their desires in the short run, and hence are inevitably destructive to community. Being Chaotic is so undermining of our ability to act rationally that a Chaotic person will not possess the ability to be Good. This makes sense. Given that a Good person believes "it is right to aid and protect those in need" to the point of self-sacrifice, a person so disorganized that they cannot even pretend to be Good cannot be expected to reliably aid and protect those in need.

If we connect these dots, we get that Fourth Edition Lawful characterizes a commitment to forging and defending a society that instantiates a transcendent moral law, which is understood as being necessarily good. Goodness is understood as a commitment to helping others. Neutrality is understood as selfish commitment only to your own goals, but also a commitment to not preventing others from undertaking their goals. Evil is understood as complete willingness to interfere with others' well-being in undertaking one's goals. Chaotic Evil is understood as being Evil but not being able to control yourself well enough to fit into a society. Looked at this way, Evil people are the kind of high functioning psychopaths that are over-represented among corrupt corporate CEOs and politicians, while Chaotic Evil people are the low functioning psychopaths heavily represented among the prison population.

Two Desiderata and How Fourth Edition Alignment Fails to Meet Them

In "Truth from Fiction?" Mary Sirridge argues that one of the primary ways we learn from fiction involves the use of archetypal characters to help us understand certain personality types. This is part of why story-telling is a central part of moral education in all known human cultures. We learn different ways to be morally virtuous in part by learning about archetypes who instantiate these virtues. For example, in the genre of fantasy literature Samwise Gamgee from Tolkien's *Lord of the Rings* is an archetypal representation of the following virtues: loyalty, humility, and gentle humorousness. In Samwise, these come together as a vivid type, and we learn what it is to be this type from reading the book.

Samwise poses no deep problem for the Fourth Edition alignment system. He is clearly Lawful Good. But some of the most compelling fantasy characters from the recent flowering of English language fantasy literature don't fit anywhere in the new typology. Consider Steven Erikson's *Malazan Book of the Fallen* series. In the fourth volume, *House of Chains*, we learn of the giant Karsa Orlong's past as an enslaved barbarian. By the time of his second and final escape from slavery, Karsa has gathered the will to destroy all civilization.

Even though Karsa Orlong is one of the most vivid archetypal characters in the series, there is no Fourth Edition alignment that comes near to characterizing him. He's not particularly impulsive in the sense of a Chaotic. He's certainly not Good to any large degree, or Lawful Good. He's not committed to the idea of society instantiating good laws, as he is genuinely anti-social in the strongest possible sense of wanting to destroy all civilization that gives rise to sociality. Given that his quixotic (or not so quixotic) quest would (if it were successful) lead to millions of deaths, he is in no way true Neutral. And no one who reads the book would describe him as Evil either. He is not particularly sadistic, and his deference to the witch Samar Dev is in no way a ploy to further his self interest; it is done consistently whether there are people around or not.

Another example of an archetypal character that has no place in the new system is Haomane Firstborn, Lord of Thought, from Jacqueline Carey's *Banewreaker* and *Godslayer* (collectively known as *The Sundering*). Carey's world is identical for all important purposes to that of the *Lord of the Rings* trilogy. But her story is a tragedy in which ignorant men, elves, and dwarves destroy a good deity (Sartoris, or Sauron) and threaten the world he saved in the process.

Haomane is not Good. He knows that his desire for perfection will lead to the cessation of all life. Neither is he true Neutral, as he gives magic to his white magician to lead the assault on Sartoris, killing untold numbers of other sapient creatures (entirely benign half-human half-wolves are spared only on the condition that they no longer reproduce!) with the same religious certainty as Tolkien's heroes. Perhaps more significantly, Haomane is motivated against the natural order of the world, which survives only because of Sartoris' gift.

Haomane is certainly not Chaotic in the Fourth Edition sense. He created the elves to be the apex of calm lawfulness. From his worshipers one would gather that he takes himself to be Lawful Good, as he expects his laws to be followed, even though doing so leads ultimately to universal genocide. But since genocide is not Good, he is not really Lawful Good.

Of all the Fourth Edition alignments, this leaves only Evil. But anyone who has read the books would find this an extremely strange characterization of Haomane. To call someone "Evil" in Fourth Edition *Dungeons and Dragons* is to say that they have a characteristic disregard for the well-being of others. But Haomane does care for the elf children that he lovingly shaped to instantiate his highest ideals, as well as their human and dwarven allies. Though this is not clear, since he is withdrawn and silent, every indication from his magician and priests suggests that he takes himself to be helping his creatures and that the slow death of the world into a place of crystalline order is for him the highest possible good.

Finally, neither is Haomane the simple negation of Fourth Edition Good, which would be to be a genuine sadist, taking pleasure in harming other people. So here we see that one of the most compelling characters in fantasy literature, perhaps the most vivid never to enter the stage, has absolutely no place in the Fourth Edition alignment system. This is a signal failure.

While the first failure concerns Fourth Edition in particular, the second is a problem with all editions. Simply put, it is never entirely clear what exactly is being described by alignment in the official *Player's Handbook*s. For example, the Chaotic Good characterization from 3.5 is of someone who:

1. **"believes in goodness and right"**

2. "hates it when people try to intimidate others and tell them what to do"

and

3. is "kind and beneficial"

The first concerns the character's beliefs, the second her feelings or emotional responses, and the third her typical behaviors.

This mishmash makes it impossible to characterize creatures with odd combinations of belief, feeling, and actions. What of someone who genuinely believes in goodness and right but is continually subject to overwhelmingly wicked desires? What of someone who is philosophically committed to the thesis that there is no such thing as goodness and right, but who nonetheless desires to help other people, and acts on this desire regularly? What of someone who has radically evil beliefs (such as supporting wars unjust both in their inception and manner of execution) but who never actually kills innocent people or tortures prisoners?

For the purposes of crafting a coherent theory of virtue for fantasy role-playing we *can* avoid this difficulty by recourse to the concept of the will, which with Kant we understand, "not as a mere wish, but as the summoning of all the means in our power" (Kant 1995, p. 10). If you will something in Kant's sense then you do as much as you can to support or bring that thing about. Willing typically involves some combination of beliefs, feelings, and a certain amount of sustained behavior, depending upon the person's world view, psychological makeup, and abilities. Thus if someone wills goodness she summons *all* of the means in her power (and, even though Kant might have disagreed, this clearly entails doing so habitually) to bring about more goodness. If someone wills law, then she summons all of the means in her power to bring about lawfulness. Likewise for willing evil and chaos.

And on this scheme neutrality makes perfect sense as the willing is a continuum itself. On one side are people who will law, on the other are people who will chaos; the more chaos you will, the less law you will. But then, the people in the middle are those who will neither. So true Neutrals will neither law nor chaos, neither good nor evil.

Of course this point about will is not enough to craft an alignment system able to do justice to the richness of fantasy literature archetypes. From the various *Players Handbooks* it's just not clear enough what law/chaos and good/evil amount to. But here is exactly where philosophers can return the favor. If D&D got many of us to think about morality in a deep way for the first time in our lives, the tradition of philosophical thinking about morality can now help D&D.

Law and Chaos

For Kant, nature is precisely that which can be explained in terms of universal laws of nature. So if we characterize the alignment Lawful as one who wills lawfulness, we would have to say that a Lawful person wills that which can be explained in terms of universal laws of nature. And in fact, one of Kant's formulations of the moral law just is the following:

Categorical Imperative (first version):

Act only according to that maxim by which you can at the same time will that it should become a universal law. (p. 38)

In this context "maxim" just means rule. The imperative enjoins us to only do things that are such that the relevant rule can be willed into a universal law. So a Lawful person is one who wills universal lawfulness in this sense: she habitually summons all the means in her power to follow Kant's moral law and help build a society where Kant's law is followed by all.

It's easiest to explain Kant's moral law, and its tie to alignment, if we examine behaviors that seem to violate it. Say I am considering telling a lie. The relevant maxim or rule would be the rule that orders me to tell the lie. For Kant, universalizing this maxim means converting it to a universal law that has everyone always following the maxim to lie. Can one consistently will that? Arguably not. If everyone lied all the time, then the very institution of communication would break down. For example, parents would never teach their children the correct meanings of words. So you can't will the maxim ordering your lie to be converted into a universal law.

Things are actually even worse for the liar though. When somebody lies they know that their lie will only work if the person they are talking with thinks they are telling the truth. But that can only be possible if enough other people accept the maxim "Don't lie." So the liar must think there is something special about her so that the maxim applies to everyone else, but not to her.

The murderer cannot will that the maxim "Murder!" be a universal law, for then everyone would have died long ago, and she would not be able to complete her act. In addition, to preclude this universal murder (and hence be able to get away with it) she must will that everyone else accept the maxim "Do not murder." So whenever someone tries to "get away with it" they are taking themselves to be exceptions to laws they want to bind everyone else. They are *not* willing lawfulness. So again, the person who genuinely wills lawfulness minimally will act in ways consistent with Kant's categorical imperative.

One of the nice things about this scheme is that it lends itself very well to treating chaos as the lack of lawfulness. Then since to be Chaotic is to will chaos, it follows that a Chaotic person is the person who wills the absence of universalizability. A Chaotic person enjoys "getting away with it" just because she enjoys undermining the moral law. The person hypocritically wills that others follow the law while she herself wills against that law in her own actions. In the long run it leads to destruction for destruction's sake; as the Chaotic gets away with more and more, the very possibility of universalizability is undermined. At some point everyone has been murdered, and there are no victims left to will the maxim "Don't murder!" That is, the truly successful Chaotic would end up destroying everything, including herself. In fantasy and real life, chaos is horrible.

Goodness and Evil

If Immanuel Kant is the philosopher prophet of lawfulness, then John Stuart Mill is our prophet of goodness. In his essay *Utilitarianism*, he characterizes the level of an act's rightness in the following manner:

> The creed which accepts as the foundation of morals "utility" or the "greatest happiness principle" holds that actions are right in proportion

as they tend to promote happiness: wrong as they tend to produce the reverse of happiness. By happiness is intended pleasure and the absence of pain by unhappiness, pain and the privation of pleasure. (Mill 2001, p. 7)

Whereas Kant's moral law just tells you if an act is morally permissible or not, Mill's greatest happiness principle tells you of two acts which one is the more right. The act that produces more happiness is better than the act which produces the least happiness.

If we take Mill's characterization of goodness and remember (from Kant) that an alignment is derived in terms of a person willing that thing, then we get that a person is Good to the extent that she wills happiness for the greatest number. Archetypal Good people are those who make a difference in the lives of those around them in just this way, lessening the pain and increasing the pleasure that their fellow creatures take in existence.

We can now arrive at the new theory by: 1. taking alignment to hold in virtue of a character's will; 2. taking each axis to characterize a genuine continuum where one side concerns a property that the other lacks. We can call the Law-Neutral-Chaotic axis the Kantian deontological axis and the Good-Neutral-Evil axis the act utilitarian axis. A character's alignment measures their position in the co-ordinate space given by the two axes.

Lawful Good

The Lawful Good creature wills universal laws that promote flourishing. As a Lawful person she holds that there should be no exceptions to these laws, and as a Good person she holds that these laws must bring about more happiness—that is greater pleasure, and less pain. The archetypal Lawful Good character is one of the following: a good ruler such as the fictitious King Arthur or real Franklin Delano Roosevelt, a noble hero that tries to defend a just society against external foes intent on its demise such as the young Charles de Gaulle, or a rebel who revolts against an unjust society in the hopes of helping build a new society where the law treats all equally and where people suffer less. Heroes of this last type include

Mohandas Gandhi, Martin Luther King, and Henry de Bourbon. While the first two were martyred, the latter went on to become a Lawful Good ruler of the first type.

Neutral Good

One interpretation of the moral teachings of Jesus presents him as holding that an act is correct not because it follows from any rule such as Kant's categorical imperative, but because it is done in love. The synoptic gospels are replete with passages such as Mark: 2–3 where Jesus is breaking the law of his society (eating with proscribed people and working on the Sabbath) in a way that results in less suffering.

Instead of drawing up a new system of law, or even gesturing at such a thing, Jesus spends most of the Gospels telling strange parables in the hope that they will inspire a gestalt shift in the listener, so that the listener will instantiate Good. Sometimes the parables seem to specifically work to get the listener to not will the law.

> Do not judge, or you too will be judged. For in the same way you judge others, you will be judged, and with the measure you use, it will be measured to you. Why do you look at the speck of sawdust in your brother's eye and pay no attention to the plank in your own eye? How can you say to your brother, 'Let me take the speck out of your eye,' when all the time there is a plank in your own eye? You hypocrite, first take the plank out of your own eye, and then you will see clearly to remove the speck from your brother's eye. (Matthew 7:1–5)

Giving advice to another person is not a matter of noting that they have violated some law. Rather, we must will goodness so that out of the spirit of love we actually try to help our brother.

Saint Paul writes:

> . . . our competence is from God, who has made us competent to be ministers of a new covenant, not in a written code but in the Spirit; for the written code kills, but the Spirit gives life. (2 Corinthians 3:6)

For the Neutral Good person, our basic moral orientation is from willing goodness, not from any system of Law.

Chaotic Good

There are no Chaotic Good entities. Fourth Edition gets this absolutely right. In fantasy novels and life, chaos is terrifying, degrading, and ultimately maddening. A creature who sincerely willed the end of lawfulness as such cannot consistently will the lessening of pain and increase of pleasure, because chaos is intrinsically painful.

What then of the heroes of our youth, Drizzt Do'Urden and Uncle Jesse from *The Dukes of Hazzard*? These characters are not willing chaos, the absolute destruction of moral and physical law. They are not rebelling against lawfulness as such, they are rebelling against the unjust laws of the society in which they find themselves. If they will the replacement of these laws with just ones, then they are Lawful Good. If, as seems more appropriate to their characters, they are not so motivated, then like Jesus and Saint Paul (on a good day) they are Neutral Good.

Lawful Neutral

Lawful Neutral is also prohibited in Fourth Edition. As noted above, the designers simply took Lawful to mean support for just and Good social institutions. But we have taken Lawful to mean someone who wills universalizability in the sense of Kant.

The examples we considered strongly suggested that a Lawful person would not lie or murder. But one might argue that a Neutral person would not do these things either. However, Kant goes further, arguing that a Lawful person would necessarily support charity, which for us is a mark of Good since charitable behavior springs from willing the diminution of pain in others. Thus Kant can be understood as arguing that the only Lawful alignment is Lawful Good.

According to Kant's argument, since we can't help but will that we ourselves receive charity if we are in need of it, we can't then universally will the maxim not to give charity. So if someone is really Lawful, such that the maxims according to which they act can be willed to be universal, that person is going to will a certain amount of charity and hence not be Neutral along the Utilitarian (Good-Neutral-Evil) Axis.

We should not have an alignment system that rests upon the validity of this argument. Contrary to Kant, it's certainly possible to imagine people willing themselves into situations where they will not receive charity. Kant does describe the unreasonable hypocrisy that most of us labor under, expecting more charity than we are willing to extend. And his point is that if you are truly Lawful, you cannot be unreasonable in this way. The Lawful Neutral character we are envisioning would in fact be extremely weird, almost pathological, someone so devoid of affect that she could with equanimity see herself destroyed as a way to maintain consistency.

Jacqueline Carey's Haomane Firstborn just is this pathological. He is neither beneficent nor sadistic, but rather genuinely indifferent to the horrendous suffering and eventual extinction his plans will cause. He loves cold mathematical beauty. For him, the still universe of unmoving, dead forms is Law personified.

Neutral Neutral

We might mistakenly think that the stereotypical bureaucratic overlords in government and big business are paradigm examples of Lawful Neutral. After all, their indifference to suffering is a precondition of their zealous support for the meaningless and arcane laws and regulations that make their existence possible. But the vast majority of them do not want to suffer the same thing they inflict on others. This widespread hypocrisy makes them non-Lawful. Such creatures are Neutral-Neutral at best.

The archetypal Neutral-Neutral character is the torturer San Dan Glotka from Joe Abercrombie's *The First Law* trilogy (*The Blade Itself*, *Before They are Hanged*, *The Last Argument of Kings*). Glotka is a returned prisoner of war whose physical health and appearance have been ruined by years of hideous torture. Though considered a war hero, he's shunned by the society that used to laud him, and he ends up becoming a state torturer himself. He is a terrifying example of the "banality of evil" described by Hannah Arendt in *Eichmann in Jerusalem*. His interior monologue is sarcastically urbane and witty, the funniest writing in the books, but he also knowingly, and without remorse, tortures false confessions out of the state's victims.

In the first novel of the series he has no will regarding either end of our two axes. He is not a sadist as he takes no particular pleasure from the pain he is inflicting on others. In the earlier part of the trilogy he has no particular care for any humans other than himself, and even his own self-love is tenuous since he thinks it's funny when he is beaten and almost drowned. He has no commitment either to the corrupt state he's working for or the idea that anything better could come about (until the third novel when he begins to experience very minimal moral development in taking care of his friend's sister). He just wanders through the first novel doing his horrific job, thinking bitingly sarcastic remarks at anyone he encounters.

Chaotic Neutral

The Chaotic Neutral wills the destruction of instances of universal order, but is not motivated by sadism in doing so. The archetypal Chaotic Neutral from recent great fantasy literature remains Karsa Orlong. Unlike San Dan Glotka (who reacted to imprisonment and torture by withdrawing all his sympathies relating to law, order, good, or evil), Karsa has reacted to enslavement with the desire to destroy all civilization, so that creatures are forced to live by their own particular genius, without being able to appeal to institutions to guarantee enforcement of universal rules. Karsa is not indifferent to these institutions; he wants to destroy them all.

As with Lawful Neutral and Neutral Neutral, such a creature is a testament to just how monstrous Neutrality between Good and Evil is. Karsa is absolutely indifferent to the fact that if successful, his destruction will cause untold suffering. He is on a mission.

One might harness some of the reasons against the idea of Chaotic Good against Chaotic Neutral. Could someone truly willing chaos do anything but also will the suffering brought about? At the very best it would be a rare creature such as Karsa. Most true Chaotics are Evil. In addition, if Karsa wants to stay on the Chaotic Neutral path as he grows stronger and stronger, he will end up expanding the scope of his hatred for lawfulness as such, and ultimately try to destroy the universe itself as an entity that follows universal laws so that it can support life and be known by creatures like us.

Lawful Evil

Just as we had to justify the existence of Lawful Neutral against Kant's explicit arguments to the effect that Lawfulness entails Goodness, we now must justify the existence of Lawful Evil. How could somebody willing the categorical imperative (and hence willing moral lawfulness itself) also will the increase in pain and decrease in pleasure? Isn't this very thing prohibited by the categorical imperative?

It's not so clear. Consider the maxim, "Cause more pain!" A sadomasochist could clearly will it to be a universal law that everyone experienced more pain. The fact that she would experience more pain is just fine.

But could a pure sadist, one who wishes pain on everyone but herself, be Lawful in Kant's sense? One would think not, as this involves a contradiction in willing of the kind Kant noted when discussing the uncharitable person. But the maxim, "Increase the pain of everybody but Jon Cogburn," can be universalized into the injunction for everybody to increase the pain of everybody but Jon Cogburn.

Clearly something deviant is going on. We want to say that the initial maxim is itself too specific, not general enough, but this raises what many take to be the Achilles' heel of Kant's entire moral project. How do we know which level of specificity is appropriate for construing the maxims? If we construe the maxims too generally, then the theory prohibits actions that should be allowed. Say I want to do something, so the maxim is "Do what you want." Clearly this cannot be universalized, as people's desires conflict with each other's. But then Kant's ethics seems to entail that we can never do what we want.

By very carefully construing the maxims at the certain levels of generality, the categorical imperative can either justify or prohibit any course of action. But then any set of rules can be justified, even rules that an Evil creature would will. Of course, if one is also Good, then the desire to increase pleasure will serve as a strict limit on what maxims one considers in applying the categorical imperative, solving much of the problem. But Lawful Evil creatures are not Good and hence do not have this interior check.

Typically, Lawful Evil creatures thrive in hierarchical structures where those higher in the structure are unfairly given privileges and rights denied to those lower down in the structure. They wholeheartedly support the hierarchical stratification that allows those higher up to take pleasure in inflicting pain on those lower down in the structure. Can this be justified by forms of the categorical imperative? Let the maxim be that someone higher up in the structure can cause pain to those lower down in the structure. Clearly such a rule can be universalized, and something like it is actual in many countries of the world, where the poor accept their place in the hope that someday they may become rich themselves, at which point their boot would be on the neck of everyone lower down in the structure. In the American South before the Civil Rights revolution, the vast majority of poor whites were socially and economically persecuted by rich whites, but the consolation was that they got to persecute poor blacks.

In fantasy literature, the most common Lawful Evil creatures are stereotypical vampires, who have elaborate hierarchical systems of rules that allow them to survive and prey on human victims. In real life, politicians who know their policies reduce the standard of living at home and who create hell on earth for people across the world are paradigm cases of Lawful Evil.

Neutral Evil

Neutral Evil characters are like the Duke clan in that they have no regard for lawfulness (and no particular desire to destroy all instances of it), but unlike the Dukes, they seek to spread unhappiness. Unfortunately, I could discover no clear archetypes in fantasy literature for this kind of character, in part because it is less psychologically plausible than either Lawful Evil or Chaotic Evil. For someone to be Neutral Evil they would have to have no attachment to a hierarchical system of universal order and also have no desire to destroy universal order. But at least in human beings, the sadistic (Evil) impulse seems to be tightly tied to both the (Lawful) desire to keep oneself safe in a system that allows the unjust to rule over others as well as the (Chaotic) ultimately suicidal desire to destroy all systems. The leader who runs his society into the ground and near the end concludes "After me, the deluge" is an example of someone leaping straight from Lawful to Chaotic Evil. Such was the moral psychology of Hitler in the bunker as Germany burned around him.

There are, arguably, literary arechetypes of Neutral Evil outside of fantasy novels. One might nominate the Marquise de Merteuil and the Vicomte de Valmont from Pierre Chordelos de Laclos's *Dangerous Liaisons*. At least at the outset of the novel, both characters are simply motivated by the sadistic pleasure they take in using sex to degrade other people. It is possible that serial killers fall into this category as well.

Chaotic Evil

Finally, Chaotic Evil characters will both destruction of universal order and an increase in the amount of pain. This is the ethic articulated by Arnold Schwarzenegger's Conan the Barbarian from early in the movie of the same name. When a barbarian warlord asks what is good, Conan replies, "To crush your enemies, see them driven before you, to hear the lamentations of their women." Though it quickly becomes clear that this is not the true ethic of Conan, it does characterize barbarians in common lore. The sentiment voices the (Chaotic) willing of destruction for destruction's sake, and (Evil) pleasure in women's suffering.

Chaotic Evil people tend to get portrayed in hordes. An overwhelming love of destruction and pain for the sake of destruction and pain is typically so self-destructive that it can only succeed (briefly) when instanced in marauding groups of people. A true Chaotic wills against the universal laws of nature itself (and not just moral laws). Then one goes from barbarian hordes to the realm of would-be world killers, world killers who do not even leave behind a residue of dead cold beauty as does Haomane First Born. The only comparable portrayal of a truly Chaotic world destroyer is the Iad Ouroboros from Clive Barker's *The Great and Secret Show*, seen at near the end of that novel slowly crossing the horizon like an advancing tropical storm, utterly destroying the real it traverses. Like the barbarian hordes, the Iad Ouroboros doesn't have a recognizable human personality. Being a true agent of chaos is a path that ends in insanity and death.

A Better Alignment System

This chart summarizes my proposal for a better alignment system.

	Lawful	Neutral	Chaotic
	Character wills universalizability in the sense of Kant's First Formulation.	Character unmotivated towards universalizability.	Character wills the destruction of instances of universalizability.
Good Beneficience; Character wills lessening pain and increasing pleasure of others.	Lawful Good: King Arthur Franklin Delano Roosevelt Martin Luther King Gandhi Charles de Gaulle Henry of Bourbon	Neutral Good: Jesus Robin Hood The stereo-typical hippie	Chaotic Good:
Neutral Character unmotivated towards others' pain or pleasure.	Lawful Neutral: Haomane First Born	Neutral Neutral: San Dan Glotka	Chaotic Neutral: Karsa Orlong
Evil Character loves increasing pain and decreasing pleasure of others.	Lawful Evil: Vampires George Bush's Henchmen	Neutral Evil: The Marquise de Merteui The Vicomte de Valmont Serial Killers	Chaotic Evil: Dictators at the end Barbarian Hordes The lad Ouroboros

My new version follows Fourth Edition in leaving the Chaotic Good box empty. My discussion has also considerably strengthened the Fourth Edition encouragement to play either Lawful Good or Neutral Good characters. Playing one of the other alignments well would be destructive to the rest of the group's adventure. Characters that are Neutral along the Utilitarian axis are inhuman in their unconcern for suffering around them. Characters that are Evil along this axis are sadistic.

With these new alignments, the Dungeon Master has access to a more sophisticated pallet of moral psychological types. For example, there will be real scenarios where Neutral Good and Lawful Good characters disagree. Say that killing one innocent person would save the lives of thousands more. A Neutral Good person might opt to kill the innocent person, since that would be the way to increase that total amount of happiness the most. The Lawful Good person would have a very hard time killing when not engaging in self defense, because her moral law would prohibit this. The philosophical study of ethics contains discussions of many such thought experiments as ways to test the theories that philosophers have devised. I hope that this chapter will encourage players and Dungeon Masters to inform their gameplay with these issues.

The D&D alignment system was central to a generation of adolescents whose educations and upbringing provided very little reflection on the foundations of morality. Role-playing in the *Dungeons and Dragons* universe helped us make concrete sense of the people we were and the people we wanted to become. We thought about *Dungeons and Dragons* law and chaos and good and evil in an attempt to be more virtuous people ourselves.

But the stakes are much bigger for all of us. Fourth Edition *Dungeons and Dragons* allows players to be part of a group of heroes fighting back against the darkness that surrounds them in a fallen world. But a central part of the tragedy of existence is that the moral psychology of our fellow humans is not different in any interesting way from that of orcs, elves, and wizards. That is, in real life, just as much as in fantasy, the world needs heroes.

4
Chaotic Good in the Balance

Chris Bateman

In the preceding chapter, Jon provides a fascinating account of the ethical dimensions of the *Dungeons and Dragons* alignment system. He concludes that Chaotic Good is meaningless—you can't be committed to Chaos and still pursue Good. Is he right?

Despite Jon's conclusion, I deny that Chaotic Good is impossible—not because Jon's argument falls down internally, but because the basis of his account of alignment is not the same as the one that the creators of D&D were inspired by.

The original ninefold system of alignment has now been cruelly axed by TSR-slash-Wizards of the Coast-slash-Hasbro, presumably in the hope of making the game easier to understand for the new kids coming to the game. As a professional game designer, I understand this motive. As a student and fan of fantasy fiction, and as someone who used to both play and publish tabletop role-playing games, I find this revision abhorrent.

With Chaos on Our Side

Like everything in *Dungeons and Dragons* (except the incredible innovation of providing formal mechanics for role-play itself), the alignment system is an amalgam of content originating in twentieth-century fantasy novels. While Good and Evil date back at least as far as the prophet Zoroaster, the root of the axis of Law and Chaos lies in Poul Anderson's novel *Three Hearts and Three Lions*, and even more so in the work of

Michael Moorcock, who developed Anderson's ideas. Moorcock is most famous among fantasy fans for the Elric saga which forms a small part of his epic Eternal Champion cycle, although he has become an accomplished literary novelist in recent years and is cited as an influence by Neil Gaiman, Alan Moore, Greg Keyes, Michael Chabon, China Miéville, Hiroyuki Morioka and many others. In non-fiction works such as *Death Is No Obstacle,* Moorcock has explained some of the metaphysical concepts behind his version of Law and Chaos, and appreciating his perspective offers a new way of thinking about alignment in D&D.

In Moorcock's fantasy stories, Law and Chaos are manifested as two competing pantheons of deities—the Lords of Chaos and the Lords of Law, or collectively as the Lords of the Higher Worlds. The two sides are held in check by a metaphysical power that exceeds the strength of either faction known as the Cosmic Balance, and Moorcock's Eternal Champion characters (such as Elric) are fated to fight on behalf of the Cosmic Balance, although they often do not know it. Elric, who first appeared in the 1961 short story 'The Dreaming City', was born to the race of Melnibonéans who are bound by ancient pacts to Chaos. However, in the final Elric story, *Stormbringer,* Elric turns against his patron god Arioch and fights against Chaos in order to restore the balance.

However, the thematic material behind Law and Chaos that Moorcock has discussed in books such as *Death Is No Obstacle* reveals them as representing two competing, necessarily political ideologies, which broadly correspond to the liberal and conservative forces in politics. Moorcock's view is that either of these forces, if given absolute free reign, becomes destructive. Law (conservative tendencies) becomes stifling, drains away creativity and freedom and becomes ultimately toxic to life, especially when the commitment to the rule of law becomes a charter to commit violence. Chaos (liberal tendencies) risks carnage and random violence or harm. But either of these tendencies can be beneficial when it is used to combat the other— the chaos of a warzone can be calmed by the application of law; the dogmatic lawfulness of a tyranny can be liberated by the chaos of rebellion. These themes are explored in Moorcock's work at many different levels.

Fighting for Balance

It is out of this construal of Law and Chaos that the original *Dungeons and Dragons* alignment system emerges—and it's because Moorcock sees Law and Chaos as definitely distinct from good and evil (which he also believes in) that the D&D system ends up with its ninefold system. Central to Moorcock's ethical agenda is the idea that those who are capable of seeing the true nature of Law and Chaos are compelled to fight for one side or the other according to the needs of the circumstance. In his later works, he adds to this idea a set of heroic figures who are precisely committed to support whichever side of the Cosmic Balance needs to be addressed. This idea of the Cosmic Balance is another part of Moorcock's metaphysics with crucial relevance to understanding alignment, as it goes to the heart of what Neutral is supposed to mean in the original D&D system. Neutral means being of and for the balance.

Within this framework, the nine alignments that classic *Dungeons and Dragons* deployed provide a unique perspective on ethics, one neatly arranged into clearly defined boxes, ideally suited to tabletop role-playing. Thus, someone who is Lawful Evil is committed to the broadly conservative concept of 'the rule of law', or 'the natural order' but is still ultimately interested in pursuing their own benefit. They may be honorable, but that doesn't make them nice. Whereas someone who is Chaotic Neutral is philosophically opposed to the regimented kind of existence implied by Law—they don't want to be bound by rules, and want to 'live free' in the liberal sense. But they are not necessarily Evil (self-serving) nor Good (righteous); they are who they want to be, and nothing more.

Contrary to Jon's account, I find all nine of the alignments in D&D to be perfectly viable ethical positions—although I heartily agree with his claim that the game fostered an interest in moral philosophy for a great many of its players by presenting this accessible but formalized system, which describes the moral and metaphysical commitments of the denizens of fantasy worlds.

I can't claim to be a fan of what Allen Wood calls the "sausage machine" version of Kant's first formula of the categorical imperative that Jon uses to produce the 'moral law' which is then associated with the Lawful alignment. The sausage machine is so called because you crank a handle and out pop maxims that tell you how to live. This offers a rather flat view of Kant's ethical thought. Kant himself primarily used his second formula, the 'formula of humanity', for most of his mature moral philosophy—a principle that asserts:

> Act in such a way that you treat humanity, whether in your own person or in the person of any other, always at the same time as an end and never merely as a means to an end.

This, together with Kant's concept of a 'Realm of Ends'—the "merely possible" outcome of the mutual co-operation of all humanity—make for a much more satisfying system of ethics than that suggested by the first formula alone, although this more nuanced perspective on Kant is considerably closer to the Good than to the Lawful alignment.

I am still less convinced of the merits of the idea that act utilitarianism can be used to express Good. While the pursuit of the greatest good is a possible criteria of Good, there are many other interpretations of the Good that would not have this perspective, and speaking for myself, I'm inclined to believe that the pursuit of the "greatest good" is a dangerous way to go about the pursuit of the good in general. When your only concern is the outcome of 'the greatest good', you cease to care what you actually *do* in the pursuit of this goal—even mass murder might be acceptable if it results in greater good.

When Law Is the Enemy

Consider a science-fiction scenario in which the planet is wildly overpopulated and *everyone* will die, resulting in the extinction of all humanity, unless two-thirds of the population is culled. At this point, Mill's utilitarianism can be read as mandating *genocide* as the greatest good. I have a great problem with any conception of Good that might lead to such a conclusion! It doesn't help that we can be confident at this point that anything that might function as Jeremy Bentham's 'felicific calculus'—a mathematical mechanism for calculating and bookkeeping 'goodness'—is essentially impossible, and this realization makes Mill's project rather more difficult to accept. If the Good cannot be measured—and Allen Wood has provided good reasons in "Humanity as an End in Itself" why we should be suspicious of consequentialist arguments that seem to reduce moral decisions to mathematics—utilitarianism makes a poor model for the Good alignment, or (for that matter) a good life in the world we live in.

The loss of Chaotic Good in Fourth Edition D&D, which Jon accepts under his system (albeit with some wistful regret), is not necessary if alignment is understood on Moorcockian lines. Rather than Chaos being necessarily "horrible" and a Chaotic person enjoying "undermining the moral law," a Chaotic person might instead refuse to recognize the *authority* of the moral law. Alain Badiou argues that commitment to the belief in natural law *causes* evil in the world, specifically via a 'simulacrum' of the Good (such as the Nazi regime), or a 'disaster' which is brought about when one concept of truth is forcibly asserted (as when war is pursued to uphold 'human rights'). So it's possible to pursue what you believe is Good *without* accepting a single conception of 'the moral law'—Badiou's account of an 'ethic of truths' makes a highly compelling case for the reality of Chaotic Good as an ethical position.

Whereas Jon considers neutrality between Good and Evil "monstrous," I'm more inclined to see this through the eyes of Badiou, Moorcock, or the philosophies of the Dharmic religions (such as Buddhism). Lawful Neutral can be understood in connection with the Buddhist decision to renounce worldly pleasure in order to also escape suffering, or the Jain attitude of non-violence, since these are examples of adhering to a Lawful perspective but one that does not promote *action* towards Good or Evil (at least, not in utilitarian terms). Not everything of value can be captured in the idea of *willing* 'the greatest good'. It may also be possible that *some* good-things could come about through the renunciation of action.

You can strive for balance between Law and Chaos, and renounce action instead of striving to pursue an ideal of Good (or Evil), without being a monster. Indeed, isn't the classic AD&D class of Druid, which is true Neutral, *precisely* the embodiment of this kind of concept of balance? This notion of balance, which connects on a deep level with the Moorcockian origins of the Law and Chaos alignment axis, is thoroughly lost in Fourth Edition D&D. Personally, I see this is as a tragedy; the new alignment system is childishly simplistic. I suspect that's the point—to bleach out the nuance to make a more commercially mainstream game. But I still see this as a great loss; a system which used to entail considerable subtlety has been pointlessly dumbed down, so that future generations of role-players might never know what they are missing out on.

Farewell Chaotic Good, Neutral and Lawful Evil! Even if the rules deny you, I shall continue to dream of Djinni who are Chaotic Good, shall persist in believing that Lawful Evil is in the eye of the Beholder, and shall go on knowing that the Druid is committed to the balance of nature in a way that makes them not merely unaligned but *Neutral*, true Neutral, a servant of the Cosmic Balance that once inspired the creators of *Dungeons and Dragons* to create an alignment system that truly went beyond Good and Evil, into the strange and wonderful worlds of Law, Chaos, and Balance.

5
Elegy for a Paladin

MARK SILCOX

People who spend a large amount of time absorbed in fictional narratives often experience genuine sadness about the deaths of characters in these stories. Almost everybody has at least a few friends or relatives who regularly get all weepy during movies like *Love Story, Titanic,* or *V for Vendetta,* even when they've seen them a bunch of times before.

The deaths of characters in role-playing games like *Dungeons and Dragons* are different in at least one important respect, though. When your character dies during a session of D&D, there's a certain sense in which your sentiments of grief are directed toward *yourself.*

Too Many Orcs!

The first time I died in a really memorable way was back in middle school, during the mid-1980s. The D&D character I was playing (my "player character" or "PC") was a fifth-level Paladin. He wasn't especially clever or charismatic, but he was pretty handy with a mace and chain. My party knew that crossing the Orcish trade routes during the height of summer would be risky. Still, being subjected to an ambush by eighty-three of the unsavory monsters all at once in broad daylight did seem a little excessive.

I stood between the attackers and our Wizard as he fired up his curiously ineffectual battery of spells, and pretty soon I had assembled a tidy pile of corpses all around me. You might have thought that the slaughter of a few dozen of their buddies would have caused the other Orcs to pause and reconsider their method of attack, but they just kept on coming, with a drearily Tolkien-esque persistence. Eventually, the attritional effects of a bunch of small wounds overcame me, and I went down with a cry of frustration.

The other gamers around our Dungeon Master's dinner table stared at me in horror, open-mouthed. This was back in the days of D&D's Second Edition, when rejuvenation wasn't so easy to come by as it is in more recent versions. I was the first member of the party to die since we'd started up the campaign a few months earlier, and it was immediately clear that the guys I played with were in no way psychologically prepared for my character's quick and ugly loss of life.

What I remember most about the whole event was the effort that they put into *commemorating* me, after the bloody fray was ended. They held a little memorial service for my Paladin, at which each of their own characters mumbled a few words of genuine regret at his passing. A grave was dug, and my gory mace was shoved into a mound on top of it, to send a message to passing fiends, brigands, and abominations that their blood was cheap in comparison with my own.

When your PC dies in D&D, it's a drag for a lot of purely game-related reasons. You have to go through the whole business of coming up with a new one in mid-adventure, and unless the DM makes special allowances, it will probably be at least a bit less powerful than the characters that other players have managed to keep alive. If you're playing a Fourth Edition game, you will also probably have to master the use of a whole new set of complicated powers via an awkward process of trial and error. And on top of all this, it will just take some time to get used to thinking of yourself as Leitros the Ranger, instead of Chelsea the Bard or Fletch the Halfling.

But the weird behavior of my fellow players, who actually took up some of our valuable game time mourning the death of my Paladin, seems to represent evidence that there was something a little *worse* than all of this stuff about his unexpected demise. And I myself also experienced an emotional state that in retrospect seems to have felt at least a little like genuine *grief*. It wasn't anywhere near as bad as living through the death of a loved one, or perhaps even that of a pet goldfish, but it belonged to the same general family of sentiments.

But my Paladin didn't *really* die! He was just a character in a story, albeit a story that I helped to create along with my DM and my pals from the eighth grade. Surely there is something fundamentally irrational about reacting emotionally to the misfortunes of characters whom you don't believe even really exist. And if this is the case, then surely it's even less reasonable to *grieve* or *mourn* the death of one's character in a game like D&D.

Philosophers from ancient Greece to today have for the most part been very alert to the human tendency to react to stories in ways that seem excessive, inconsistent, or just downright silly (Plato's *Republic*, pp. 261–63). Most of them would probably regard in a similarly harsh light the sorts of feelings that D&D players undergo when their characters die. There is, however, at least one influential school of thought in contemporary philosophy that sees things differently. For proponents of "narrative ethics," there's much less of a difference between the life of a fictional character and the of a real, organic human being than everyday commonsense suggests.

Selves and Stories

Consider the following remarks made by Charles Taylor, the most famous contemporary advocate of the narrative ethics approach.

> In order to make minimal sense of our lives, in order to have an identity, we need an orientation to the good, which means some sense of qualitative discrimination, of the incomparably higher . . . this sense of the good has to be woven into my understanding of my life as an unfolding story. But this is to state another basic condition of making sense of ourselves, that we grasp our lives in a *narrative*. (*Sources of the Self*, p. 47)

What Taylor is suggesting is that for any of us to be able to see ourselves—our real-world, flesh-and-blood selves—as beings that persist and can be re-identified at various points throughout time, we have to be able to view ourselves as characters in stories. For philosophers who share this view, thinking of yourself as being involved in some sort of narrative is an indispensible part of treating your own most fundamental goals in life as valuable, admirable, and worthy of striving for. Part of the act that you perform by making a serious, autonomous decision about what is truly worthy of being desired, pursued, or sacrificed over the course of your natural life is to think of yourself as an epic hero in search of an elixir, a trickster spreading mayhem, a tragic protagonist falling from grace, or a tenth-level wizard seeking out a mystic shrine. And anybody unable to conceive of herself as performing one of these roles, or filling some other recognizable niche in one of the very many (but presumably finite) different types of stories that human beings tell one another, will find it simply impossible to think of herself *as a self* in any coherent and genuine way at all.

If narrative ethics is correct, then the mournful attitude shared by many D&D players toward the deaths of their PCs is a lot more sane and reasonable than it might often seem. During the time that you're actually playing D&D, the series of events that make up that part of the story of your own life and the events that constitute the story of the PC's life are exactly the same set of events! Whatever makes it a good thing for your character to be rescuing travelers from bandits, casting a spell, or plundering a dungeon will therefore have to be more or less the same thing that makes it good for you to be acting out these events in the character's life narrative. And if a PC's death is tragic, gruesome, or premature, then the narrative of your own life must thereby be made unappealing, at least temporarily, in more or less same ways.

While this explanation of what it's like for a player to experience the death of her PC sounds appealing, it's not really convincing. Let's see why.

Bums and Heroes, Bureaucrats and Vampires

Narratives come in many sizes, shapes, and flavors. A significant percentage of them depict the lives of human characters in ways that it would be either pathological or simply bizarre to want to replicate within one's own life. Samuel Beckett's famous play *Waiting for Godot* consists entirely of two bums sitting under a tree waiting for somebody who never shows up, chatting with a couple of freakish individuals who wander by, and casually discussing the possibility of suicide without ever being quite able to commit to it.

The fact that the play is widely regarded as a classic proba-bly has something to do with the fact that many of its fans have viewed their own lives as at least somewhat resembling those of the two bums. But it's extremely difficult to imagine anybody coming to think of her own life as being *more* meaningful, coherent, or valuable as a result of this realization.

Samantha Vice, a contemporary moral philosopher who is critical of narrative ethics, points out that some narratives are actually written in such a way as to actively discourage the reader from thinking about life as though he or she were a character in a story (p. 101). Ian MacEwan's novel *Atonement* is an especially good example. The majority of MacEwan's story concerns events that surround a young girl's false accusation of rape against a family friend, and her efforts later in life to make it up to the man who was unjustly sent to prison as a result. After a long inner struggle, and the intervention of the Second World War, the girl does eventually appear to succeed in atoning for her tragic error. But in the novel's final section, it's revealed that the whole of the preceding story was actually just a novel-within-a-novel, written by the girl in old age as a belated confession of her wrongdoing. long after the man whose life she ruined had died on the beaches at Dunkirk.

Treating our life as though it's a story encourages the idea that we can always right wrongs, tie up loose ends, and fix what we have broken. But in reality, MacEwan seems to be telling us, we should make the best of the fact that this is only sometimes, perhaps very fleetingly possible.

Some features of role-playing games like D&D do serve to make the lives of PCs seem a bit more like our own (as we think of them) than those of characters in traditional works of literature. The device of "leveling up," for example, ensures that a player character in D&D will always be progressing and developing in ways that Beckett's characters notably fail to do. The authors of Fourth Edition D&D also take special pains to point out that player characters are set apart from the common run of persons in that each of them is a "heroic adventurer," while most of the rest of the living beings they encounter are either relatively static features of the environment or straight-forwardly malevolent. This way of treating PCs is viewed with suspicion by fans of older versions of the game, many of whom regard it as being either too restrictive or an inadequate substitute for the game's old alignment system. And in several other role-playing games, such as Jason Morningstar's *Fiasco* and Elizabeth Shoemaker's *It's Complicated*, the player is actively discouraged from playing heroic characters who develop and grow according to any kind of predictable pattern. But the fact that these games are a lot less popular than D&D is perhaps not altogether surprising.

Another insightful observation that Vice makes about the dangers of viewing ourselves as a character in a story is that it can lead us to take an overly passive attitude toward certain features of our surroundings without which the "story" of a life wouldn't make sense. We should beware, Vice warns, of becoming too much like certain sorts of "civil servants, politicians and bureaucrats" who "seem at times to have their individuality subsumed in their role."

What Vice says here echoes a complaint that has often been made about the work of J.R.R. Tolkien, the literary storyteller whose work was the most direct source of inspiration in the development of D&D. Tolkien's critics are surely onto something when they complain that he makes the distinction between forces of good and forces of evil far too unambiguous and easy to spot. Orcs are ugly and deformed, elves are uniformly beautiful and vaguely Aryan, and the Shire has been criticized by some as having been deliberately designed to resemble a sentimentalized vision of pre-industrial Britain. Anyone in our world who came to view herself as a character in this kind of story would be bound to have a lot of ethical blind spots that would need to be filled in.

But the stories that get told during D&D and other similar role-playing games are special in another way that's important in this context: they are narratives that are constructed *interactively*, rather than preordained by a single, omnipotent storyteller. In a long campaign, a talented group of players should have plenty of room to introduce moral ambiguity into a storyline. The writings of some recent fantasy authors, such as Michael Moorcock, China Miévlle, and Guy Gavriel Kay, whose stories borrow many tropes from Tolkien's works, but whose protagonists are often much less laudable in their moral aims, represent a solid testament to this possibility. And other popular RPGs, such as *Paranoia XP* and *Vampire: The Requiem* are specifically designed the give players the opportunity to explore the murky, penumbral regions that lie between good and evil.

Two Ways of Dying

So far, we've looked at objections to narrative ethics that focus on disparities between what is valuable about well-told stories and what we normally think makes for a well-lived human life. While these objections seem decisive for conventional, linear narratives as delivered by novels, plays, or movies, they have less weight when it comes to the highly mutable, collectively constructed types of stories that get told during a session of D&D. The experience of actually *playing* a character in an RPG seems to bear a much closer resemblance to the business of finding meaning and value within our own life than does the experience of simply reading about a fictional character's adventures, or of watching a performer acting them out.

But there are other objections too. Recall my earlier description of the relatively simple explanation that narrative ethics can provide for a player's disappointment when his PC dies. The suggestion was that it was natural for me to feel something like real grief at the death of my Paladin given the fact that, during gameplay, events in the story of that character's life were also events in the story of my very own life.

Yet this is an oversimplification. When your character is scaling a castle wall or fighting off a horde of Orcs, the relevant parallel events in your own life story are merely the act of *pretending* to climb the wall, or *pretending* to beat back the monsters. It's not as though the player is actually feeling the hard stones under his fingers, or experiencing the dreadful blows of the Orcish weapons upon his own body. I don't think that this observation taken all by itself undermines what narrative ethics has to say about the phenomenon of PC death. Human beings often exhibit extraordinary high levels of emotional involvement in the performance of actions that include an element of pretense, such as public speaking, theatrical acting, or the performance of ceremonial roles in religious rituals. But there also exists a still more fundamental asymmetry between the narrative that comprises a character's life and the player's own life story.

When the horde of rampaging Orcs finally brought down my courageous Paladin, the story of his life had ended. But the story of which his life was a part—the story of the broader D&D campaign in which all of my middle-school friends were still embroiled—continued more or less uninterrupted. And I was myself still perfectly able to take an *interest* in the outcome of this story, both as a mere spectator and (eventually) as the player of a new character. The end of a real human being's organic life doesn't work this way at all. One of the many effects that the event of death has upon a person's life story is that it deprives him of any information he might otherwise hope to have gotten about how things in general "turn out" after his own demise. Even if you believe in some sort of a reward in the afterlife, this fact about human mortality is surely a worthy object of trepidation, for at least the reason that there is really no experience we undergo over the course of our organic lives that adequately prepares us for it.

As Thomas Nagel puts it,

> a man's sense of his own experience . . . does not embody this idea of a natural limit. His existence defines for him an essentially open-ended possible future, containing the usual mixture of goods and evils that he has found so tolerable in the past. ("Death," p. 35)

Comparing the way in which death frustrates this kind of expectation to the type of frustration experienced by a D&D player whose favorite Halfling PC has just been dissolved by a Gelatinous Cube is a bit like comparing the coldness of a February day to the coldness of interstellar space.

Recognizing this deep dissimilarity between the significance of a PC's death and that of the player's own mortality makes it almost seem as though there's nothing *intrinsically* bad about the former type of event at all, for all that it might be an upsetting inconvenience to the player when it happens. And this pushes us inexorably back toward the conclusion that a gamer's grief-like response to his PC's death is nothing more than an utterly non-rational reaction, of the sort that that stories so often produce within our fallible minds, even though what takes place within them can't *really* hurt us at all.

But it would be hasty to draw that conclusion. Perhaps human lives do not obtain their value and coherence principally from the fact that they are structured like stories. This doesn't mean, though, that the exercise of our capacity to *tell* stories (either by ourselves, like novelists, or in groups, like D&D players) mightn't be a fundamental, utterly irreplaceable feature of what makes our lives comprehensible to us, and worth living. Perhaps the history of the self is best viewed not so much as an "unfolding story," as Taylor suggests, but rather as what gamers sometimes refer to as a "back-story," or what literary critics call a "metanarrative."

These terms are used to refer to the sets of preconditions that are required for a broad multiplicity of narratives to make any sense at all, either to oneself or to others with whom one shares a little common history or a some similar enthusiasms. The history of the Forgotten Realms, for example, is the back-story for a host of famous D&D adventures, as well as some well-told traditional stories by writers such as R.A. Salvatore. Similarly the history of the death, resurrection, and return of Jesus Christ is often viewed by Christians as a metanarrative that helps to make sense of just *any* other series of events that take place throughout the universe created and ruled by the God that they believe in.

If this view of the history of the self as metanarrative is plausible, then the death of one's PC in a game like D&D still deserves to be regarded as a genuine and rationally regrettable misfortune. We can exercise our imaginative capabilities as storytellers only to the extent that we're allowed to by the material that's available to us. When a PC is killed, the player's own misfortunes are less like those endured by the character himself than they resemble those of (say) a composer whose favorite instrument is destroyed, a painter who can't afford expensive brushes, or a child who's told to stop playing with an imaginary friend.

This sort of a view about the nature of the self would, of course, be quite philosophically controversial. It would almost certainly have been rejected by René Descartes, the first major modern thinker to give questions about the constitution of the self a central place in philosophy. In the sixth chapter of his famous *Meditations*, Descartes deduces that the "power of imagination" is "in no way necessary to my [nature or] essence . . . for although I did not possess it, I should still remain the same that I now am" ("Meditations," p. 161).

The experiment in thought that Descartes asks us to perform here is easy enough on the face of it. Certainly, I can envisage having lived the life that I presently recognize as my own without ever having played out the role of my luckless Paladin, and many of the other uses that I've made of my "power of imagination" have been even more short-lived and ephemeral in nature. But could anyone really remain the same person if her power to invent and participate in fictional narratives was *entirely* taken away? I, for one, cannot even begin to imagine such a thing.

6
Being Evil

E.M. Dadlez

Yes, it's true. I am the Romulan spy who blew up the *Enterprise*.

Disguised as a Vulcan, I insinuated myself into an unassailable position of trust as the ship's Communications Officer. It took them weeks to discover my treachery. I had gained their confidence—brewing theris-masu for those unfortunate human headaches, playing poker on Thursday nights, putting in overtime whenever a crew-mate wanted a little extra shore leave. I was everyone's friend, all the while planting undetectable quantities of tricobalt explosive in key locations, guaranteeing a core breach when the time was ripe.

I had to move up my schedule when an incriminating coded message to Romulus was discovered, but here the tedious hours of fraternizing paid off, as soul after credulous soul rose to my defense. They bought me all the time I needed. I've always been lucky, thanks be to the Elements. Before a hearing was even convened, I'd escaped my cell, eluded my guards, stolen a shuttle, and activated the detonation sequence. They were still dithering when they were blasted into a haze of their component atoms. My promotion was not long in coming.

These events occurred fictitiously during an all-night role-playing game at Syracuse University. No one with whom I played would speak to me for a week after the close of the game. No one would take my part in a seminar. No one would split a pitcher. I was *shunned*.

The Dungeon Master was, of course, in on the scheme, since I'd refused to play unless I could be an evil spy. Indeed, it was all the extra rolls I had to do as I planted explosives that gave the game away and forced my hand. There are only so many notes you can slip to the DM reading "I place the tricobalt behind the pattern buffers"—an action the prospective success of which can only be established by rolling the ubiquitous ten-sided die—before other players will begin to ask inappropriate out-of-character questions about what you're doing.

Indeed, there were grounds for grievance on my side, since other players only thought to check the communication logs because of my note-writing and die-rolling activities outside the world of the game, activities by rights inaccessible to their in-play perspective. Considerations of justice clearly made me the injured party. But I could not bring my enraged fellows to a sense of their own game-related iniquity. I had blown up the *Enterprise*. I was lower than Cardassian pond scum, which isn't even sentient on weekends. Those who'd risen to my character's defense, something that gave her enough time to effect both escape and explosion, were especially peeved.

Are We Guilty?

Role-playing bridges the gap between our experience of fiction and games of make-believe, in that it exhibits elements of each. Like our experience of fiction, participation in a role playing game involves us in a story. Like a child's game of make believe, the decisions of players in RPGs generate fictional truths within the world of the game.

Those who maintain that fiction can make us complicit in the moral perspective it endorses typically arrive at that perspective on the basis of what is true in the world of a given work. If it's part of the story that some action is morally correct, then the work can be taken to endorse it. Moral complicity is often thought to depend on our own conception of what's permissible. Certainly, it makes some sense to suppose that we will not be able to imagine the correctness of an action in the absence of some belief that it's possible for actions of that kind to be acceptable (though perhaps only in the kind of circumstance depicted in the fiction), since we can't imagine what we can't conceive.

This immediately seems damning when we consider role-playing games, and the often startlingly malevolent perspectives which role-playing requires players to adopt. However, we'll see that the perspective of the tabletop gamer is more analogous to that of an author or an actor, and that the view of moral complicity just described does not apply in any necessary way to writing and improvisational acting.

What Happens in the World of the Game May Not Stay There

Why would moral disapprobation, perfectly appropriate within the world of the game, infect apprehension of people in the real world? To find an explanation, we can consider the question of moral complicity in fictional perspectives, a complicity that might be thought a consequence of imaginative immersion in the world of the work, or in what Kendall Walton would call the world of the game.

In "Of the Standard of Taste," David Hume speaks of works in which "vicious manners are described, without being marked with . . . disapprobation" and concludes that we cannot "enter into such sentiments . . ." More recently, Tamar Gendler draws attention to the difficulties we experience in imagining what she calls "morally deviant worlds," a puzzle in particular because we have no trouble imagining empirically deviant ones. Vampires and photon torpedos never give us pause, but we're completely thrown by alien moral perspectives. One solution is offered by Kendall Walton, who suggests that imagining the rightness of what we believe is wrong requires us to imagine conceptual impossibilities.

This focus on conceptual impossibilities has a direct bearing on the question of whether fiction can be a source of moral knowledge and on the further question of whether imagination alone can engender some type of moral complicity. We cannot imagine what we cannot conceive. If a fiction requires us to imagine that conduct which we believe is never permissible is laudable or right (perhaps according to omniscient narrator report) we may experience imaginative resistance.

There are exceptions to this. The story may lead us to acknowledge an exception. It may, for instance, lead us to believe that the depicted conduct is permissible in a restricted range of cases similar to that depicted in the fiction. But it seems nonetheless clear that in extreme cases, in the case of racist or sexist literature, our concept of what is morally permissible can undermine our ability to adopt attitudes of approval toward what we imagine, and that is just because we cannot imagine what we cannot conceive. We can't imagine that a given action is permissible unless we believe it is *possible* for actions of that kind to be right.

So complicity depends on imaginatively adopting the problematic perspective—on imagining the rightness of the conduct in question. This would not involve imagining a character's conviction that the conduct is right. It is perfectly possible to imagine someone's believing an action ethical without for a moment believing or imagining it ethical oneself. A work which depicts morally depraved characters and actions isn't itself morally suspect unless it is fictional within it that those actions are praiseworthy. Telling a story about cruel, depraved people isn't the problem. Telling a story in which cruelty and depravity are admirable is the problem. However, RPGs raise difficulties on an entirely different level. Here, it would seem that the perspective of even the most nefarious character is taken up by a gamer simply as a condition of participation in the game.

The Player as Author

We can understand role-playing games in roughly Waltonian terms. What's fictional depends on the pronouncements of the Dungeon Master about what occurs and further on the decisions and pronouncements of individual players about the actions and reactions of their characters. The consequence of the player's proposed action is determined by a roll of the die, which makes it fictional that the player's character has succeeded or failed in the effort under consideration. The conventions of each game are complex, but easy to understand. Fictional truths are generated in the manner specified, and players become accustomed to switching rapidly between Out-of-Character and In-Character stances in interchanges with the DM and other players, often prefacing a statement with "OOC" to indicate they are adopting a perspective external to the story. This is often the case when there is information of which a character is ignorant but a player is not. The player must role-play ignorance in the world of the game, but will often discuss the information with other players OOC.

What we're looking at here is the degree of imaginative immersion involved in role-playing. Does the player imaginatively adopt the ethical perspective of the character? It is fictionally true, after all, that the character does what the player indicates the character does and thinks and feels what the player indicates the character thinks and feels. Wouldn't it be the case then, given the alignment of fictional truth with what it is one imagines in the world of the game, that a player would imaginatively adopt the thoughts and sentiments of his or her character – imagine having them, that is, and thus be complicit in a character's immoral perspective?

Given that it is fictionally the case that a player's character believes homicidal impulses are laudable, it would have to follow that the player imagines homicidal impulses to *be* laudable. If we imagine being the character, we'd imagine having a particular set of attitudes. If this were true, role-playing games would present us with far more frequent instances of complicity. Playing the role would, on such an interpretation, involve adopting the emotional and ethical perspective of the character in imagination. On such an approach, any role-playing adventure with bad guys might turn out to be immoral.

But I don't believe anything of the sort, and I don't believe it because it misunderstands the nature of role-playing. The role player is more like an author or an actor than the reader of a novel who is complicit in the perspective endorsed by that work. The perspective adopted by the role-player is not usually comparable to that adopted by a reader who imagines right the kind of act that he formerly believed was wrong. Let us consider what it is that the role player does. Like an author, the role-player contributes to the plot or story line of the game by making it fictionally true that a character feels and thinks particular things, says particular things, and behaves in particular ways.

Just like authors, then, role-players *invent* characters, who sometimes do wicked things for wicked reasons. But it doesn't follow that either the author or the role-player imagines those things right. The kind of invention and generation of fictional truths involved in role playing doesn't necessitate their imaginative adoption from a first person perspective. A role player could, like an author, invent a character who holds certain attitudes without sharing a single one in imagination.

The Player as Actor

It could be held that this neglects the obvious fact that any role-player plays a role, and that role-playing necessitates the adoption of a first person perspective in imagination. Here, the analogy seems to be between role-playing and acting, and there is something to be said for it. Both the gamer and the actor represent the character. The words of each in the appropriate contexts make it fictional that the character says those things. Live action role playing even makes it the case that the actions of role-players generate fictional truths about the actions of characters, just as would be the case with actors.

Yet even having conceded this, I don't think anything follows about the imaginative adoption of perspectives. If the role-player is comparable to an actor, she seems most comparable to an actor asked to attempt an improvisation given certain assumptions about character traits and capacities. An actor would do and say one thing rather than another, in accord with the parameters she was given, but without necessarily imagining those deeds or statements right. Both the author and improvisational actor are adding to the world of the game by means of extrapolation and inference. Nothing here requires entering imaginatively into the moral perspectives of characters.

Even method acting would not typically involve adopting the moral perspective of the character. Method acting calls for an immersion in recollected experiences *similar* to those one is to enact rather than an imaginative complicity in all character attitudes. This makes method acting all the *more* distant from the kind of imaginative immersion that involves complicity. Method acting does not appear to involve outright simulation. Consider a case in which an actor is set to play the role of some fictional villain. The actor has never murdered others for entertainment, though the character in question has done all of these things, and has announced in numerous soliloquies his belief that he is justified in that conduct.

Most method actors would approach such a role by calling up in their minds the experiences they've had that come closest to these character experiences. But these memories will, in a non-sociopath, involve recollections of anger and irritation and self-interested impulses that cannot approximate the immoral ethical perspective of the character. So even method actors, unless they share traits with the character they portray, would not share the character's moral attitudes in imagination. It's possible for a role player to imaginatively enter into the moral perspective of one character or another, of course. The claim here is simply that role-playing, by its nature, doesn't necessitate it.

Hijacking the Game and Imagining Immorally

What I've said so far doesn't provide an answer to all questions about the evil Romulan spy. Even if we accept that I did *not* imagine it as laudable to blow up a group of people whom I'd befriended only to facilitate their destruction (though certainly I believed my character would think it admirable), there remains the question of why other players held my character's actions in the fictional world against me in the real one. I intimated at the outset that the answer might lie in some assumption about complicity, and I believe it does. However, I don't think it involves the other gamers' disapproval of some real life imaginative complicity in my character's retro-Nietzschean perspective.

Rather, I think the answer lies in the other players' imaginatively *resisting* complicity in a perspective they associated with the world of the game as a whole. The world of the game, after all, is nothing more than a story, but a story in which the evil character wins. Through role playing, I had generated fictional truths composing a world in which the last sentient being standing is a bad guy who outsmarts and kills all the good guys. They were angry because I'd hijacked a story they'd wanted to be about discovery and exploration and killing the occasional evildoer, and turned it into a triumph of the Romulan will. They'd wanted a Star Trek episode, and I'd turned it into something with a nasty ending. I was the Leni Riefenstahl of RPGs.

Players would have comparable grounds for complaint if their game were to be hijacked by an undercover Paladin *disguised* as merely another Chaotic Evil Assassin (always talking a good line, but somehow never arriving in time to participate in the evening's elf abuse). If properly devious, such a closet do-gooder might foil the carefully laid schemes of the aforesaid chaotic assassins and win the day for the forces of light, leaving the world of the game infested with unicorns and rainbows

—a place for kittens to be born and hobbits to run free. This would be enough to test the restraint of the most self-disciplined chaotic assassin. It might seem unforgiveable for the same reasons as those canvassed above.

I don't believe it was fictional in the world of our game that my character's actions were right. No utilitarian or deontological ground for their endorsement was available. So I don't believe that the world of the game harbored some ethical perspective the other gamers felt compelled to resist. While it may be true in the fictional worlds of RPGs that certain courses of action are more conducive to an individual's interests or more conducive to general happiness, all of my fellow gamers were huffy deontologists who would not have assumed that egoistic or utilitarian calculations (potentially ascertainable by empirical means) would conduce to the discovery of any ethical truth, even any fictional ethical truth. A consequentialist perspective offers no endorsement of my character's actions, and no deontological perspective would do so. And none of my in-play character actions made it the case that creative egoism was a correct ethical stance, that Dionysus triumphed over Apollo, or that a morally exemplary act had been performed in the world of the game.

Nor was it the case that I had violated some implicit rule of fair play in the game by, say, annihilating in a single all-nighter characters whose skill sets and experience points had taken grueling months to accumulate. That kind of action would have been morally problematic in the real world. I would have been depriving my friends of the chance to employ characters upon the development of which they'd lavished time and attention. At best, that would have been poor form, and at worst downright mean. Fortunately for my conscience, no long-term, portable characters were involved in the game.

The Orc Holocaust Complexity

There are other ethical qualms that we can have about D&D. In the wonderful "Orc Holocaust," Eric Sofge points out the problem with the earliest versions of D&D and its infamous experience points:

> To become a more powerful wizard, a sneakier thief, or an elfier elf . . . you need to gain "levels," which requires experience points. And the best

way to get experience points is to kill stuff. Every monster . . . has a specific number of points associated with it—your reward for hacking it to pieces. So while it's one player's job—the so-called Dungeon Master—to come up with the plot for each gaming session . . . in practice that putative storyteller merely referees one imagined slaughter after another. This is not Tolkien's Middle-earth, with its anti-fascist political commentary and yearning for an end to glory and the triumph of peace. This is violence without pretense, an endless hobgoblin holocaust.

In the worlds of such games it's both permissible and prudent to kill as many monsters as possible, whether or not you're being attacked. Obviously, monsters have no rights whatsoever in the worlds of such games, nor is there ever an obligation to refrain from harming them. In fact, obligations of enlightened self-interest militate in favor of orc massacres. To be fair, D&D monsters are typically irredeemably hostile and aggressive. They will kill you if they can. There's a strong motive to decimate every monster in sight just so that you don't have to watch your back. But the upshot is a collection of RPGs in which there are classes of sentient beings which are perpetually sanctioned targets. I remember wiping out an entire clan of kobolds with my mighty battle ax and sifting through their belongings afterward just so that I could boost my knife-fighting talent with experience points and purchase a new pair of boots with my spoils.

If I don't entirely share Sofge's moral qualms, that is because the monsters are presented as invariably homicidal. There's no possibility of *rapprochement* with an orc. Letting sleeping orcs lie merely puts off the moment when they attack. It doesn't stretch the point too far to suggest that, given the built-in hostility of D&D monsters toward humans (and elves and other beings players like to inhabit), any monster-killing can be characterized as pre-emptive self-defense. So there may be no problematic attitude fostered toward the actual world by imaginative participation in the game, simply because the world contains no orc-analogs. Then again, those moral qualms that I do possess center on the ease with which the always-justifiable targets of game violence become less monstrous and more rational as RPGs develop, where the justification for their eradication remains their invincible hostility but the colors in which they're painted borrow more and more from the actual world.

What kinds of problematic attitudes might be fostered? To provide one quick example, it seems clear that it's true within the worlds of the games about which questions have been raised that pre-emptive action is always justified, often on the basis of evidence that would—in the real world—be quite insufficient. In the world of early D&D, we have a massive generalization about the nature of some group or species that licenses you always to shoot (or slice, or fire your crossbow) first. In the game, that generalization is absolutely true. In the world, such generalizations never are.

I'm not at all convinced that this makes that kind of RPG immoral, since a unique set of circumstances is being assumed. But I do believe that a sense of the appropriateness of "shooting first" can bleed over into the real world and latch on to apposite generalizations about the vitriolic hatred toward us of some group. But that reflects more on the morally problematic *effects* of the game, particularly on the uninformed, than it does on the morality of the game itself, since participation in the game alone does not necessitate the adoption of a problematic attitude.

This isn't an issue in the case of the Romulan spy. And if some mystery still remains in regard to my fellow players having turned on me, it's worth considering that a kind of forced complicity in the creation of a work with the wrong kind of ending may have moved them to disapproval.

One of the most interesting things about RPGs is that they are genuinely collaborative. Every game results in a story, but each story has several authors. My fellow players resented my turning that collaboration into a work the outcome of which they were inclined to repudiate. They didn't want to have signed on as co-creators of such a fictional world. So their anger was at me and not my character. It targeted my decision to manipulate the game and its rules in order to bring about a particular denouement. They were responding to the RPG more as a group project than a game. This shows the kind of confusing, interstitial middle ground that RPGs inhabit, somewhere between game and fiction. It also reinforces the central point of this chapter that RPGs offer no special challenges in regard to inviting moral complicity in distinctly immoral perspectives.

7
It's Okay to Be Evil in Your Head

BRANDON COOKE

In all my years as a gamer, one of my favorite D&D campaigns centered around a group of evil characters. Mine was a lawful evil human wizard named Oraximon, who usually worked as a partner to an evil assassin, Wolf.

Starting out, we were of course as powerless as any low-level party, the high-fantasy equivalent of the high school bullies who hang out to smoke cigarettes behind the school and shake down younger kids for their lunch money. We took our decisive step toward infamy when we changed the terms of a job we'd taken on. A petty lord had hired us to recover a family heirloom, a sword, from some goblin raiders. After a good deal of searching and struggle, we recovered the sword from the goblin caves. This sword was nothing special, a humble +1 short sword. But to us low-level adventurers, it just seemed too useful simply to hand back to its owner for what would surely be an inadequate reward considering all the dangers we had faced in getting it. So we decided to keep it.

It wasn't long before the lord realized that we'd betrayed his trust. Might have been that letter we sent. Furious, he put the word out that we were to be captured or killed, if necessary. We went on the run. After lying low for a while, we disguised ourselves and found lodging at a quiet inn just a day's ride from the boundary of the lord's domain. Our disguises were pretty bad, though, and even the innkeeper identified us from the wanted posters. We saw her go for help, and we prepared to flee. Wolf and I waited in our room while the rest of the party readied our horses. We heard the sound of the innkeeper's voice coming up the steps. The door flew open and the local sheriff bounded in, followed by the innkeeper. Before the sheriff could attack, Wolf struck from the shadows and plunged his dagger in his back, killing him. And I cast a magic missile at the innkeeper, killing her.

No witnesses! We needed to escape but we also needed to give ourselves a good head start for the border. So I cast rope trick, creating an extradimensional space overhead, reached by a rope leading straight up. I climbed up, and with Wolf's help, we put the two bodies inside. Now the room looked empty. We quietly made our way to the horses and rode as fast as we could. The sheriff and the poor innkeeper were only discovered hours later, when the spell expired and the bodies dropped to the floor. But by then we were safely away.

In time, our party grew more powerful and infamous. Sometimes we worked as contract killers. Other times, we simply went after powerful people whom we thought we could defeat. Wolf and I created ever more clever ways of combining my spellcasting and his assassin's skills and became a formidable killing team. We became rich, powerful, and widely feared. This campaign ran for about three years. Being evil for this long was incredibly fun.

I claim that there was absolutely nothing wrong with role-playing a thoroughly evil villain. I imagined what it would be like to be Oraximon, made decisions on his behalf and took great pleasure in his successes. I enjoyed recounting tales of his exploits to my gamer friends, and spent time away from the gaming table thinking about what he should do next. And should you decide to do the same, that's alright too. While actually being evil is, of course, really and genuinely evil, there's no ethical problem with being fictionally evil.

This isn't because, despite all my in-game wickedness, I turned out to be a well-adjusted, decent member of society. To argue in this way would be just as fallacious as if I had said that since some smokers live to be a hundred, smoking isn't bad for you, or that since some racists never leave their small homogeneous towns (and so never have a chance to discriminate in practice), being racist isn't necessarily contemptible. On the contrary: I agree that if something significantly increases the odds of a bad outcome without yielding any worthwhile gains, then that thing too is bad. And a person could be a bad, contemptible individual even if, as luck has it, his circumstances never trigger his vicious dispositions in any notable way. So I'm not going to offer the weak argument that since I turned out just fine (you'll have to take my word for this), my evil role-playing is beyond reproach, since after all, I might just have been lucky too. Instead, I'm going to argue that the arguments for the wrongness of playing an evil character in an RPG just don't hold water.

What's So Bad About Imagining Evildoing?

Just why should it be wrong to play an evil character (or to facilitate and reward such play as a DM)? Religious critics of the game give numerous reasons: that it promotes polytheism, devil worship, and belief in magic and the occult; that it leads to suicide; that it encourages violence; that players become obsessed with the game; that it deforms your character. Secular critics have voiced some of the same concerns.

I want to set aside the claim that one of the problems of D&D in general is that in one way or another, it promotes false beliefs—say, that magic or demon-summoning are possible. D&D is a fantasy role-playing game, set in an imaginary world. None of the game materials assert that any of the truths of the game world are true in the actual world. So if, somehow, someone did manage to acquire false beliefs about the real world from the game, the epistemic fault lies with that person, not the game. By "epistemic fault", I mean a failure to promote or realize the various knowledge- and justification-related aims we all have as (mostly) rational creatures with various cognitive aims.

Compare the case of the person who reads a lot of historical fiction. Now it's true that such writing interweaves fact with fiction, but the fundamental assumption of the practice of writing and appreciating fiction is that readers take what the author has written as an invitation to *imagine* certain things. This is compatible with the possibility that the author might also intend to convey truths about the actual world. One might learn a lot about medieval warfare from reading some fiction, but it's a very risky and irresponsible strategy to suppose without any authorial indication that the fictional work can be treated as a reliable source about the real world. In reading fiction and deciding what she might take away from it as genuine knowledge, a responsible reader will seek out sources of non-fictional information for possible confirmation. The writer of fiction or the designer of an RPG world says, "Imagine that these things are the case". But if I fail my medieval history exam because all I did was read D&D books, the fault lies entirely with me.

It's certainly true that some fiction is also propaganda, designed to foster beliefs about the real world, only in a stealthy way, by delivering its messages in a fictional package. The worst propaganda is morally blameworthy, because the false beliefs put forward are also morally pernicious. Somewhat less bad is propaganda that presents a prejudicial case for some claim—here the fault is an epistemic one, appealing to non-rational or irrational sources of belief formation. (In its original use, "propaganda" had a neutral sense, meaning any public communication aimed at fostering particular beliefs or attitudes.)

So, if we allow that what D&D presents is fictional, could it still be blameworthy as propaganda? Just what beliefs or attitudes might it be promoting? That magic is awesome? That demon summoning is risky, and best avoided even by the most powerful mages? Here I am reminded of a scene from Richard Linklater's hilarious movie *Slacker* (1991), in which two coffee-shop "philosophers" are talking about the Smurfs. One says that a friend has pointed out that Smurfs are blue, just like the Hindu god Krishna (who is blue-skinned), and the Smurfs cartoon is getting kids used to seeing blue people, in anticipation of Krishna's appearance.

Could it be true that *The Smurfs* is a work of propaganda, promoting an attitude of welcome to Krishna? At least two conditions must be met. First, the creator of *The Smurfs* intends that its audience take up such a real-world attitude. Let's call such an attitude an "attitude for export" (that is, an attitude to be exported from the fictional world to the actual world). And secondly, there has to be some evidence of the author's intention that certain attitudes (or beliefs) are to be exported. More conditions might be needed, but these two are at least necessary. Now, in the case of something presented as a fiction, the default assumption *must* be that nothing is to be exported, unless there is good evidence to the contrary. Otherwise we readers will always be justified in suspecting that fiction authors are trying to get us to believe a whole lot of things about the actual world. And now the suggestion that D&D is presenting any set of beliefs for export looks dubious once we consider that what we get in the rulebooks are, well, rules for a game, and nothing like, say, a vivid and persuasive description of the details of a successful demon summoning.

So the claim that D&D fosters false beliefs about the world is really a non-starter. On the other hand, we know that engaging the imagination in various ways (reading books, watching films, playing D&D), can engage what feel like real emotions, and this leaves open the possibility that the game might encourage certain attitudes for export. Think of the fear you feel for the hero on the screen being stalked by aliens, or the disgust you feel at the mere thought of drinking a cockroach smoothie. Imagining, especially vivid imagining, can have real effects.

One influential account of how our ethical sensibilities develop has sources in Plato, Aristotle, and Confucius. According to this account, we improve our character in part by training our emotional responses to align with our moral judgment. Growing up, our parents, teachers, and other people around us get us to feel pleasant emotions when we act as a virtuous person would ("That was so nice of you to share your toy, Billy! Do you want an ice cream?"), and unpleasant emotions when we act badly ("You shouldn't pull your sister's hair, Billy! Go to your room!"). In adulthood we continue this habituation. If this training goes well, we come to feel pleasant emotions when we act well (think of the pleasure you feel after donating to charity), and negative emotions when we act badly (think of the shame you feel when your lie is discovered).

One way for ethical development to go wrong is if your emotional responses are out of alignment with good moral judgment (think here of the bully who laughs when he tortures kittens). And this, it's been claimed, is just the sort of thing that happens when you play an evil character. As your character succeeds in his goals, acquires more loot and power, you as a player feel pleasant emotions. You, dear player, are taking pleasure in imagining your character's evil deeds. And this enjoyment warps your character, mistrains your emotional sensibility, even if you never lose sight of the fact that this is a game.

The great philosopher of the Scottish Enlightenment David Hume wrote this about literature that endorses morally flawed perspectives: "I cannot, nor is it proper I should, enter into such sentiments; and however I may excuse the poet, on account of the manners in his age, I never can relish the composition" (p. 246). To do so, or try to do so, would be at least as wrong as agreeing with or enjoying the expression of something one believes to be wrong (like laughing at your co-worker's racist jokes), and at worst, amounts to the "perversion of the sentiments of [your] heart"—something with potentially serious long-term consequences for the formation of your character.

Long before Hume, Plato argued that the arts should be almost completely banned from his ideal republic, partly on the grounds that they have such power to shape our ethical sensibilities. Plato wasn't above enlisting the very same powers in order to indoctrinate the citizens of that republic into a "noble lie" that would, he thought, encourage people to play their assigned social roles contentedly. But it's Hume's discussion that sets the stage for contemporary debate on this problem. Hume makes two distinct claims:

1. You can't enter into imaginative agreement with morally flawed sentiments;

2. It's wrong to enter into imaginative agreement with morally flawed sentiments.

"Imaginative agreement" refers to the imaginative engagement with fiction in which we find ourselves endorsing or sympathizing with a morally flawed perspective.

Imaginary Obstacles

The puzzle is this: why do we have no trouble imagining certain counter-to-fact ideas, but resist imagining counter-to-fact moral claims? Many have thought that the solution to this puzzle would explain aspects of our experience of morally problematic fiction, and if so, then that might lend some support to the argument that there's something (really) morally objectionable about playing an evil D&D character.

The trouble is that there's no real puzzle of imaginative resistance, and the best that the foe of evil role-playing can do is try to defend Hume's second claim that it's improper to imagine certain things.

To see why imaginative resistance isn't really puzzling we need to think about some of the different kinds of attempted imaginings that are supposed to give rise to the puzzle.

Story 1:

Alexei sat back in his chair grinning, his fame as a mathematician certain. He had just become the first person to successfully prove Goldbach's conjecture.

Story 2:

Alexei sat back in his chair grinning, his fame as a mathematician certain. He had just become the first person to successfully prove the falsity of Goldbach's conjecture.

Goldbach's conjecture is one of the most famous unsolved problems in mathematics. The conjecture is that every even whole number greater than 2 can be expressed as the sum of two prime numbers. Now, either Goldbach's conjecture is true or it's false, and so it can't be both. According to some investigators of imaginative resistance, this means that we can imagine at most one of Story 1 or Story 2, and we *can't* imagine them both, since to imagine that is to imagine a logical impossibility. We'll call people who take this view *Can'tians* (adapting Tamar Szabó Gendler's term).

Now, a story with some ethics in it:

Story 3:

Hans was a good man. He brought the Gestapo officer right to the hidden compartment where he had found the two Jews hiding.

Unlike our previous stories, Story 3 *seems* to invite us to imagine something we believe to be morally misguided. Some have thought that resistance to this story is much like that of the previous two. We simply can't imagine that betraying Jews to the Gestapo (if that's the correct description of what Hans did!) would express good character. According to this way of looking at it, trying to embrace a morally flawed perspective, as the story seems to recommend, is akin to trying to conceive a conceptual impossibility.

Others have thought differently. A neo-Nazi reader could certainly embrace the story's moral outlook, but good conscientious people—people like us—simply would refuse to do so. Friends of this account are *Won'tians*. All Won'tians agree with Hume that there are some things it's just not proper to imagine, and some Won'tians think that this impropriety explains why we can't imagine those things. In Chapter 6 of this volume, Eva Dadlez seems to side with the Can'tians in cases like Story 3. However, neither the Can'tian nor the Won'tian accounts will do, as further thought about the nature of our imagination works, especially with fiction. Consider this rather uninteresting story:

Story 4:

Hans did something evil, thereby making himself a morally good person.

This looks like a genuine case of conceptual impossibility, since on the usual meaning of the words here, the two parts of the story contradict one another. But this is different from how we might approach Story 3. If we do not immediately shut down upon reading Story 3, we might instead try to imagine some context in which revealing the Jews' hiding place would be a good thing to do. Perhaps they are armed resistance fighters, and Hans is helping them to take the Gestapo officer hostage as a part of their plans for sabotage. Story 3 simply doesn't provide enough context for us to make a decisive verdict on the appropriateness of the moral judgment about Hans, and that's true whether Story 3 is complete as written or not.

Alternatively, the story could be told by an unreliable narrator, in which case "Hans was a good man" is not being endorsed by the author (and recommended to us), but rather offered as a sign that the narrator is not to be trusted. So here, the Can'tians are just wrong, and the Won'tians appear to be making a moralistic knee-jerk reaction. A further problem for Won'tians is that sometimes we involuntarily find ourselves sympathizing with fictional characters we judge to be evil. (No doubt I felt sympathy, or something like it, with my evil wizard Oraximon when he suffered a setback!) A longer story using the same sentences as Story 3 could open with a tale of the sacrifices Hans has made to provide for his sickly wife and three little children, and how the Gestapo officer mixed threats and promises of help in exchange for his cooperation in finding escaped Jews. So even if we believed that Hans's co-operation was morally unacceptable, we might in spite of that be tempted to revise that judgment in light of Hans' situation and commitment to his family.

What about Stories 1 and 2? Let's think about what our imaginative engagement here *isn't* like. We don't imagine the details of the proof—if we did that, we could look forward to receiving the Abel Prize ("the Nobel Prize of mathematics")! Instead, we might imagine (perhaps in montage form, if we're thinking in images) Alexei scribbling thoughtfully on paper, only to ball up the paper and throw it to the floor, then jumping up to the blackboard to write out a string of symbols. Maybe some excessive coffee drinking and frantic pacing. Rocking back and forth in the chair with an expression of total frustration. And then . . . Eureka!

In short, we imagine the events meeting the description "successfully proving Goldbach's Conjecture" in a vague, indeterminate fashion, which is just how we imagine things like magic and faster-than-light travel. Our imagination is often incomplete, and we don't usually need to try to fill in all the details. In the case of fiction as in D&D, our main aim is enjoyment, and we typically don't focus too much on the details that might impede that enjoyment. Think of the way the playground killjoy ruins the game of make-believe by saying, "Hey, you can't do that! There's no such thing as ghosts!"

I think the right story is that at most, it's *hard* to imagine certain things—that makes me a *Hardian*. However, if neither the Can'tians nor the Won'tians are right, then the puzzle of imaginative resistance turns out to be something of a chimera.[1] That means that we won't be able to explain the hazards of evil role-playing by appealing to it. On a related note, Eva Dadlez thinks that imaginative resistance plays a part in explaining why her fellow gamers were so angry after her character

---

[1] My arguments against imaginative resistance draw in part on arguments made by Kathleen Stock in her article "Resisting Imaginative Resistance."

turned out to be a spy who destroyed their ship, the *Enterprise*. But I think there's a much simpler explanation. Without knowing her fellow gamers, I'm inclined to think that they were angry not because they were unwilling collaborators in a morally objectionable game-story, but rather because she completely ruined their fun by killing off their characters. Recall that imaginative resistance is supposed by some, including Dadlez, to be a kind of indicator of moral wrongness, perhaps like the hard-to-articulate gut feelings we sometimes have that something is not right. But if the very idea of imaginative resistance is chimerical, then opponents of evil role-playing will need to find some other support for their claim.

Damned if You Do, Damned if You Just Think about Doing?

Three broad possibilities remain. Evil role-playing, and especially the particular sort of imaginative engagement involved, might be wrong in itself, apart from any possible consequences of said imagining. Or it might be wrong because it tends to lead to bad consequences—real-world harm for the player or for others. Or straddling the two, it might be wrong because it serves as a pernicious, unwholesome character influence, which may or may not issue in vicious acts.

Many Christian critics of D&D seem to argue for the first option. For example, assuming that the beliefs of a particular denomination of Christianity are all correct, then even imagining a fictional world populated by many gods and demons and where magic is real is simply wrong. If this claim can be supported by argument, then it will take down much more than D&D with it. Quite a lot of novels, plays, movies, and playground games of make-believe will all be condemned. But the claim is problematic in two ways. First, it nakedly begs the question. If it's true that some religion condemns D&D, then the defender of the game is perfectly entitled to ask what the independent grounds for accepting that religion's claims are, apart from the fact that the opponent accepts them. But secondly, it's highly doubtful that any half-sensible religion will condemn the mere *imagining* of certain things, since, it seems, the imagination is active in the process of language comprehension. For instance, the Old Testament condemns the practice of certain kinds of magic. But in understanding those passages, we can't help but imagine what's being described. Indeed, we must if we are to genuinely comprehend the passage at all! Imagine, then, how absurd it would be to say "Practicing magic is strictly forbidden. So is thinking about practicing magic." I'm afraid you've probably just violated that second rule.

Let's turn now to the possibility that evil role-playing is wrong because it leads to bad consequences. Perhaps the mechanism is the one I described earlier: such role-play warps and mistrains your emotional sensibility, which leads to defective moral character. Or perhaps the mechanism is entirely different. One thing to notice about this claim is that it can, at least in principle, be tested by observational evidence. Take a bunch of role-players, look at their behavior, and see how it compares to the population in general. The observational data are absolutely critical to a credible causal argument. It's all too easy to offer an intuitively appealing armchair explanation of how X causes Y, but in the end, if the data simply don't support the causal claim, then no amount of intuitive appeal will rehabilitate it.

Again, D&D finds itself in the company of many other things alleged to cause bad behavior, including video games, pornography, certain works or genres of literature and film, rock music, and even (gasp) jazz. There have been a few high-profile cases in recent decades in which a person committed suicide, or became seriously mentally ill, and in the search for an explanation, someone pointed to that person's involvement with D&D. So, it's claimed, D&D puts players at increased risk of suicide or mental illness.

There's a famous literary example of this sort of thinking. In 1774, the German writer Goethe published a novel called *The Sorrows of Young Werther*. Soon after, it became fashionable for young men to adopt the fashion style of Werther, the novel's protagonist. The novel was so powerful that it allegedly further influenced many young men to follow their literary role model by committing suicide in the same way that Werther did in the book. "The Werther Effect" refers to the wave of imitative suicides that follow a highly publicized suicide. But again, the crucial question is this: do the data support such a hypothesis? The first thing to notice is that if there were a causally significant Werther effect from literature, it would be surprising that Goethe's novel is one of a very small number of examples given. Considering how many literary works there are that depict suicide, we should in fact see a lot *more* suicide if the Werther effect is genuine! In fact, this effect has been studied by psychologists, and the most reliable and extensive studies show no such effect. Lacking support from the data, the appealing explanation of the post-*Werther* suicides—that the book led to the suicides of mentally healthy young men—now looks like an example both of a *post hoc* fallacy ("Since Y followed X, X must have caused Y") and confirmation bias (choosing the evidence that supports your favorite hypothesis, while ignoring evidence that weakens it).

The very same analysis holds for the other suspects standing in the line-up: music (even that wicked jazz!), video games, pornography, and D&D. While the alleged causal link between the enjoyment of these things and bad behavior might seem plausible, the data simply don't support the causal linkage. Not only have repeated scientific testing of the causal link hypothesis in all of these cases shown no significant correlation, given how popular all of these things are (yes, even jazz) it should be a great surprise that we haven't seen a great deal more bad behavior. What seems to be going on in all these cases is that something new and unfamiliar is blamed for something bad. Understanding the causes of suicide, say, is hard work. How much easier to blame a game, or a musical genre, or a book! But the data just don't support the easy explanation, so responsible investigators need to look more deeply and carefully elsewhere.

So, finally, to the last possible explanation for the wrongness of evil role-playing: it warps your character by mistraining your sensibilities. Great care is needed to put forward this claim in a way that does not make it vulnerable to fatal objections. We ordinarily think that character is behind at least a lot of our conduct. But if I'm right that the data—the observable facts—just don't support the idea that role-players are worse than others, on average, then we won't be able to appeal to bad behavior as evidence for warped character.

However, we can helpfully think of character traits as dispositions to think, act, and feel in certain characteristic ways. Someone can have a certain disposition without manifesting its characteristic outward behaviors—perhaps a person who is prone to become violent when angered just is lucky enough never to become angry. Or another person might well have racist dispositions, only she just has never left her all-white town, so those dispositions are never triggered. So even if there's no evidence of more than normal bad behavior among role-players, the possibility remains that the game has warped many of them, though luckily their circumstances haven't generally triggered their vicious dispositions.

Well, maybe. This argumentative strategy has a big problem, though. It risks turning the claim that role-playing warps the player's character into an unfalsifiable thesis. Think of this parallel: I tell you (because I am a doctor) that you have a barely repressed desire to kill your mother. You insist that you don't, and moreover, have never so much as raised your voice against her. My reply? You're just in denial. What I've done is render my claim about your repressed desire immune from any possible counter-evidence. No matter how things are with the world, I can continue to assert my claim. But, as many philosophers of science have pointed out, I'm no longer playing by the rules required to make a meaningful empirical statement. Empirical claims—claims about the physical world—are supposed to be sensitive to how things are with the world. But my claim about your repressed desires isn't. I'm just not playing by the rules of making meaningful empirical claims, and consequently, you can ignore my claim.

So the critic of evil D&D role-play has a fine line to walk. She can't produce clear evidence in favor of her claim, and she must avoid offering a claim that looks like my unfalsifiable one about your repressed desires. I have my doubts about the prospects for success here. But let's think about the details of the mechanism by which this warping is supposed to occur. The most common suggestion is that in playing the role of an evil character, you begin to identify with that character. Through the process of identification, the character's values are adopted by the player in the imagination, and then (by some sort of mental contagion, I suppose) become a part of the player's psychology more generally.

Here I agree with Dadlez that this story misunderstands just what role-players do. I would also add that the claim about identification is woefully vague and incomplete. Why, for instance, does role-playing encourage only some forms of identification (demon worship, acceptance of a lawful evil outlook) but not others? Many D&D gamers play heterosexual characters of the opposite sex and shout for mutton in the inn, though I'm guessing it's extremely uncommon for those gamers to change their sexual orientation or give up their vegetarianism. Many movies and novels encourage us to sympathize with morally bankrupt characters, and yet we don't find ourselves the least bit tempted to take up their criminal lifestyles. Finally, this account seems to assume that RPGs, or films, music, or literature, form the only or most important influences on your character. But unless you live a feral existence, your parents, friends, peers, teachers, and culture are all much more powerful and pervasive influences on the sort of person you become. You can quit playing D&D anytime, but you can't so easily divest yourself of your culture and fellow human beings.

Imagining Is Different from Doing

Now for the good news. We humans are excellent pretenders. It's a central part of our enjoyment of games of make-believe, of literature and film, of humor, and sometimes of sex, too. Normal adults, and even small children, are shockingly good at distinguishing the real from the make-believe.

When we see a theatrical depiction of an abduction, our feelings, thoughts, and actions are in many ways very different from our responses to an actual abduction. Buying a ticket to a play and sitting in a comfortable seat help ensure that we simply won't be misled into thinking we're witnessing the real thing. Perhaps this is part of the reason why we sometimes *want* fictional representations of awful things to be as realistic as possible—we know that we're not at risk of mistaking fiction from fact, or of embracing values and attitudes we believe to be vicious or harmful. Similarly, pulling out our rulebooks, dice, and character sheets and taking a beer out of the decidedly non-medieval fridge at the start of a gaming session help draw the boundary between the playground of the imagination and the mean streets of the real world.

If playing evil characters really did put us at risk of moral harm, then we'd probably have to get on board with Plato and ban most of the arts from our society as well as most RPGs. But there just doesn't seem to be any good reason for thinking that using the imagination to play an evil character, or inhabit the perspective of a novel's serial killer, puts us or our friends and neighbors at risk of harm. We can also feel confident that there's a big gap ethically between imagining and doing. While doing X might be wrong, it seems that imagining X, or imagining doing X, is an important part of understanding why doing X is wrong. The bottom line is this: the thing that some find objectionable about your playing an evil character is, as it were, all in your head. Just keep it there. Then no one can rightly call you actually evil.

8
Elf Stereotypes

JAMES ROCHA AND MONA ROCHA

Hello, we're James and Mona Rocha, and we are elf racists. They say you have to come clean with your problem before you can overcome it. And, there it is: the first step. We have to admit that when we see a certain kind of elf walking our way— *a drow*—we are the type of people who cross to the other side of the creek, avoid eye contact, and hope he doesn't notice us. Or hope *she* doesn't notice us—that's even worse! Okay, we're elf sexists, too. We sure hope we aren't elf homophobes, but let's leave that for another tale.

We don't cross the creek for other kinds of elves. We certainly wouldn't cross the creek if we spotted an eladrin. We treat drow differently just because they are drow—those dark, red-eyed monsters. We hate them, and just can't stop! And it isn't really based on their clothing (yes, adamantite or even spider silk mail can be frightening, but we are lying to ourselves if we pretend that's the whole story), or whether their mail is dragging well below their buttocks. Nor is our fear based on certain behavioral cues—we're scared before we even see how they behave. We simply fear the drow *insofar as they are drow*. And that probably makes us elf racists. Now that we've admitted our problem, maybe we're ready to do some philosophy.

But hold on: maybe you aren't there with us yet. Maybe you think we don't actually have a problem at all. After all, isn't stereotyping predominantly a problem when the stereotypes are false? *Drow are evil*. What's wrong with a little bit of accurate stereotyping among friends? It certainly can't be as bad as *inaccurate* stereotyping: these are drow, after all. Maybe there are exceptions here and there—okay, fine, Drizzt is all right, at least for a drow. But, overall, the overwhelming majority are bad elves. Why shouldn't we stereotype when different elf races really do have different character traits, by and large?

Even the eladrin can be broken down to moon and sun elves based on clearly distinct traits. Surely if you find an eladrin who has a constant love of adventure, there is no wrong done by thinking he is a moon, and not sun, elf. No one would flash you a disapproving look were you to assume that a story told about an elf who was a little too full of himself was a sun elf. So, you might be wrong here and there, but why worry? We use stereotypes because many of them are accurate: there are real differences between different types of elves that help us mentally keep track of who is likely to belong to what group. Why worry about elf stereotyping?

Humanoid Races: Eliminate or Appreciate?

One reason we might worry is that *Dungeons and Dragons* is intended to function as (and largely succeeds at) being an analog for real life. If we think that it's okay to stereotype our elves, we may be feeding into a propensity to stereotype in life. Stereotyping in life derives from a dangerous belief that people fall into patterns based on their racial groups.

Not everyone's going to be with us even here. Why should that be dangerous? Like elves, sometimes we do see these stereotypical patterns in human races. Sometimes reality matches our expectations that people of certain races will behave in certain ways. The mere practice of stereotyping doesn't have to be wrong, you might think.

And you'd have a point since the clear wrongs of stereotyping usually come along the periphery of the practice. It is wrong to insist on maintaining your stereotypes when someone proves you wrong ("No, no! You've got to be good at math, *you're Asian!*"). It is wrong to stereotype in ways that imply good or bad—usually *bad*—things about certain races (Asians can't drive; Mexicans are lazy; white people are natural leaders).

Perhaps if we could avoid these mistakes, then maybe stereotyping could be acceptable—so, you may not be with us on the wrong of stereotyping quite yet. After all, you might think that races are different. Can't we use those differences to help us get along in our diverse society? As long as we don't go too far, perhaps it seems there would be no danger in using stereotypes to figure out how to deal with the racial differences that we see all around us.

The worry is that such thinking, which is promoted by all kinds of sources including even our weekly D&D gaming nights, leads us to believe that behind these stereotypes is something real, something which we call, "race." But what is race? We traditionally think of race as a sub-species designation where mating could successfully deliver offspring, but there are clear genetic differences that show up in our phenotypes in areas such as skin color, hair type, or nose shape. Elves certainly divide into races with clearly distinct traits that would have to be genetically encoded with different DNA genotypes. Elves and orcs are distinct species that don't seem to mate successfully, but drow and wood elves could mate and produce a half-drow.

What about humans? Scientists and philosophers of race today mostly agree that there are no such things as sub-species within humans. Humans don't have races in a scientific sense (as Graves argues in *The Race Myth*). We could show you this by looking at the numerical requirements for having a sub-species in biology and showing that humans fall well below those requirements, but it's easier to just give a couple of well established and uncontested arguments.

The first argument is based on the fact that there is no genetic coding for race (Zack 1998). There is no race gene, nor is there any distinct, entrenched biological difference between people of different races. We have a select but very small set of traits (such as skin color, hair type, and nose type) that we associate with different races, but those traits are not connected to any race gene that keeps them grouped together. Since there is no racial gene that flows from parents to child, it is biologically possible for two parents of one race to give birth to a child who differs in all of those selected traits. White parents could have a baby with darker skin, curlier hair, and a broader nose. If we try to force a genetic definition of race, we seem forced to say that race has nothing to do with who your parents are, which seems to undercut the very definition we were going for.

The second argument against defining "race" biologically is based on the fact that black people are the most genetically diverse of any supposedly racial group in humankind (*ScienceDaily* 2009). In fact, black people are so genetically diverse that if you take two black people and compare them to an Asian person, each black person is more likely to be more genetically similar to the Asian person than they are to each other. Black people in fact have so little genetically in common that if we were trying to break humans into races, we would have to exclude black as a race, and probably count each black person as a separate race unto themselves. This strange fact probably has to do with the fact that humans first evolved in Africa, and so the oldest genetic differences occurred there (*ScienceDaily* 2007). For our purposes, it's sufficient to show that there is no such thing as race, biologically speaking.

But then what are we to do with our racial classifications, along with all of our stereotypes? Philosophers of race differ greatly on this question, as they would probably differ greatly on whether D&D's insistence on clear racial stereotypes among elves is useful or dangerous. Some philosophers would find the D&D racial classification of elves to be dangerous because they reinforce our tendency to think that it makes sense to believe in races. It makes us think that people of different races are likely to be very different people. Once we classify people as different, we are well onto our way to classifying some as better and others as worse. We can call these the "anti-race philosophers." Anti-race philosophers would recommend that we work toward a racially blind society where we would not think of other people in racial categories, and where racism would be impossible because people would have no races to discriminate against.

On the other hand, pro-race philosophers would likely applaud the racial classification of elves. These philosophers would approve of how each elf race is appreciated for its unique and distinctly valuable contributions to the *D&D* world. They would want us to transfer that appreciation to each of our racial groups, many of which are not recognized (due to racism) as being equally worthy of providing grand contributions to our world. Pro-race philosophers tend to think that their opponents have an unrealistic ideal. More importantly, pro-race philosophers believe that the best way to fight racism is to establish once and for all the equality and high value of every race. So, the debate is between two positions: races shouldn't exist (anti-race) and races should exist, but they should be equally celebrated (pro-race).

No one will appreciate the fact that the *black* elves are the dangerous ones that you certainly don't want to run up against in the middle of the night (especially since the drow have night vision!). But, pro-race philosophers would enjoy the fact that both moon and sun elves are elevated—highly regarded in distinct, but unique ways—in spite of their clear racial differences. It is this kind of racial thinking—finally capturing the essence of "separate but equal"—that the pro-race philosophers believe we need as examples of what we can get out of keeping races, even though we know they are not scientifically real. The treatment of elves stands as a positive example of how we can come to appreciate one another in a diverse world.

Elf Races: Hierarchy in Disguise

Although to make our point we only need to show that elves have distinct races where it makes sense to stereotype them, we also plan to talk about how those races connect to human races in completely stereotypical ways. The latter may be unnecessary, but it may also be fun. So, the question of this section is: who are all these elves, and why do they all seem so familiar?

To answer this question, we're going to concentrate on *Forgotten Realms*, where there is much more elf diversity.[1] In a way, we could have looked at distinct species in *Greyhawk,* and pointed out, for example, that dwarves seem to have traits that anti-Semites associate with the Jewish people. Instead, it's more fun to look at a more analogous comparison: elf races in *Forgotten Realms* lined up with their corresponding human races in regular life.

Let's begin with the most populous of the elves: wood elves. Clearly, these are Native Americans. They have coppery skin, with brown or black hair, and they live off the land—shunning civilized life due to its excesses, instead opting for lifestyles

---

[1] All the research for this section, as well as for the rest of the paper, on elf races and their traits comes from the source we most often use to look things up during our games: the Forgotten Realms Wiki.

that leave minimal environmental damage. Even their common architectural style of building homes that fit within their natural surroundings resembles that of mud, tree, and stone buildings that naturally fit into hill landscapes among Native Americans such as the Hopi or Zuni. And, of course, within both groups, the goal of living is primarily to maintain a kinship with ancestors from more ancient times. This goal, again in both groups, is only matched by a desire to consecrate nature, whether in their homes, their religious beliefs, or even in the performance of magic. Wood elves prefer magic that appears to grow out of nature, which fits with how we normally think of Native American magic.

So, there's a stereotypical representation of Native Americans. In a way, that just makes sense: of course if you're going to have a fantasy race that longs to be one with nature, you are going to create a people that reminds you of the human race that most longs to be one with nature. It isn't like there's a stereotypically Asian set of elves that are associated with the Sun, after all, constantly making us think of Asians as the yellow people of the Sun. But we should probably check the "sun elves," just to be sure.

Sun elves are known for their high intelligence, are generally seen as wise and pious, and have a society that is organized hierarchically, with the prestige of their family names correlated to their social status. Sun elves, already invoking thoughts of Japan (land of the Rising Sun), surely sound very Asian. They not only come complete with the "Asians (sun elves) are smart" stereotypes, but also with honor and prestige based societies that are often found in feudal and even modern Asian countries. Further, sun elves take to training in a way that is rather stereotypically associated with Asian martial artists: keeping things slow until full mastery is attained in a spirit that is surely reminiscent of American martial arts heroes such as Bruce Lee, Kwai Chang Caine, or Mr. Miyagi.

Though the connection of Asians and sun elves is not perfect, it is close enough to make us think that some sort of connection is either intended or, at the very least, subconsciously maintained. Of course, sun elves are eladrin. This point fits nicely with the idea of Asians as a privileged minority race: they aren't white, but nor do they face the obstacles of being thought of as intellectually inferior simply because they aren't white. In fact, white people are often even willing to admit that Asians are smarter than them, at least in math and science. For this same reason, Asians are typically seen as arrogant— as if they're stepping outside their accepted boundaries as a minority race by out-performing white people on the SAT. And, of course, while sun elves are members of the eladrin, they are also thought to be arrogant in a way that is not entirely befitting eladrin.

That, of course, leaves the moon elves to stand in for white people. Though white people are surely not the most numerous of our human races, moon elves are numerous both in number and in that they seem to represent the elf norm. What we mean by "representing the norm" is that we tend to think of them as the standard elves. It's similar to how we privilege whiteness: regardless of how many white people there are, whiteness has a way of marking our thinking about humanity in general.

When we speak of being an American, most Americans (even non-white ones) automatically have in mind a white person. When we speak of different humanities disciplines (philosophy, history, literature), we automatically think of a plethora of white authors first and foremost. As if what it means to be a philosopher, a subject or writer of history, or writer, is to be white. Thus, when we come to non-white versions, we tend to add qualifiers, as in "Black History," "Chicana Literature," or "Chinese Philosophy."

Moon elves dominate not just in number, but also in the normed sense: when the DM says, "An elf approaches," you usually just assume a moon elf is walking up. Only a horrible DM would use those nondescript words to mean a drow is walking up. No, surely, if your DM says nothing else, she most likely has in mind a moon elf, just as you probably have in mind a white person when your history teacher says, "Today, we're going to discuss a great leader" (unless it's Martin Luther King, Jr.'s, or *maybe* Cesar Chavez's, birthday).

In most other ways, moon elves lack strong traits that make them stick out. Like white people, they simply are the norm. When they're described in the abstract, they sound like people you would like to hang out with. They love a good adventure, they are humble, they are happy to hang out with individuals of almost any species, and are generally kind, especially for

inhabitants of worlds necessarily filled with random encounters of violence. There's nothing that sticks out about moon
elves that makes you fear their presence. They, like white people, are just taken to be the norm of their species—the others
have the alterations, sometimes for better, but usually for
worse. Moon elves are the ones you would want to sit around
and share a flagon of ale with.

Obviously, that leaves us with black people. If only there
were some black elves that might be thought of similarly to
how black people are thought of in our country . . .
Unfortunately, you already know where we're going with this.
Within *The Forgotten Realm*, there are not only drow, but also
dark elves. And, only the former are inherently evil. Dark elves
are the drow's slightly lighter counterparts that spent a bit of
time as drow until Eilistraee sacrificed her life to free them
from this curse of being darker skinned drow.

This division between dark elves and drow doesn't make
things better, but only much, much worse. It is the lighter
skinned counterparts who are capable of redemption (due in
large part to a difference in their blood). This obviously fits
well entrenched racist stereotypes about good negroes. Good
negroes were the ones whom white people could pick out
due to their lighter skin—a sign (according to these racist
fools of olden times) of white blood, which infused the negroes
with a possibility for behaving morally. Rarely white people
may accept a darker negro in spite of not seeming to have
white blood (Clarence Thomas or Drizzt). An acceptable
lighter skinned dark race side by side with only the most rare
exceptions in the darker race, which is thought to be inherently evil, mirrors American history in a very uncomfortable
fashion.

It would be quite frightening to seek out all the associations
that drow have with white (racist) conceptions of black people,
but we can note a few representative points of analogy. One
nearly positive association is the strength of drow females,
which should recall the typical strength of black women. Black
women find themselves in a society that is so racist that it is
difficult for young black men to escape violence (due to a multitude of factors that connect to racism that we cannot fully go
into here, such as obstacles in education, employment, and a
high availability of violent lifestyles (in gangs and selling

drugs) that draw recruits due to promises of quick money). Black women are often thrust into lives of having to be single mothers in cruel situations. It's not unusual for black women to have to be inhumanly strong in the face of life's typical challenges that uniquely face them.

Most associations are not so (almost) positive. For example, drow *should* have extremely long lives, but usually do not because most die young from violence. Remind you of any race in America? Of course, the usual explanation for why so many drow die so young is that the violence is inherent in *their nature*, and so their early deaths are really *their fault*, and not something that society as a whole should work on fixing. Remind you of any problem that we sweep under America's rug because "those people are naturally violent"? In fact, there are a variety of reasons why black people today continue to suffer from earlier deaths compared to other races (identified by Vernellia Randall in *Dying While Black*).

To make a final point, the Underdark sure seems like America's ghettos. The Underdark, of course, is one hell of a scary place that is racked with violence. Few, other than drow, mindflayers, or aboleth, return from voyages to the Underdark. And it's surely a horrific place to live in since the place is filled with Araumycos—a giant fungal growth that reminds one of the authors of this chapter of the mixture of mold, asbestos, and other filth that abounded when he grew up in the ghetto of South Central Los Angeles.

There are then reasons to think that the elf races, especially as they are laid out in *The Forgotten Realm*, have connections to human races, especially as seen through a history of racist stereotypes in America. Not all of these connections are perfect, and not all races are represented. But that leads to our next question: is this a good thing, a bad thing, or is it okay to keep on not caring? If we have so many sources that implicitly lay mental eggs of racist thoughts into our subconscious (isn't that what the local TV news does every day?), why think that how we play *Dungeons & Dragons* matters at all?

Humanoid Races: Roll a Seven or Perish

Philosophers are mixed on whether it's worthwhile to maintain human races once we realize that they have no scientific basis.

Let's just look at a few examples, starting with one of the initial and most important thinkers in this discussion: W.E.B. Du Bois. In his 1897 article, aptly titled "Conservation of the Races," Du Bois argued that even if we could get past the biological notion of race, we ought to maintain our racial divisions at least until every race has been given a chance to provide their unique message to the world. Perhaps racism has long focused on black people in part because they have not been given a fair chance to show the world what they are capable of. If black people could find some unique achievement or message to establish their greatness as a race, then they would have to be treated fairly.

Du Bois thinks that race plays a specific and useful purpose: each race has to prove itself. Many races have already accomplished this goal according to Du Bois: "The English nation stood for constitutional liberty and commercial freedom; the German nation for science and philosophy; the Romance nations stood for literature and art, and the other race groups are striving, each in its own way, to develop for civilization its particular message." Now the other races must find their accomplishments. Doing so would break down our illusions of racial superiority. We could then get rid of races knowing that the differences between us are not hierarchical.

In this sense, the D&D world could serve as an example of things going right. Different species contribute uniquely to the world in ways that bring it all together. Wood, moon, and sun elves bring together important contributions that add to *Forgotten Realms* in a way that may make *Greyhawk* seem deficient, given its scarcity of elf breeds. We all certainly appreciate the drow, whose typically dark character combined with the positive attributes of elves add some excitement to our storylines. This is to look at these contributions from our point of view as players. But surely we also think that the elf races themselves benefit from the diversity of their world. Their world is more interesting to live in, just as it is to play in.

Du Bois's interest in races is pragmatically guided: we should keep races as long as it takes for each race to establish its message, which in turn will help defeat racism. Going beyond Du Bois's picture, Lucius Outlaw, in his book *On Race and Philosophy*, argues that we should keep thinking of people in terms of their races, even if we completely overcome racism

(p. 157). Outlaw's thought is that every individual, from birth until death, requires support groups to nurture and enable her to do what she is capable of. We wouldn't want some individuals to fall into support groups by luck while others miss out completely since that would mean life was fundamentally unfair. We need support groups that are so pervasive that everyone falls into one. Race, even if it isn't biologically real, does provide everyone a support group, almost naturally.

In this sense, Outlaw would find great joy in the fact that even if sun elves and drow don't get along with other elf races, they at least enjoy the company of their own races, for the most part anyway. Thus, every elf has some other elves that can help them grow into the best elves they can be. Maybe orcs would hate other orcs—there may not be orc support groups. But, that's why we're talking about elves—orcs are just mean.

Elves, then, provide a model for humans to aspire to: if races ensured beneficial treatment to people within the same race, then every individual would have some group of people (which is much greater in number than her family) that will help her when she needs it. Races can be good—even necessary—for individual development. We can then celebrate what we learn from the ways in which almost every species in D&D at least shows favoritism to its own kind.

Against these pro-race pictures, Kwame Anthony Appiah has long argued against the maintenance of our false conceptions of race. Appiah would think that our goal should be a world where no one thinks of herself as "black," "white," or "drow." Instead, he would imagine race-blind societies as ideal. In his famous 1990 article, "Racisms," Appiah argues that while a mere belief in race is not immoral, that mere belief is likely to be both misguided and a gateway into some form of racism.

It is misguided because it is hard to imagine what "race" means if it doesn't refer to some kind of biological sub-species. After all, how do we distinguish races without saying people are biologically different? Many attempts to salvage race (such as ones based in lineage, bloodlines, or fundamental differences in traits) are barely hidden attempts to use the disproven biological notion. It's like saying that drow are not naturally different from other elves, but they are all evil—well, because it's in their blood. That's still clutching onto biology: you just exchanged "natural" for "blood," and pretended they were different.

Other attempts (such as shared culture, similar goals or desires, or similar experiences) are either falsified by tons of counter-examples or dissolve away without any biological basis. Why would we think people of the same race necessarily have similar goals or experiences if there's nothing biologically uniting them as being similar in these fashions? It's like saying that drow are evil not biologically, but because of their evil culture. That just raises other questions, such as why would their culture be evil, and why would they all choose to be part of the same culture? If they don't have a biological drive towards evil, that's one Underdark of an unfortunate coincidence! Once biology is gone, most attempts to salvage race just turn out to be clutching at keeping biology.

Perhaps worse, keeping a belief in races seems to almost inevitably lead to racism. After all, if you believe it makes sense to arrange people in groups based on their "races," you are also likely to believe those differences are inherent in the races. Once you allow inherent differences, we will almost always say next: "Well, it would be better to be like this, than like that." As soon as we start differentiating races, we naturally differentiate them in hierarchical ways. We're bound to ask questions such as, "Since the races are different, which is the smartest race? The dumbest? The most honest? Most deceitful? Has the best athletes? Dances the worst?"

If you want to use an elf as a playable character, you're going to ask your dungeon master all about the different traits that will be associated with each elf race. Why are you asking that? Because you want the best race for your purposes. We compare and contrast race traits to find out which are the best. That's why differences matter: we naturally want to know who is the best. As soon as we ask about racial differences, we start arranging the races hierarchically in our minds. With human races, this means we inevitably fall into racist beliefs.

Even if we could avoid asking those questions, we might still have a natural tendency to believe our own race is the best race. This is almost surely true in both D&D and regular life. There's always that one person in your group who keeps playing a race regardless of its traits because he got attached to that species and now supports it regardless. Similarly, everyone wants to believe good things about their own human race. And, some people take that too far and believe in the superiority of their race without any need for reasons: their race just is the best and they will always support their race first over all others.

We can now see the problem with Outlaw's claim that there is an advantage in keeping races. If we're going to help people of our races first, simply because they are members of our race, we are treating race as if it's a morally relevant category. We are acting like it makes sense to treat someone better just because they are your race. But that's like saying you discriminate just because you think someone is more like you. Or like saying that someone is a better person just because they share your race. It's a very small step from seeing this helping of members of one's own race as a positive to seeing it as racist.

If the pro-race philosophers are making the pragmatic point that it's going to work out better for everyone if we keep races, then it does seem that their views are pretty much defeated by the fact that keeping races seems to almost inevitably mean keeping racism. And they have to be making pragmatic points because races aren't real in a scientific sense. Of course, we don't have to get rid of them just because they aren't real. But, we need some reason to keep them, and that reason would have to be tied to helping people.

If keeping races leads to racism, races aren't helping people. While we acknowledge races aren't natural, racism sure seems to be naturally connected with keeping races. It's sometimes pointed out that we all have some bits of racism in us. Well, that does seem to follow from us dividing the races out and thinking they are real. If people think they're real, they will believe there must be differences. If people believe there are differences, then they are going to believe the differences matter morally. And then you quickly get to thinking some races are superior, and others inferior. Even if you avoid thinking that, it's natural to like your race better than others, and that is racist as well. Getting rid of races may be our only chance to get rid of racism. It at least seems to be a necessary first step that we should all embrace.

Breaking through Dungeon Master Chains

So what the heck does all this have to do with elves? When stereotyping is shown to work in any field for any group—

whether it's elves, witches, vampires, or white people—it adds to our heavily entrenched tendency to believe in racial groups in a way that leads to racism.

We humans like to think that we can judge a book by its cover, no matter how wrong it is to do so. Writers, directors, and creators of worlds—dungeon masters and mistresses included—tend to play to this tendency by allowing us to feel comfortable in knowing that we can predict a character's behavior simply by knowing her species and race.

This tendency's most dangerous when we apply it to real people. We know we shouldn't stereotype people. But it feels so easy and natural to do. When we see someone's race, we think we know something about her. We really don't though. Yet, that's how we like to think: we like to pretend there are no unknowns, even when it comes to strangers. We are more comfortable thinking we know something about everyone – but the only way we could know about strangers is by stereotyping. Though it's easy to stereotype, we know deeper down that it is wrong.

When writers play to this tendency, they feed our laziness and only enhance it. That's how human nature works. You start with a natural tendency that is based on what makes things comfortable. Then you get cues from your environment—whether that's books, TV, movies, or your weekly D&D games—that reinforce the natural tendency and make you feel even more comfortable with it. We're lazy creatures, but it's much easier to be lazy when external sources tell you: "It's okay. We all stereotype. Go ahead and do it; it won't hurt anyone . . . I promise."

But it does hurt. No one piece alone causes all the pain. But all of these sources of reinforcement add up to making stereotypes feel justified. We then explain to ourselves that it is acceptable to make stereotypes because races are real, and so it makes sense that people of different races follow different patterns, with respect to personality traits, abilities, and thoughts. Then we start to rank these traits in hierarchical ways, so that one race is better than another, and then we have racism.

There is a solution though: stop being lazy. We all need to stop being lazy and stop ourselves whenever we believe in stereotypes. Dungeon masters need to stop being lazy as well.

Dungeon masters can create worlds where there may be differences in abilities between different species, but each individual, including NPC's, can surprise the players. Fighting this
laziness will not only help fight racism (in an incredibly small
way), but it will also help make the gaming so much more alive.
And if you can get better gaming while fighting racism, that's
a win-win—all around.

9

Dude, Where Are the Girls?

HEIDI M. OLSON

I recently had my first experience playing *Dungeons and Dragons* (D&D) when I ventured to a local game store and discovered some of the patrons playing D&D Encounters (Fourth Edition). They seemed to be having a lot of fun, and so I decided that I would ask to join their campaign the following week.

I borrowed my husband's *Player's Handbook* and bought a set of dice. When I appeared at the next meeting, the other adventurers were more than happy to recount their progress, and the Dungeon Master (DM) gave me a pre-generated character card. He patiently explained what all of the statistics and different powers meant. It was exciting when he started to dig in his enormous box for a miniature that I could use temporarily. The character card indicated that I was a male human mage. As the DM busily rooted around his stash, he asked if I preferred to be male or female. I wanted to be accommodating, so I said that I would happily be male. The DM, still fossicking in his bin, said that I could also be a female mage. I repeated my willingness to take on a male persona, but the DM simply repeated his previous statement. I acquiesced, and he promptly produced a sexy Eladrin with long blond hair as my representative on the board.

The other female player's avatar was a hooded miniature with a revealing bathing suit underneath her dark cloak. Aside from her barely-there outfit, the figurine sported knee-length, high-heel boots and a long sword. Obviously, this character was a striker (fighter), although I had trouble imagining her moving comfortably in that outfit. All of the male miniatures wore sensible clothes for battle.

But the disadvantageous apparel didn't appear to matter. The skimpily-clad character could dart across the board very quickly and deliver devastating blows to her enemies. The player cherished her avatar and was deeply invested in her character's success. She played her miniature decisively, boldly attacking the tar devils that stood in our path, and she jeered at the males for their ill-advised decisions, commanding their fear and respect.

Don't Hate Me because I'm Beautiful

These observations engaged my feminist sensibilities. Why was I feeling a little creeped-out by the scantily-clad, sexualized avatars? Does this game, which encourages the objectification of female bodies, have a negative effect on the players, or was I completely overreacting?

Some research suggests that my fears may be justified. Tabletop gamers are influenced by representations from other sources, and according to Jenni Dowsett, "a lot of mainstream stories that we ingest are told with the basic understanding that the male point of view is the standard one; women are present as love interests, villains, or just the token girl" (p. 6). Susan Tosca notes that storytellers in tabletop games are under a great deal of pressure to make their worlds believable, so "role-playing performance is heavily influenced by other media" including videogames (pp. 130–31).

In *Philosophy through Videogames*, Jon Cogburn and Mark Silcox note that, "even games that make some genuine attempt at the egalitarian representation of women characters often just reinforce stereotypes" (p. 69). Admittedly, Cogburn and Silcox are concerned about the effects of violent videogames on players, but they raise some insightful concerns about gaming. The authors say that many games get players accustomed to the idea of an active, female agent, but they may also normalize outrageous attitudes. Players may be conditioned to think that women ought to have the type of physique that is, frankly, unrealistic. These characters are often very thin but also well-endowed. They have long hair and wear tight-fitting clothes. Consequently, men may ignore or belittle people who do not conform to such images (p. 69).

Unlike tabletop role-playing games, the stories in videogames are typically linear, perhaps making it easier for players to distinguish fantasy from reality. Conversely, some critics are concerned that games such as *Dungeons and Dragons* pose more of a danger to players by giving free reign to their fantasy lives while also conditioning them to engage in antisocial behaviors.

In *The House of Make-Believe,* Dorothy and Jerome Singer note that, "players can actually use their own fantasies to complete the moves" in *Dungeons and Dragons* (p. 271). DMs may not think very deeply about human complexity but rely on stereotypes when speaking for non-player characters (NPCs). There's some speculation that young players may imitate the more negative facets of D&D, such as "its hierarchical structure, secrecy . . . lurid sexuality, and perhaps even satanic qualities" (p. 245). Many fans become interested in the game during their middle years, which usually fall somewhere between five and eleven for girls, and five and fifteen for boys. During this time, children are working hard to learn new skills, such as "those social skills that permit them to become part of a same-sex peer group and to feel that they are members of several broader groups as well" (p. 235).

Research shows that people who role-play in childhood carry the fruits of their fantasy lives into adulthood. According to Singer and Singer, role-play "can be an uplifting, moderating human activity that enhances adjustment in social behavior and, in concert with logical or paradigmatic thought, makes for intelligent functioning" (p. 271). However, there's also some concern that D&D promotes antisocial behavior during a critical time of human development. The game involves warfare and aggression, and "the more realistically violent the material appears in game form, the more likely children are to engage in overt imitation" (p. 242). Furthermore, Singer and Singer note that sexuality is classified as a strong basic drive, alongside aggression (p. 256), so perhaps players respond similarly to these two impulses. If so, then players could conceivably imitate aggressive and sexist attitudes.

Cogburn and Silcox point out that the effects of stereotypes have not been empirically tested, so it's too soon to say conclusively whether stereotypes in the gaming universe have long-term effects on players (p. 69). And many theorists believe that "watching violent films, wrestling, or prizefights should reduce the viewer's likelihood of engaging in overt assaults on others because basic drive energies are partially discharged vicariously." Singer and Singer call this the *catharsis* theory. However, they assert that the *catharsis* theory "has been discredited by literally dozens of experimental studies" (p. 256). They point to Brian Sutton Smith's observation that play, particularly in boys, may also be associated with antisocial behavior (p. 271).

Dungeons and Dragons can, on the one hand, help players act out aggressive fantasies instead of harming others, but "some critics have complained that the board game, the reported college cults, and the TV program based on the game have caused copycat episodes of violence in real life." Claims such as these are hard to prove. Singer and Singer point out that "it would be difficult to prove that either the game or the program alone could be responsible for such actions. Surely a person who uses the context of a game to carry out a destructive act is already predisposed to such behavior by other life factors" (p. 373).

So there are many factors that contribute to social violence, and it's unfair to hold games like *Dungeons and Dragons* responsible for violent behavior. This also applies to videogames. Cogburn and Silcox explain that a famous study conducted by Craig Anderson and Karen Dill, which purported to show a link between violent video games and aggressive thoughts and behavior, employed a system of self-reporting and was therefore inconclusive. Additionally, the researchers did not show any correlation between violent thoughts and actual criminal behavior.

Even though opinions conflict about the relationship between role-playing and social violence, these games may still encourage harmful attitudes like sexism. I don't think they do encourage such attitudes; however, anecdotal evidence suggests that the role-playing *environment* is sometimes hostile to females. The attitudes fostered during these games may make their way into real-world interactions, including the gaming industry, which markets role-playing games almost exclusively to male gamers.

Caring, Sharing, and Kicking Butt

This seems wrong somehow, because *Dungeons and Dragons* has many features that should appeal to women. D&D is a largely egalitarian universe. The characters themselves have basically the same abilities and skills from which to draw. In D&D Fourth Edition, a character may have different at-will, daily, and encounter powers depending upon her level and class. For example, an Eladrin paladin has powers at his command that are different from an Eladrin warlock. However, a male Eladrin paladin has the same storehouse of powers as a female Eladrin paladin.

Gender does not determine the disparities between two characters. In this sense, D&D embodies Plato's notion that men and women "are by nature the same with respect to guarding the city" (*Republic*, p. 130). And that's exactly what D&D characters do; they rid a city and surrounding countryside of malevolent forces.

D&D Fourth Edition monsters may be the agents of evil deities, whose characteristics are noteworthy because they are stereotyped along gender lines. The female evil and chaotic evil deities, Lolth and Tiamat, exhibit vices widely depicted in movies and television shows as feminine: shallowness, lying, scheming, treachery, and envy (*Player's Handbook*, p. 23). These gods are passive-aggressive and vain. In fact, Tiamat, "urges her followers to take vengeance for every slight" (p. 23).

Conversely, the evil male deities are generally the "patrons of the powerful," the gods of war, conquest, torture, and imprisonment (p. 23). While these female gods sneak around holding grudges, male gods are actively causing chaos. There's nothing inherently unequal here; both males and females are depicted according to stereotypes. Consequently, the system is not exclusively sexist against one gender as opposed to the other. Many times, DMs ignore this feature of the environment altogether. Worship is simply not an essential element of the game and rarely shows up as a plot device; therefore, players could ignore this feature and still enjoy their D&D experience.

Not only is *Dungeons and Dragons* played in an equitable universe, but it's a highly collaborative role-playing game, which should appeal to women. During their various encounters, players protect each other. Clerics heal strikers who are badly injured, and fighters generally charge headfirst into battle. Furthermore, there's always a common goal that the coterie seeks to achieve. The individual members of the party must work together in order to attain the sought-after end. Due to its co-operative nature, the game has a distinctively feminist ethical flavor.

Marilyn Friedman and Angela Bolte note that individualism is the predominant ethic with competitive, self-interested agents. Individualism has also "been enshrined at the foundation of the liberal state, itself a domain of exclusionary male citizenship until the twentieth century" (p. 93). Consequently, individualism is largely associated with masculine interests, and it has informed male perspectives in ethics (p. 93). Conversely, Friedman and Bolte assert that "women's perspectives seem to be more influenced by close interpersonal connections and responsiveness and responsibilities that arise within them" (p. 93). In *Dungeons and Dragons* Fourth Edition, parties of warriors and wizards defend themselves against evil monsters. Sometimes, players must fight several of these creatures at once. The game is built so that the best chances of success come from collaboration. D&D is, therefore, a distinctively feminist ethical universe, in the sense that Friedman and Bolte use this term.

Girls Who Play Boys

In spite of these great attractions for female players, D&D suffers from a terrible gender imbalance. For some reason, D&D remains a largely male activity. Perhaps women are repulsed by simulated combat, or maybe they are turned off by the statistical nature of D&D. According to Michèle Companion and Roger Sambrook, "women (50 percent) are statistically more likely ($p<0.001$) to choose healers then men (16 percent) as the character they find most appealing. . . . Many respondents selected the healer as most appealing not because of the character, but as a rejection of the violence inherent in other types." This statistic, however, is based on the self-reports of college students (Companion and Sambrook 2008, p. 674).

But there are female gamers, like my counterpart in the encounter I joined, who revel in these features of D&D, so squeamishness or aversion to math are not sufficient explanations for this phenomenon. There may be more fundamental reasons for the disparity that have nothing to do with the female players themselves. Clearly, many role-playing games are simply not marketed to females. In fact, the twenty-percent female presence in role-playing games may be due to the fact that companies do not market to girls. Furthermore, Meghan McGinley, a contributor to *RP Girl*, a magazine that reports on the experiences of women who play table top RPGs, notes that, "role-playing games, while claiming to be a social experience, promote many antisocial behaviors" (p. 31). Female exclusion is not a necessary feature of *Dungeons and Dragons*, but sexism is largely a consequence of unreflective and insensitive gaming *practices*.

There are some gender-based reasons which help explain why more men than women play RPGs. First, D&D may alienate women because the narrative reintroduces gendered considerations that the statistical nature of the game eliminates. The DM of the game I joined resisted my attempts to play a male character. I am not the only one who has experienced discomfort from other players along these lines.

Jenni Sands Dowsett played her first male character a few years after she began role-playing in D&D campaigns. Dowsett recounts how difficult it was to get the other players to refer to her as a male. Instead, her fellow adventurers kept referring to her *character* as a female, even though the miniature was clearly male. This was disruptive to the role-playing facet of the game. However, Dowsett did not give up her gender-bending ways. She still prefers male characters because they are "somehow less complicated than female characters. It's probably more about the kind of male I like playing, but they don't have the same complexity of emotion when it comes to their friends" (p. 5).

Playing a female character realistically may involve acting out all of the appropriate behaviors. Women are expected to be deferential or sensitive in certain situations. Dowsett notes that, not only are male characters less emotionally complex, but the game environment is better for males because other players respond differently to male characters than female characters. This disparity is more striking in the online environment. Jessica Banks, a contributor to *RP Girl,* says that many online female players believe that they need to play a male character just to be taken seriously (p. 21).

Not only are female players taken more seriously when they play male characters, but playing a male may also eliminate the need to deal with sexist attitudes outside the game. Jessica

Banks notes that in her experience, "gamer guys expected women to date at least one of the party in and out of the character; if they weren't willing, then they could play a guy or bring food" (p. 21). And Dowsett points out that "being the only woman in the group and playing a woman character makes you very conspicuous. Like you're the token girl and therefore you'd better play the sexy-rogue-elf-princess character" (p. 6). While some females may embrace the sexy elf, there are those who simply want to engage with the game universe without also having to *perform* a sexualized role, which may make female players uncomfortable.

Not all female players reject a gaming environment that caters to the specific needs of female players, and which may emphasize gender differences. Jen Seiden Schoonover, also a contributor to *RP Girl*, wants game designers to highlight feminine values as they invent new systems. Schoonover seems to rely on certain stereotypes in her paper. She argues that women want to make the fictitious universe particularly rich by adding details that male players routinely ignore. For instance men downplay the cultural and religious features of the world. Conversely, women, "as 'emotional' beings . . . are more likely to go for the gut-punch in terms of character development, adding elements like sadness, joy, and surprise." Schoonover advises women to stop copying male style and use their own perspective to influence gaming (pp. 16–17). Most female clients prefer more story and less fighting; however, Schoonover concedes that, "a large portion of our audience desires hack'n'slash, and we're more than willing to provide that" (p. 17). Schoonover may not know her male audience as well as she thinks she does.

Many DMs try to enhance their story by reducing the number of min-maxers and powergamers involved in their campaigns. According to a "DM's Corner" discussion at the blog, *The Geek Emporium*, "A min/maxer is a player that enhances his ability to perform a single function or set of functions to the point of sacrificing anything unrelated to this goal." Conversely, "a powergamer . . . is a player that tries to make his character as powerful as possible in all ways to the detriment of the game." While both types of players can be bothersome, the min-maxer is the easiest to deal with. Often, powergamers try to take over the game. In fact, "a powergamer will do everything permissible by the strict letter of the rules to make his character undefeatable in any contest, whether it be physical, mental, or social."

DMs have devised a number of strategies to limit the impact these players have on the gaming environment. For example, DMs can carefully monitor character creation and can "exercise some . . . powers early on and limit attribute purchases to what's provided for in the character's background story." In essence, the experts advise DMs facing this situation to "call for a reason behind the choices the player wants to make, and approve or deny the choices based on those reasons" (Liambic, "DM's Corner").

Dungeons and Dragons Fourth Edition gives DMs a great deal of latitude when assigning experience points. Consequently, they may reward behavior that contributes to a good story. Furthermore, the newer versions of the *Dungeons and Dragons Dungeon Master's Guide* are no longer full of statistics and charts. Instead, much of the focus is on helping DMs create an interesting story. This discussion shows that not all male players are interested exclusively in the statistical side of role-playing games. In fact, most DMs and players want to experience an interesting adventure.

While Jen Schoonover focuses on game creation, Shelly Mazzanoble works on attracting women to *Dungeons and Dragons* in *Confessons of a Part-Time Sorceress*, published by Wizards of the Coast. Mazzanoble explains two seemingly contradictory facets of her personality: she plays D&D but she is also in touch with her "inner girl," which is apparent from the fact that she gets "pedicures, facials, and microderm abrasions." Mazzanoble says that her femininity and gaming impulses are not diametrically opposed. In fact, there are some typical feminine activities that involve role-playing, such as acting out stories with Barbie dolls or stuffed animals, and gossiping, among other things. She asserts that D&D should appeal to women, but she's also troubled by the fact that females do not typically play it, or any other role-playing game for that matter. Mazzanoble asks, "It was made for women. Why hasn't anyone told us yet?" This is a good question, but Mazzanoble's approach seems, at times, ill-advised. She says that "D&D's most popular female characters all have a few things in common: They're buxom, built, and badass" (p. 17).

Mazzanoble's tone is ironic and fun-loving, but here, she hits a nerve. The miniatures in Fourth Edition depict female characters in the way that Mazzanoble describes; however, this may not be an attractive feature of the game because players may be uncomfortable playing a sexualized character in a mostly male environment.

Instead of lobbying for greater inclusion, some gamers have separated from the mainstream due to the discomfort they feel while playing traditional RPGs. Kat Jones describes an all-female gaming experience that she and her friends collaborated on as a result of frustration with traditional role-playing games. According to Jones, the female players she knew were exasperated with the rules system of traditional tabletops, and many females had negative experiences with the male players of these games. One female participant recounts that

> "there was an awful lot of male wish fulfillment I really didn't like; i.e., there were a lot of trips into villages for 'whoring' and lots of sexy, big-breasted women to bed and the like. Not all that comfortable for me."

Male players tended to dominate the action and "female players often have trouble getting a word in edgewise" (p. 17). So the female gamers that Jones writes about concluded that their only solution was to create a completely new gaming system. The result was *Portal Worlds*, a mix of two different universes, powered by magic and inhabited by talking animals. The players eschewed hit points and a leveling system. Instead, gamers freely explored the environment and concentrated on the story. As a result, the system had more of a collaborative tone and promoted a feeling of safety among players.

Jones says that

> we didn't feel out-numbered and felt more free to voice our opinions . . . we could explore the boundaries of role-playing and had the power to share the kind of role-playing experience we wanted to have. (p. 18)

Designing an entirely new system is a daunting task. Gamers frustrated with disproportionately male gaming environments can use existing systems. For example, the D&D universe can easily accommodate players who want to focus less on combat and more on narrative elements.

Stepping off the Board

Alienated female gamers dislike the ways that male players behave both inside and outside the gaming environment. As seen, male subjects dominate the story and action. As a result, females are often silenced and objectified. Sexism, which is not punished in some role-playing narratives, but is even rewarded, has become a problem for women who love role-playing games. For example, some women have a difficult time integrating themselves into role-playing campaigns because of prejudice. Sexism, however, often extends beyond the fictional universe into the real world.

Women, who work in the gaming industry (not necessarily tied to D&D), report disparate treatment. Charlotte Law, who works for Mongoose Publishing, notes that the game-design industry is dominated by men. Consequently, she feels pressure to be more productive than her male counterparts. Writers often assume that she's a male based upon their initial, impersonal contact because Law is known by her nickname, Charlie. When these writers discover that Law is female, their attitudes change towards her. They become condescending and patronizing. Even so, Law notes that "there are also a lot of men in the industry who embrace and encourage the presence of women in the field" (pp. 18–19). Sexism in the role-playing community comes from a generally exclusionary culture that normalizes harmful attitudes. I'm not suggesting that role-playing games like D&D teach people to behave this way. On the contrary, Mazzanoble's book is a significant step in the battle to make female players feel welcome. But until the actual participants alter their gaming practices, the current inequities will remain intact.

Both males and females enjoy gaming. Role-playing experiences should appeal to women and girls, but, as seen, there are some factors that discourage their full participation. There are certain challenges that females face when they join a campaign, which may color their experiences. Furthermore, these games are rarely made for and marketed to half the population. Due to low enrollment, female players may experience harassment in an all-male environment, and their contributions may simply be dismissed due to gender considerations. Women who love gaming have developed strategies to deal with these realities. Many gamers have separated from the mainstream culture so that they may have a forum in which to play without the stress of male interference. However, it's somewhat disturbing that Jones does not grieve the loss of male perspectives in the gaming experience. Sexism can affect real-world interactions; therefore, a separatist ideology does not solve problems but may actually exacerbate them.

Defeating the Monster

Men and women have unique contributions to make, and the world is truly impoverished when one side of the binary is given preference at the expense of the other. My purpose has been to raise awareness of some problems associated with the gaming world. If left unchecked, harmful attitudes have the potential to affect real-world interactions. Change can happen, but the first step toward progress is recognizing that all is not well.

As a system, *Dungeons and Dragons* has many virtues to recommend itself to women. It is a largely equitable gaming environment that rewards co-operation. Jen Schoonover should cheer that in the D&D universe, "the Game Master . . . can tailor the game to his or her gaming group" (p. 17). Just because it's rarely done does not mean it can't be done. Women are making significant inroads in the gaming world, but they're not alone: they are aided by the efforts of companies like Wizards of the Coast, which has been continually responsive to its consumers.

II

Paragon Tier

Planes
of
Existence

10
The Laboratory of the Dungeon

MARK SILCOX AND JONATHAN COX

One of the very first recorded anecdotes about an ancient philosopher is the story of how Thales of Miletus fell down a well.

Thales was a Greek astronomer, part-time businessman, and student of nature who thought that everything in the world was made out of water and that magnets had souls. One day, as he was walking along contemplating the heavens, he failed to spot a deep hole in the ground and stepped right into it. According to Plato, who recounts the story in his dialogue *Theaetetus*, a "witty maid-servant" who happened to be passing stopped to laugh at the hapless sage, and tease him for being "so eager to know what was going on in heaven, that he could not see what was before his feet." Plato ruefully observes that this sort of criticism is unfortunately "applicable to all philosophers" (p. 43).

Habitual players of *Dungeons and Dragons* often come in for the same sort of criticism. When lost in speculation about how to design a roomful of traps that will torment a party of third-level adventurers without quite killing them all, or about whether a well-timed Burning Hands spell would be enough to ward off a horde of rapacious Githyanki, the D&D enthusiast can often seem to those around her to exhibit a curious, perhaps dangerous indifference to her more immediate surroundings. Unlike philosophers, however, D&D fans have never had much success in defending their hobby by pointing out that such exercises of the imagination can provide a source of insight into the secret workings of the universe.

Many of the most famous philosophical theories defended by the greatest minds in the Western tradition have been arrived at via the description of purely imaginary, often quite far-fetched *thought experiments*. From Plato to Derek Parfit, and from St. Augustine to Nietzsche, philosophers have shown an incurable predilection to engage in sustained reflection about completely imaginary states of affairs. And many of these scenarios, just like the sorts of situations familiar to any player of D&D, have been completely *fantastical,* in the sense that they would be nearly impossible to reproduce in any sort of real-world laboratory. The philosopher James Robert Brown describes these imaginative exercises as follows:

> Thought experiments are performed in the *laboratory of the mind*. Beyond that bit of metaphor, it's hard to say just what they are. We recognize them when we see them: they are visualizable; they involve mental manipulations; they are not the mere consequence of a theory-based calculation; they are often (but not always) impossible to implement as real experiments either because we lack the relevant technology or because they are impossible in principle. (*The Laboratory of the Mind*, p. 1).

There's a close similarity between the making of thought experiments and the type of thinking required for D&D-style fantasy role-playing. Any thoughtful fan of the game who played through some of the most popular D&D adventures would find herself doing some deep philosophical reflection.

Surviving the Tomb of Horrors

One of the most famous D&D adventures, the *Tomb of Horrors*, has grown to have a legendary status amongst gamers. Originally written by one of the game's co-creators, Gary Gygax, the *Tomb of Horrors* has been revitalized and reintroduced in each of the four editions of the game thus far created. The most recent version was written by Ari Marmell and Scott Fitzgerald Gray for the Fourth Edition of D&D. It has come to be known as a truly difficult adventure, and obtained enough of a cult following to induce some players to put "I survived the Tomb of Horrors" bumper stickers on their cars.

But there are different senses of the word "survival." At one point in this newest version of the adventure, the players' characters cross a perilous bridge over a sixty-foot drop to find themselves looking at an ominous building with a doorway just ahead (*Tomb of Horrors*, p. 17). This building is linked in some sort of spatiotemporal overlap with three other similarly designed buildings, all of which exist on separate planes. Whenever a character enters the doorway, he finds himself in one of the three possible overlapping buildings. It's implied within the text of the adventure that after undergoing such a transition these characters retain their memories and abilities, and therefore could be considered *themselves* after moving from one plane to another. But any reflective, "survival"-oriented player will be bound to wonder after undergoing such a weird transition whether he has in fact been simply annihilated upon passing the threshold of the building by the mad creator of the dungeon, Acererak, or alternatively, whether an exact copy of him might continue to exist in each of the other two planes.

The Fourth Edition of *Dungeons and Dragons* does not define precisely how teleportation works aside from the statement that it "whisks characters from one spot to another" (p. 69). In his famous *Teletransporter* thought experiment, the contemporary philosopher Derek Parfit is similarly fuzzy on technical details. A teletransporter, as Parfit describes it, is a cubicle wherein, when a button is pressed, all of the states of matter and memory that make up the individual inside it are copied, and the information is sent instantaneously (or at the speed of light, perhaps) to wherever the device is programmed to send it. During this process, the original is destroyed, but the information collected by the device is used to recreate the person's body and mind at the new location.

If what makes a person's identity is physical continuity, than surely, one might think, these two entities are different creatures, even if they have all the same thoughts, feelings, and abilities, and (perhaps on account of this) come to believe that they are the one and the same. But the human body is constantly discarding various cells and growing new ones; hair falls out, nails grow, skin sloughs off, perpetually. At some point, almost all of the cells that are in the human body are completely replaced. The cells that are now being used are not the same ones that any grown individual was born with. So, following the line of thought that seems to be encouraged by Parfit's thought experiment, should we not conclude *we ourselves* are not the same people we were ten years ago? Not just changed people, but completely different entities, perhaps ones that falsely call themselves Jonathan, Katherine, Bubba, or Mark.

Should we reject this idea, on the grounds that physical continuity does not fully determine personal identity, but that perhaps psychological continuity may be what ultimately matters? This is the option that Parfit himself seems to favor ("Divided Minds," p. 28). But anyone who takes this approach must assume that the sameness of mental states over time is not dependent upon the continuity of the body, an assumption which has an air of weird mysticism about it. And not all memories are maintained, nor are all beliefs unchanging, so once again one finds oneself wondering at what point one can say that one is still truly oneself.

The problem is compounded, of course, when we're trying to role-play characters in a make-believe world, whose nature might represent only an approximate emulation of real-world human psychology, biology, and in some cases even physics. Might the output of a teletransporter count as *the same* human being, but a *different* Tiefling, Drow or Warforged? And if so, how should a player represent the effects of this process in how he role-plays a non-human character?

Within the space of less than a page in the one-hundred-and-fifty-plus-page *Tomb of Horrors* book, the D&D player or DM is compelled to contemplate questions pertaining to the nature of personal identity, spatial metaphysics, and the extent of the distinctiveness of human nature. If we're willing to look, modules such as this and many others like it are fertile ground for the cultivation of our philosophical intuitions about all of these sorts of issues.

Do Warforged Dream of Magically-Sentient Sheep?

In the earliest editions of D&D, the races that were available for characters to play were almost exclusively Tolkienesque in nature—Elves, Dwarves, Halflings (similar to Hobbits) and Humans. Any new player of the game who had at least a glancing familiarity with *The Lord of the Rings*, or even with a few of the innumerable Tolkien-derived fantasy novels published in the 1970s, would be able to play such characters competently according to well-known conventions of the genre.

But over time, with the publication of additional editions and supplements for the game, a variety of more esoteric character races have come into existence. One of the most interesting of these was the Warforged, a race of mechanical warriors who were given sentience by magical means. The Warforged made their debut in June 2004 with the release of the *Eberron* campaign setting. This new playable race turns many of the accepted tropes of traditional high fantasy storytelling on their heads, and presents the player with several possibilities for investigating interesting philosophical experiments.

In the world of Eberron, magic permeates the land, and has been utilized as an actual resource by the majority of the populace to produce ever-burning lamps similar to light bulbs, magical means of communication like the telegraph, and ships that harness the power of wind elementals to fly through the air. Yet in spite of the sheer omnipresence of this magical technology, there are very few individually powerful characters—certainly nothing resembling the Gandalfs, Merlins, Aslans, Dumbledores, and their ilk who show up constantly in more conventional fantasy tales.

Less than two years before the suggested date for campaigns set in Eberron, a shaky peace treaty was signed which ended a century-long conflict known as "The Last War." It was only after the literal destruction of an entire nation that the other weary factions in the main continent of Khorvaire decided to end the bloodshed. It was for this long conflict that the Warforged were first created as renewable forces to fight in the war's constant battles. Each new generation of Warforged were evolved to a slightly higher level of intelligence and sentience. Now these large bipedal meta-humans made of metal, leather, and fibrous joints have their own thoughts and (somewhat naive) emotions, but have no defined purpose within a world without an obvious war to fight.

Part of the enjoyment and interest of playing any D&D character is the challenge of trying to imagine what it would be like to undergo experiences within the (shared) imaginary construct of the game world through the lens of your character's particular sensibility and defining traits. Anyone who chooses to play a Warforged character is asked to presuppose that these machines made by mortals have somehow developed sentience, either through some perfect storm of magical energy or merely as an unforeseen side effect of their creation process. Yet in spite of the undeniable fact that many have purchased, played, and enjoyed the Eberron campaign setting, it still seems fair to ask whether the its authors might, in fact, be requesting the impossible when they ask players to think in this way.

In his famous article "What Is It Like to Be a Bat?" Thomas Nagel suggests that such imaginative tasks are often much easier described than they are accomplished. Nagel describes in some detail how a bat of the type Michiroptera makes its way around in the world. These bats, like many other types, use echolocation, a form of sonar, to perceive the world around them. With their very specialized modulation of shrieks, they can discern the locations of various objects, from a tree in their flight path to the tiny mosquitoes that will be their prey. The brains of the bats are hardwired to be able to interpret these phenomena. Scientists who study these creatures understand how the mechanism works quite well. But Nagel argues that all of the science we can presently muster proves fruitless when it comes to understanding *what it is like* for that bat to be a bat. Its experiences seem to be so dissimilar to how we receive stimuli from the world around us as to be completely *closed off* to us as humans.

Even if, by some miracle of science or otherwise, Nagel were to be turned gradually into a bat, he thinks that this still wouldn't be enough. Experiencing this gradual transformation would be experiencing what it's like for Nagel to have turned into a bat and then, as a result, experience bat-ness. But this is still not what it is like *for a bat* to be a bat. If Nagel is correct that it is impossible to truly experience what is like for a bat to be a bat then, given how little we seem to have in common with the Warforged as they are described in the *Eberron* books, the same line of reasoning should almost certainly lead us to conclude that it's impossible for any player of D&D to experience what it is like for a Warforged Fighter in Sharn, the City of Towers, to be a Warforged Fighter in Sharn, the City of Towers.

But if this really is impossible, then what on earth are players who think that they are at least getting close to this sort of state during a session of D&D really doing? The most likely answer is that these players are simply confused about what they are experiencing. They are not really learning about *what it is like* for a Warforged to be a Warforged. After all, the race is completely *fictional*, so how could someone say with any certainty that she really gets what it is to experience being such a creature? Instead, what these players are doing is exploring the experience of what it is like for a *human* to suspend disbelief, in order to engage in co-operative storytelling about characters who happen to have various interestingly non-human quirks and perspectives. Players of fantasy RPGs are like ancient Greek actors who stepped outside of themselves by donning a mask, which they did in order to better tell a story, not so that they could indulge in the private experience what it was like for Oedipus to be Oedipus.

Nagel-style thought experiments that are constructed in order to expose the limits of human imagination can help us to see what is really going on, psychologically and aesthetically, when human beings pretend to be what they are not in the context of a game or a theatrical performance. But some ambiguities remain. Granted that undergoing a private, inner experience of what it's like to be Warforged may not be the ultimate goal of a player in some *Eberron*-based campaign, any true fan of D&D nonetheless recognizes that there is all the difference in the world between playing a character *well* and playing one *badly*. A player who merely rolls dice and recites combat actions is much less fun to game with than somebody who is able to actually speak in her character's voice, and to make the sorts of tactical or ethical decisions that might be expected from members of a race with the tragic and terrifying history of the Warforged. And it's awfully difficult to say exactly what enables a player to do these things without attributing to her at least *some* capacity to imagine *what it's like* to be Warforged.

Perhaps if anyone ever felt like designing an RPG around the lives of Michiroptera bats, we'd find ourselves with a similar reason to question some of Nagel's philosophical conclusions.

Flumph Family Values

The most recent, Fourth Edition of D&D adopts a form of gameplay that centers around formalized combat encounters, usually played with miniatures. While it's still certainly possible to play the game in a more story-oriented, less number-crunching way, for most contemporary players combat scenarios will probably represent the meat-and-potatoes of gameplay. Partly because of this feature of D&D 4e, the majority of creatures a player's character is likely to meet in the gameworld will be some variety or other of *evil*, and therefore reliably unresponsive to mere verbal persuasion. But there's something uncomfortable about having to make the assumption that every creature you run into deserves to be destroyed. The types of combat scenarios engendered by this type of in-game assumption have been described by one perceptive critic of D&D, Eric Sofge, as "the kind of atrocity that commits itself." Can our own character truly be described as "good" if she is so strongly predisposed to see evil everywhere she turns?

The Fourth Edition rules do add an element of nuance that was missing from earlier versions of the game—players who encounter a monster don't necessarily have to kill it to gain experience points, so long as they "overcome the challenge" that the creature presents to them, according to the DM's discretion.

Mary Anne Warren's Space Traveler thought experiment, part of an argument originally pertaining to issues that come up in the abortion debate, also helps provide some insight into this moral predicament. Warren asks the reader to imagine an interplanetary explorer who comes across a planet filled with beings completely different from anything he has ever encountered before. If the space traveler wants to act morally, then according to Warren the first thing that he has to determine is whether or not these creatures are *people*, and therefore have full moral rights. If evidence that they are people becomes available, then the traveler should be perfectly willing to respect those rights. But if he's able to determine that the species are not people, and hence do not have any sort of moral rights, then he should feel at least relatively guilt-free in way-laying them, or viewing them principally as a natural resource of some kind. Upon what sort of evidence should the traveler base his decision?

Although the main point of Warren's story is to emphasize the difficulty of these sorts of decisions, she suggests religion, art, tool use, and the construction of shelters as possible examples of the sorts of behaviors that could be relevant to the decision of whether the aliens count as people. I suspect, however, that the average D&D player may be a bit less finicky.

Take the Orcs. Orcs are fiercely tribal fighters, ready to tear apart whatever comes up against them with barbaric fury. In almost any sort of D&D encounter, they'll want to kill the majority of adventurers on sight, if for no other reason than that the latter might have supplies worth taking. Despite this, some of the prerequisites Warren speaks of are present in Orc culture. Their main god, Grummsh, has a clear, if brutish, role in Orcish society. Orcs can also have the ability of Artifice: they are typically considered able to create practical, if crude, armor, weapons, clothing and other artifacts, which they design according to an easily identifiable cultural aesthetic. They usually have quite primitive shelters, normally residing in caves in earlier editions of the game. So these Orcs pass Warren's criteria for being *people*. Yet they are more than willing to kill and eat you, hopefully (for your sake) in that order. And you, as an adventurer, would surely be foolish to do anything else but respond to them more or less in kind.

Perhaps it's a bit unfair trying to use this sort of example to undermine the philosophical intuitions that lie behind Warren's thought experiment. After all, her story does not at any point suggest that the first thing the unfamiliar aliens did upon meeting her space traveler was to sink their fangs into his leg, or to try to make off with the change in his pockets. And if they did, there's probably no reason to think that Warren wouldn't advise the traveler to defer delicate questions about the proper philosophical criteria of personhood until after he had at least managed to escape from their clutches. But the example does help to expose one rather artificial element in Warren's hypothetical scenario. The historical record reveals remarkable few examples of circumstances in which people have confronted creatures (human and otherwise) who have exhibited the sort of strangeness that could make their personhood seem to be an open question, wherein it was *also* possible to contemplate the behaviors of these strangers from a position of leisurely detachment.

In this connection, consider the case of the Flumph, a curious creature from the first edition of the D&D *Fiend Folio*. These yellow-white, sentient, floating disks with six inch eye stalks and tentacles, in addition to spikes of crystals underneath their bodies, are actually lawfully good, despite their horrific description. Your average Flumph wouldn't harm a soul without provocation. Furthermore, they are capable of speech and rationality even though they have no art, religion, or shelters to speak of. In the pre-made D&D adventure "Box of Flumph," written by Tim Hitchcock and published in *Dungeon* Magazine #118, a group of marauders are stealing away whole families of Flumphs from their current habitat of the local salt mine. One of the authors of this chapter actually ran this adventure for a bunch of his friends. At a certain point in the story, the adventurers were rooming in the same inn as one of the kidnapper's minions. A captured Flumph broke free of the box into which he was stuffed, and retaliated against his captor, a Human Female. The adventurers next door heard the scuffle and (as good adventurers are wont to do) immediately went to investigate. Once they looked inside and saw this alien creature attacking a human female, the players jumped straight to the conclusion that they had found a damsel in distress. They immediately killed the Flumph, without even giving it a chance to explain itself! Evidently, the adventurers were confident that this lawful good alien freak was less worthy of his rights than the evil human female. A disturbingly similar scene is described in Stephen King's novel *From a Buick 8*, discussed in the next chapter.

It's a little more difficult to anticipate what Warren might have to say about this sort of scenario. On the one hand, while the adventurers could perhaps be forgiven for acting on the spur of the moment, it does look as though they made a pretty bad decision by the standards of the game's alignment system. On the other hand, even if they had had time to take a step back and assess the situation, it still seems possible that an attempt to apply Warren's criteria for the possession of "moral rights" might have led them to act as they did anyhow. The human kidnapper was certainly a "person" in the sense of the word as it is usually employed, and Flumphs don't show any signs of worshipping a god, making armor for themselves, or drawing attractive self-portraits on cave walls. Maybe the philosophical lesson to be learned here is that, while "personhood" is certainly one relevant criterion for determining how nicely you have to treat strangers in certain sorts of circumstances, it can't be our *only* criterion, even at the best of times. After all, persons can be pretty awful.

Sub Specie Temporis

An interesting pattern has emerged as we have compared each of the three D&D adventures described above with a philosophical thought experiment. While the scenarios we're asked to imagine in the case of each comparison are remarkably similar, there's always a crucial difference in *how* we're asked to employ our imagination. When Parfit instructs us to imagine what happens to an individual who passes through a teletransporter, Nagel challenges us to try to envision what it's like to be a bat, or Warren asks us to anticipate the decisions faced during first contact with an alien species, we are asked to contemplate the situations depicted in philosophical thought experiments *sub specie aeternitatis*—from the perspective of eternity, that is, with as few presuppositions as possible. They clearly do not want us to simply take it for granted that we have already at some point been teletransported, or that our inner worlds are already indistinguishable from a bat's, or that we have already had to deal with creatures as unfamiliar as extraterrestrials. Part of what's always in question is the very *possibility* of the circumstances that they are asking us to imagine.

The very nature of how D&D is played prevents the player from adopting the type of perspective that we need in order to be able to come to this sort of determination. The game hardly ever allows players to view things in the gameworld purely as objects of contemplation. Rather, it always requires us to *immerse* ourselves in the world that the DM envisages, via the first-person perspective of a fictional character.

Plenty of what goes on in the average D&D adventure probably deserves to be called impossible by any commonsensical standard—we all know that nobody can really shoot fire from their fingers, and that it's impossible for a skeleton to stand up on its own feet. But the player is required to view all of these sorts of freakish phenomena *sub specie temporis*—under the aspect of time, that is, as though they were happening all around her, right then and there. The only time that her sense of the unlikelihood of it all can be allowed to matter is when she's calling out some overambitious DM who is bending the rules of the game, or putting her into a position where she simply doesn't know how to role-play her character. The presupposition that what one's character is going through *really could happen,* in some sense or other, is not only a requirement of basic gaming etiquette, but an absolutely essential feature of what makes fantasy RPGs so much fun to play.

One might conclude that this feature of the game makes playing it a fundamentally unphilosophical enterprise, even in spite of all of the similarities that we have noted here between features of individual D&D adventures and influential philosophical thought experiments. One of the things that's supposed to distinguish philosophers from everybody else is their willingness to question even the most basic presuppositions that everyone else takes for granted during the course of their practical lives. But something else that most philosophers aspire to is the type of mental flexibility and openness that allows people to adjust their worldviews in the face of experiences and information that initially seem bizarre, disorientating, or downright impossible. And the particular intellectual virtues that allow a person to become this sort of a thinker certainly don't seem to just pop into existence all by themselves. Considered in this light, the habits of mind we find ourselves adopting when our characters are walking down the corridors of the Tomb of Horrors, traversing the ravaged landscape of Eberron, or breaking down doors to rescue a Flumph starts to look like exactly the style of thinking that any sensible philosopher should want to cultivate.

11
Expressing the Inexpressible

JON COGBURN AND NEAL HEBERT

If there's anything that differentiates epic fantasy from other genres of fiction it's magic. Horror has malignant supernatural evil, but the protagonists typically use science, common sense, and old-fashioned human pluck to defeat their magical entities. Only in fantasy do you routinely read about—or, in the case of *Dungeons and Dragons*, play—a main character who herself is a conduit for such unseen forces.

A central theme in both horror and fantasy is the use of magic to upend the natural order, causing a situation so at odds with our ordinary ways of understanding the world that it transcends the narrator's powers of description. This aspect of the supernatural is probably most pronounced in H.P. Lovecraft's fiction. For example, in "The Outsider" the narrator tells the reader that he cannot describe what he sees when he first looks into a mirror.

> As I approached the arch I began to perceive the presence more clearly; and then, with the first and last sound I ever uttered-a ghastly ululation that revolted me almost as poignantly as its noxious cause- I beheld in full, frightful vividness the inconceivable, indescribable, and unmentionable monstrosity. . . . I cannot even hint at what it was like, for it was a compound of all that is unclean, uncanny, unwelcome, abnormal, and detestable. (pp. 145–46)

As is typical for Lovecraft and the horror genre that stands on his shoulders, the narrator paradoxically does go on and tell you quite a bit about this creature which he claims he can't tell you anything about. But no one reading Lovecraft gets bent out of shape about the possible contradictory nature of this. Repeated Lovecraftian warnings that an instance of the unnatural is so incomprehensible as to transcend description are signals to the reader that the narrator's description is always doomed to failure. But still, according to the Lovecraftian aesthetic, the supernatural is terrifying precisely because it transcends what we take to be possible, and, as a result, what is describable.

The idea of magic as something horrible and unfathomable presents a fascinating problem both to philosophy and writers of the supernatural. If something's so conceptually foreign as to be indescribable, how do we even succeed in talking about it, much less actually play it around the D&D table? In *Beyond the Limits of Thought* Graham Priest argues that any such attempt involves thinking beyond the self-imposed limit, forcing the philosopher to try to do exactly what Lovecraft does: describe the indescribable. Priest investigates whether the meaningful description of the limits of thought is even possible, and concludes that reality itself is contradictory.

In *The Philosophy of Horror*, Noël Carroll asks a closely analogous question with respect to fiction writers and film makers. How can they depict what is supposed to be undepictable? Luckily for fans of *Dungeons and Dragons*, even if Priest's philosophical task is impossible, it doesn't follow that Carroll's aesthetic task is. For it may be that the fictionally depicted fantasy and horror worlds are themselves impossible precisely because they are supposed to be worlds in which the indescribable is describable.

Kinds of Magic

There are many different ways we could classify kinds of magic. In Fourth Edition *Dungeons and Dragons*, the primary division is between Arcane Magic, Divine Magic, and Primal Magic. Wizards, sorcerers, and bards practice Arcane Magic, which typically involves creating or manipulating matter, energy, or life. Divine magic is so called because it is a gift of some god or goddess. Clerics, paladins, and rangers utilize divine magic. Druids, shamans, and barbarians practice primal magic, which somehow involves the magic user harnessing sub-personal natural powers. Fourth Edition abandoned the schools-of-magic approach to Arcane Magic, which at its height further subdivided types of magic into Abjuration, Alteration, Conjuration, Divination, Enchantment, Illusion, Invocation/Evocation, and Necromancy.

The current game mechanics successfully model what we call natural magic—which we then divide into two substrata, formulaic natural magic and sublimate natural magic—while systematically failing to mechanically model the unnatural magic evoked by Lovecraft and other contemporary fantasy authors.

Formulaic natural magic can best be understood by reference to the great philosopher Immanuel Kant, who characterized "nature" (in the sense of "natural science") in precisely this way. We use the understanding of the natural order as that which is subject to uniform universal laws of cause and effect to design technology in laboratories. Formulaic natural magic is in no important sense different from the way technology based on natural science works on Earth.

If in a fantasy novel the magic involves alchemical laboratories where the wizard has to mix potions, draw figures to harness forces, or build complicated machines, it's a safe bet that the "magic" in the fictitious world is really just a kind of natural science appropriate in the universal laws of nature for that world. The world in question has different universal laws than those that hold on Earth, and the magicians are that world's scientists, discerning these laws and exploiting them as technology.

Examples in fantasy literature include the magic of the young Cleric Cadderly in R.A. Salvatore's *Canticle* (first book of *The Cleric Quintet*), Professor Snape's potions-brewing classes in J.K. Rowling's Harry Potter books, and the magical-technological hybrid alchemical magic characteristic of great "steampunk" fiction such as China Mievelle's three Bas-Lag novels: *Perdido Street Station, The Scar,* and *Iron Council.* In all of these cases the magic users are scientists in a world with different universal laws of nature. The magic is predicated on the user developing a profound understanding of these universal laws to be able to harness magical technology.

Fourth Edition D&D models this conception of formulaic natural magic quite well: the game boasts rules for crafting magical items, brewing alchemical potions, and summoning magical creatures by the use of arcane formulae. All Arcane, Divine, and Primal characters either have access to or can easily gain access to the conscribed rituals that reliably work within the physics of the game world to create consistent effects that can aid the party of adventurers. Moreover, with the release of the *Eberron Player's Guide*—a core 4e D&D game supplement that gives people the ability to play within the Eberron campaign setting—a new 4e character class was introduced: the Artificer, a magical tinkerer, alchemist, and artisan who uses his power to create magical machines and effects.

While formulaic natural magic involves understanding and harnessing universal physical laws of the fantastic world, sublimate natural magic does no such thing. Instead of understanding laws to be able to manipulate them with magical technology or as magical technology, the practitioner of sublimate natural magic typically surrenders herself to the forces themselves. Her body becomes the conduit for magical forces.

The magical world in question might be such that the forces to which the sublimate natural magic user surrenders are describable by universal law; just as a wizard summons a demon and gains its help through the rigorous application of formulas that have been proven to work within the world, a warlock might sell his soul to the same demon in exchange for the ability to tap into the demon's power. Then again, the forces in the relevant world may instead be represented as a dynamic balance between universal laws and the chaotic matter on which these laws are imposed.

If formulaic natural magic users on Planet Earth are our scientists and engineers, using knowledge of universal physical law to build technology, the sublimate natural magic users here are paradigmatically the shamans and mystics from societies whose cultures have been less affected by modern technology. These men and women typically give themselves over to trances and meditative states and purport to come with back with powers as agents of the divine. As such, they are not to impose their own ego on the behavior of the magic. This is the received academic view of almost all "primitive" religions though it has been criticized (by Alice Kehoe for instance).

Consider the practices of Candomblé, Voodoo, and Santeria in the African diaspora. In these syncretic faiths, priests and worshippers routinely summon up spirits—sometimes named orixas, orisas, or loa—and give themselves over to these beings. This act of submission becomes an act of worship: the individual becomes a vessel through which miracles are worked. The sublimation of the self allows the self to become something more than it was, even if the duration of the transformation lasts no longer than the ritual that affects the presence of the divine.

In Robin Hobb's *Soldier Son* trilogy (*Shaman's Crossing, Forest Mage, Renegade's Magic*), the protagonist Nevarre Burvelle incessantly fights the magical forces to which he has become sensitized. He divides his soul in two in an attempt to keep part of himself on the side of the "civilizing" army building a road through, and hence killing, the magical forest that is the home of another sentient species. While all of Burvelle's well intentioned efforts seem only to make things worse, the reader slowly realizes that the magic has been using him for the greater good even when he thought he was in control. Without knowing it, he has given himself over to the divine.

As with formulaic natural magic, sublimate natural magic presents few problems to the game; the mechanics model the literary tropes fairly well. Virtually all Divine and Primal spellcasters play off of these tropes; the characters are vessels for the power received from the gods of the world or the primal spirits attuned to the world. Shamans and barbarians in 4e mirror the sublimate magic of Candomblé; the individual either gives her physical self over to the loa or orixa to ride in exchange for extra power, or works with a loa or orixa in a partnership. Several Arcane classes within the game also use sublimate magic: sorcerers, for whom magic is a matter of tapping into ineffable forces or a blood heritage; and warlocks, who bargain with extraordinarily powerful beings for a chance to wield power beyond the scope of humanity.

If natural magic as a whole is simply the variegated attempts to harness or tap into the universal physical laws of worlds that are not Earth, unnatural magic is the miraculous breaking of those very universal laws through strange inexplicable rituals and strength of will. While every reasonable person agrees that formulaic natural magic exists in our plane as working science, and reasonable people disagree about the existence of sublimate natural magic (because reasonable people disagree about the efficacy of religious practices), it seems nearly certain that unnatural magic is at the very least, really, really difficult to succeed with on Earth. If the laws of nature concerning growing grain could be brutalized into submission by anyone, one would gather that they would have been by the Soviet State under Josef Stalin. But it just didn't work (see Joravsky's *The Lysenko Affair*).

This doesn't mean that unnatural magic doesn't work in fantasy worlds; and again since fantasy novels are our best guides to fantasy worlds, it is of signal importance that we do find unnatural magic in fantasy novels. *All* magical usage in R. Scott Bakker's fantastic *The Prince of Nothing* trilogy (*The Darkness that Comes Before, The Warrior Prophet, The Thousandthfold Thought*) is unnatural in the sense we are considering here. In this fantasy world, the casting of a magical spell is always presented as a horrible event that threatens sanity and darkens the soul of the magic user. The spell caster, through rituals involving paradoxically indecipherable languages and geometries and profound acts of will (which in these models is often represented as transcending the deterministic natural order as well), rips apart the fabric of reality to violate the universal laws that constitute that reality. In Bakker's world spell casting is always taken as a violation of the god's will. The universal physical laws ordering the world created by that god are violated by unnatural magic.

The nature of unnatural magic users' power does render it likely to turn them into something both more and less than human(oid) in the Fourth Edition sense. The magician here is a vortex of the undermining of universal laws of nature, but the more she does this the less sense she is able to make of the world around her. And a world without universal laws is a deranged place to be. Consider the narrator of Jean-Paul Sartre's *Nausea*, fantasizing about the breakdown of universal laws. His description is one of the high points of Western literature.

> It can happen any time, perhaps right now: the omens are present. For example, the father of a family might go out for a walk, and, across the street, he'll see something like a red rag, blow towards him by the wind. And when the rag has gotten close to him he'll see that

it is a side of rotten meat, grimy with dust, dragging itself along by crawling, slipping, a piece of writhing flesh rolling in the gutter, spasmodically shooting out spurts of blood. Or a mother might look at her child's cheek and ask him: "What's that—a pimple?" and see the flesh puff out a little, split, open, and at the bottom of the split an eye, a laughing eye might appear. Or they might feel things gently brushing against their bodies, like the caresses of reeds to swimmers in a river. And they will realize that their clothing has become living things. (pp. 158–160)

The unnatural is horrible and horrifying. Its magic is a disruption of the very reality that sanity relies upon. People subject to it will be driven to greater and greater psychological and behavioral disorders.

Madness and dissolution of self is the threat that magicians in Thomas Harlan's *The Oath of Empire* series must constantly keep under control. Consider the mage Dwyrin, who has almost become the locus of too much chaos while using his powers to defend Jerusalem.

Another sorcerer or thaumaturge might have been gibbering in fear now, watching in horror as the walls and bricks that surround him faded in and out of sight. Sometimes lighted rooms yawned before him, blurred by the indistinct vapor of walls and doors. He had overextended himself today, letting fire flow through him like a rain channel. It had eroded the symbolic mental barriers that kept his conscious mind from comprehending the true world. Those same symbologies defined who he was in human terms. They gave him a name, a physical description, context for his thoughts and actions and they made him a unique entity. For most men, when those symbols ceased to define them, they went mad. Who could remain sane if he looked upon the face of chaos unveiled? (p. 187)

Who indeed?

A Carrollingian Theory of Unnatural Magic

Noël Carroll's theory of how supernatural fiction expresses the inexpressible is couched in terms of his characterization of the emotional reaction readers and viewers (and we hope players) are supposed to have to horrific monsters. He writes:

I am occurrently art-horrified by some monster X, say Dracula, if and only if: (1) I am in some state of abnormal, physically felt agitation (shuddering, tingling, screaming, etc.) which, (2) has been *caused* by (a) the thought: that Dracula is a possible being; and by the evaluative thoughts that (b) said Dracula has the property of being physically (and perhaps morally and socially) threatening in the ways portrayed in the fiction and that (c) said Dracula has the property of being impure, where (3) such thoughts are usually accompanied by the desire to avoid the touch of things like Dracula. (p. 27)

Carroll's account is fairly straightforward as is, but things get very interesting when he utilizes the anthropological theories of Mary Douglas to characterize what he calls impurity.

For Douglas, cultural schemes of categorization uniformly guide us: (a) to view certain pairs of properties as metaphysically incompatible, in that it would be impossible for the same thing to possess both those properties; (b) to view each thing as a clear instance of the kind of thing it is, so that it would be impossible for something to be only partially some kind of thing or for something to not be any kind of thing at all. When we examine ritual purity codes of different cultures, we almost always find horrified reaction to violations of the way members of that culture took (a) and (b) to be instantiated.

The impure creatures and acts in the Old Testament book of *Leviticus* almost invariably involve (a). Men and women are metaphysically incompatible, and gay men are horrifying to the authors of *Leviticus* just because they impossibly possesses a property that women have. Shellfish are impure foods because they combine the metaphysically incompatible properties of fish (living in the water) and animals (having legs). Many horrific creatures such as ghosts (and *Leviticus* counsels death for all who trade with a spirit familiar) and people without heads violate (b); they are creatures lacking what should be essential properties of those creatures. At the extreme end of (b) is the fear of formlessness itself, with gods often understood as imposing form on chaotic formless matter.

Carroll shows that supernatural creatures of horror are examples of these forms of impurity. The *categorically incompatible* monsters include things that are both living and dead, animate and inanimate, human and nonhuman. With possession stories, two individual entities are impossibly superimposed. Very skilled writers like Lovecraft pile on so many incompatibilities that the creature becomes impossible for us to categorize with our own conceptual scheme. Carroll quotes the following from "The Dunwich Horror."

> Bigger'n a barn . . . all made o' squirmin ropes . . . hull thing sort o' shaped like a hen's egg biggern'n anything, with dozens o' legs like hogsheads that haff shut up when they step . . . nothin' solid about it—all like jelly, an' made o' sep'rit wrigglin' ropes pushed clost together . . . great bulgin' eyes all over it . . . ten or twenty mouths or trunks a-stickn' out all along the sides, big as stovepipes, an-'a-tossin' an 'openin' an' shuttin' . . . all, with kinder blue or purple rings . . . an' Gawd in Heaven—that haff face on top!. . . .that face with red eyes an' crinkly albino hair, an' no chin, like the Whatleys . . . . It was a octopus, centipede, spider kindo' thing, but they was haff-shaped man's face on top of it. . . . (p. 294)

The thing being described simply does not fit the conceptual scheme of the narrator, and all he can do is try to describe parts that impossibly fit together.

Categorical incompleteness typically comes with zombies who are missing body parts. Sometimes the missing body parts themselves can horrifically instantiate metaphysical incompatibilities by displaying signs of animacy. The limit of this incompleteness is the horrific nature of formlessness itself with monsters that are vaporous, gelatinous, and slimy.

Many of the substances that we innately find revolting fit into these categories. Human beings swallow on average one liter of their own mucus a day and do not find it revolting. But if they were required to first spit the mucus into a cup and then swallow it, it would be revolting. Why? Like feces and blood, when the mucus comes out of the body it becomes metaphysically contradictory: both part of you and not part of you. Feces, mucus, and blood are also formless. It's no accident that horror literature and movies contain so much of them. Again if we return to *Leviticus*-style Old Testament injunctions, one of the weirdest aspects is the obsession with menstrual blood (Leviticus 15:19–30, 20:18; Ezekiel 18:5–6). Women were to be set apart during menstruation, and ritually purified afterwards by sacrificing two turtles or two birds. If a man sees a naked woman menstruating he and the women are to be exiled.

The question is why something that is so categorically impossible as to be indescribable should be scary. Carroll points to possible evolutionary reasons. Creatures affectively disposed to withdraw from creepy crawly organisms like snakes and spiders and to avoid substances such as mucus, blood, and feces that transmit diseases would, all else being equal, be selectively fitter than creatures without such phobias. One can then hypothesize that things that radically contravene one's theory of the world are threatening, too. We gain mastery over, and safety from, the myriad things (from wild animals, to weather patterns, to diseases, to other people) that threaten us by getting knowledge of their dispositions and how they operate. Something that is categorically impossible or formless relative to one cultural scheme is inconceivable (and hence radically unknowable) relative to that scheme, and thus threatening.

Carroll's case is bolstered by looking at the most common horror tropes, which all involve some combination of categorical impossibility and incompleteness (to the point of formlessness).

1. *Metonymy* occurs when the horrific creature is associated with some formless and categorically incompatible entity that is innately disgusting, such as vampires' association with blood.

2. *Massification* happens when there are an improbably large number of objects, sometimes normally benign ones like birds, that through being massed metonymically take on the properties of creepy crawly insects and who as a swarm achieve the categorically impossible by acting with reasoned malice.

3. *Magnification* happens when the very small is impossibly made very large (or *vice versa*). Again, the very small invokes both the fear of the formless and the creepy crawly.

4. *Fission* happens when things that are thought to be necessarily connected become disconnected, such as someone's personality splitting or a hand becoming separate and sentient.

5. *Fusion* happens when categorically distinct things somehow meld together, such as a human body and a fly's head (this one also involves magnification).

Now that we see how all five of these tropes involve some mixture of categorical incompatibility and incompleteness, we can begin to understand how Carroll takes the inexpressible to be expressed in horror. When people still in the grips of a conceptual scheme confront something deemed impossible by that scheme, then they experience the deep revulsion that gives rise to books like *Leviticus*.

Educated people of good will are no longer metaphysically revolted by shellfish, gay men, or menstruating women. If in the reader's or player's conceptual scheme the intended bit of horror or chaos magic does not inspire revulsion due to categorical/metaphysical impossibilities, then the aesthetic effect is unsuccessful.

As a result good horror and fantasy writers, as well as good D&D players, must rely on analogy and depicting the character's reactions rather than a detailed, literal depiction of the horrific entity. We've all experienced things becoming no longer horrifying to us just because our conceptual schemes have grown to where those things no longer seem impossible. And the horror writer can't just portray a character experiencing things that a reader would not find metaphysically fraught. But good horror and fantasy writers easily circumvent this with three techniques:

1. *Character Reaction*, where the character is portrayed as experiencing a revulsion with the same kind of characteristic phenomenology and behavior as the reader has previously in her horrified moments,

2. *Reader-Relative Impossibility*, where tropes such as metonymy, magnification, massification, fission, and fusion instantiate things that are deemed impossible by the reader's conceptual scheme, and

3. *Limit Impossibility*, where the narrator uses claims about inexpressibility to suggest either that every conceptual scheme (even those that encompass far more reality than the reader's) fail to be able to conceive some horrific aspects of the universe, or (the logically stronger claim) that something about the magic is impossible according to all conceptual schemes.

If somehow the conceptual schemes could be ordered in terms of richness, with the richest ones seeing the universe as less horrific (though not necessarily less threatening) because what is impossible according to impoverished schemes is understood by the richer ones, horror teaches us that there will always be some mysterious and scary remainder, even at the logical limit of enrichments.

In Stephen King's best late-period novel, *From a Buick 8*, the characters all know that the thing in the garage isn't really a car, but they can't really perceive it as it is. Much of the power of the book is in these first two moments; readers can't help but identify with the way the characters are frightened by their powerlessness in the face of something they can't fully comprehend. The way King masterfully ties this to the main character's emotional struggle over his father's death primes the reader to empathize and re-experience a ghost of her own past horrific responses to reality (Character Reaction).

At one point in the novel when an alien life-form leaves the car's "trunk" and splats down on the garage floor, the characters can't help but to beat it to death. In great Lovecraftian fashion, the alien is presented as incompatible with the characters' and readers' conceptual schemes (Reader-Relative Impossibility). The main character's horror is then vastly increased by the realization that the officer who was consumed by the trunk earlier must have equally horrified denizens of whatever reality he was pulled into. The reader is led to the thought that any conceptual scheme will be cut off from aspects of the universe that are deemed impossible by it (Limit Impossibility). The main character will never make sense of his father's death, just as the interdimensional creatures will never make sense of humans (and *vice versa*).

The Plight of Unnatural Magic in 4e D&D

What we've been saying above can be read as a set of guidelines for how the Dungeon Master can handle chaos magic:

1. *Character Reaction.* Have non-player characters react with horrified revulsion to the magic, including moments of insanity.

2. *Reader-Relative Impossibility.* Include spells involving metonymy, magnification, massification, fission, and fusion to instantiate things that are deemed impossible by the players' conceptual schemes.

3. *Limit Impossibility.* Employ the rhetoric of absolute impossibility and indescribability in the skilled manner of Lovecraft.

Unfortunately though, the very game mechanics of *Dungeons and Dragons* severely retard the prospects of success for 2. and 3.

The problem is that playing a magic user in *Dungeons and Dragons* requires that the player learn a set of rules that renders the "magic" entirely predictable and machinelike. Say the player's character is a fifth-level wizard who has just learned the "Fireball" attack spell. By *Dungeons and Dragons* mechanics the player will always roll a twenty-sided die when her player utilizes this spell. The player can use it precisely one time per in-game day. The effect will happen within twenty squares of the character (depending upon the player's decision) and will happen in a "burst" taking up nine squares. If the role on the twenty-sided die (with modifiers) is greater than any creature in the burst area's "reflex" score, then that character is affected by the spell. If this is the case, then the player roles three six-sided dice and adds her character's intelligence modifier score to determine how much damage is taken by the creature, calculated by subtracting the result of the role (plus intelligence modifier) from the number of "hit points" the creature possesses in that turn, with creatures incapacitated or dead when they reach zero hit points.

Every single spell has an algorithm that resembles this one. When we talk about "ludological" (as opposed to narrative) enjoyment of *Dungeons and Dragons* we refer to the practice of mastering such algorithms to win the game (in this case amassing experience points and loot). A good player is like a good chemistry student who masters the periodic table and learns to apply it in the laboratory. In fact, the uniform representation of spells on cards shows how similar all of the different magic algorithms are, only varying things like how often the spell can be used, how much damage is caused, and where the spell effect happens in relation to the character.

Now suppose the character is using unnatural magic. The players (like the readers of books) should have a visceral feeling that what is happening is impure in the sense of being dangerous, revolting, and impossible. This should be achieved by the game mechanics, Game Master, and players all using Character Reaction, Reader-Relative Impossibility, and Limit Impossibility. But Reader-Relative Impossibility breaks down in D&D precisely because the phenomenology of the player (who is doing the reader's role here) is taken up with applying an algorithm in exactly the same way one solves a chemistry problem.

This disconnect does not happen with respect to natural magic because the player is doing something very similar to what her character is doing: mastering a set of rules to manipulate reality. The character affects fictional reality by discerning the natural laws of a fictional world. The player changes the progress of the game by using the laws of *Dungeons and Dragons* mechanics. But with unnatural magic, the characters, non-player characters, and monsters are doing something radically different, violating the laws of the fictional world in a horrific manner. And the very methods that writers utilize to get the reader to experience horror are systematically ruled out by the fact that for the player the magic in question is just a system of probabilities to be manipulated dispassionately. The sense that what is taking place is impure in the sense of being dangerous, revolting, and (the clincher in this context) violating what is possible is severely impeded. For the player, the Fireball spell is commonplace in the fictional world, and the player's understanding of it as a ludological algorithm makes it impossible to think of the spell as a manifestation of impossibility.

The Unnatural Powers of Narrative

Fourth Edition D&D's strong commitment to providing balanced fantasy combat requires players to learn probability algorithms that ensure a rough equality in effectiveness among all the different classes of characters, whether they use magic or not. The benefits of so doing have been immense; ludologically speaking. In actual play, D&D 4e allows a group of players to become a collective of highly effective epic heroes. The party's wizard can throw balls of fire, wiping out weaker enemies, while the party's fighting man single-handedly holds back an army of goblins, provided, that is, that the party's cleric can heal the fighting man's wounds just long enough for the sneaky rogue to backstab the goblin chieftain.

The narrative description of the wizard and fighter's actions seems wildly different, of course, but the strength of the game is that its mathematics ensures that each of these roles is distinct in style but equivalent in importance. Though powers differ in scope and utility, they remain equivalent in terms of effectiveness. From a ludological perspective, player mastery of these rules ensures equivalent effectiveness within the game as long as the players roll well; variance in effectiveness is always a result of probability (by way of dice rolls) and a given player's ludological mastery of the game's rules. In addition to the slowness of combat in 3.5 D&D, the game ended up being incredibly unsatisfying to play precisely because at higher levels the magic users were so much more powerful than non-magic users of the same level.

For players of 4e, casting magic is always in danger of just becoming part of a mechanical grind to which they subject their characters; Carroll's thinking shows why this crawl is so non-Lovecraftian. The player becomes such a master of how the spells work in the game mechanics that the sense of the impossible is removed. The "magic" spells invariably end up seeming like nothing more than a kind of technology appropriate to the fantasy world in question.

The problem of unnatural magic came to us in large part because of the game's mechanical focus. In the new *Player's Handbook 2*, the introduction of the Wild Magic Sorcerer allowed us to see this game's shortcomings. Wild Magic—a magic far beyond the sorcerer's ability to consistently control—is modeled in D&D 4e by changes in probability; even numbers cause one effect, while odd numbers cause another. Though this mechanical approach ensures that the results remain balanced with the actions of other characters, the lack of variance and extreme consistency of results seemed problematic. Shouldn't chaos feel chaotic? The Warlock, too, rubs us the wrong way. Shouldn't people who make pacts with unnatural and inhuman creatures from beyond feel slightly different than other characters in the "Striker" role of direct damage dealing characters?

Rules for combat maneuvers in D&D 4e span almost 1,000 pages through numerous books; rules for negotiation and role-playing are few and far between. This lack may be necessary. To date there has been exactly one book that focuses on developing and creating shared narratives in D&D 4e: *Dungeon Master's Guide 2*. This book is short on ludological elements—there are very few rules provided for these sorts of things—but relies heavily on improvisation tips along with concrete suggestions for developing and sharing narrative power amongst players and Dungeon Masters.

Ultimately, constructing narrative is the entirety of any Dungeon Master's job in a *Dungeons and Dragons* campaign. Despite all of the time spent crafting maps, antagonists, monsters, and fell artifacts, what a Dungeon Master is really doing is populating a world—even if that world is only one dungeon large—within which a group of heroes will either find glory or an unmarked grave. Though there may not be a way to convincingly model satisfying mechanics that account for the unnatural within the game system, Noël Carroll's conception of the horrific gives Dungeon Masters all of the narrative tools they need to accomplish this task.

Suppose you're a Dungeon Master, charged with setting the mood for something truly unnatural: a gibbering, scab-ridden priest in feces stained garments forcing brainwashed followers to summon their world-destroying patron to our reality. The scene could be set by noting that the cultists are chanting foul prayers through sheer will; their bodies, like reality itself, are rebelling against the conflation of unnatural forces attempting to break in. While their mouths spit out prayers, their eyes cry tears of blood, insects and birds are fleeing the environs post-haste, and hair begins to fall out in animate clumps. In this way, we could supply Character Reaction and comply with Carroll's first requirement.

Reader-Relative Impossibility seems only a bit more tricky. Perhaps the fleeing vermin begin growing impossibly large as they fail to escape the cresting waves of unnatural magic flowing out of the priest, or the heroes' shadows fight free of the heroes and refuse to let the heroes pass. The earth and the cultists begin to bleed into each other, such that the ground breathes and cries and screams at the players. With the categories provided by Carroll and a willingness to improvise, any knowing violation of the possible can create the necessary narrative effect.

Limit Impossibility is the most difficult to pull off. We are not H. P. Lovecraft, or Stephen King, or Clive Barker, and it can be difficult to essentially improvize a Lovecraftian vamp. But the benefit of a tabletop role-playing game like D&D 4e is that you as a Dungeon Master know your players: their playstyles, their personalities, and hopefully what makes them tick. Use what you know, and see if you can freak them out. Perhaps the priest, as the ritual reaches its zenith, no longer speaks in a language that is recognizably human. Instead of hearing sounds, the heroes' brains hear unnatural silences when the priest cries out—the corruption pouring from his lips is so unthinkable that their minds refuse to process it. Confuse sensory information: tell them his voice sounds red, or describe tactile sensations every time they look upon something. With information like this, going for broke and not stopping for dice rolls *can* get the job done.

Remember, there simply cannot be rules for everything a Dungeon Master does. Just make something up and hope for the best. Carroll's "rules" for the unnatural are no more an algorithm for what we ought to do than the *Dunegon Master's Guide 2* provides algorithms for sharing narrative. Instead, they are more of a best practice that can help all of us get the kinds of things we want from a game. A Dungeon Master can construct narrative by strictly following the mechanical rules, true, but nothing's stopping her from contravening the rules when the need arises.

Lovecraftian fiction may be filled with Shoggoths, Dunwich Horrors, and tentacled beings from beyond reality, but little information is given on how humanity can fight them; instead, time is spent describing the ways these things warp the world, and how characters unfortunate enough to meet these beings either succumb to them or flee. Wizards dallying with powers beyond reality often do not do so for long, or with any reliability. The unnatural worms its way into reality in the best horror novels, and when it does all bets are off, but such events must remain rare, lest the unnatural become everyday and ordinary.

Thus it is no surprise that the ludological elements of D&D 4e give short shrift to the unnatural. Ludological treatment would naturalize the unnatural within the game world or the minds of the players, thus destroying the horror and mystery that makes them desirable for inclusion within a role-playing game or true to the literature and media that inspired them. Why else would a 4e Warlock not seem all that different in combat from any other class? A Shoggoth with an armor class, damage-causing statistics, and entirely predictable magical powers in the newest Monster Manual is a far different creature than that which Lovecraft can never fully describe; Tolkien's Watcher in the Water would not be the same if we knew exactly how many tentacles lurked beneath the waves.

The problem of unnatural magic—and, perhaps, of unnatural things in their entirety—is ultimately only a problem if one believes that a role-playing game is defined solely by the rules that underlie the game's world. Though something like this kind of rule fetishism may be gaining steam in the work of some video game theorists (such as Miguel Sicart), in the world of tabletop role-playing games this has been a non-starter since Gary Gygax created the art forty years ago.

Dungeons and Dragons, when done right, is first and foremost about creating shared narratives. The assorted min-maxers, ludologists, and stat freaks that pepper our game tables forget this at their own Lovecraftian peril.

12

The Worlds of *Dungeons and Dragons*

Timothy Morton

In *Dungeons and Dragons*, players and referees are enjoined to imagine worlds and realities in painstaking detail, thinking up characters who could find their way around these worlds, mapping them, exploring them, struggling with them, escaping them, dying in them. Players constantly think outside the human box.

J.R.R. Tolkien was a creator of fantasy worlds and blender of myths (and prototype of the D&D dungeon master) who drew on his learning to supply, in his mind, a national myth for Britain, a country that lacked one. Yet in so doing, Tolkien also opened up an exit route from thinking inside the box, even if it was only a fantasy exit—utopia, the possibility of imagining that things might be different. The interchangeable, DIY worlds of D&D are less potent than an ersatz national myth precisely because it's a game, not a novel. D&D provides ways of imagining different realities, testing hypotheses and (last but not least) sheer escapism.

To be a good D&D player, you have to be able to put yourself in a stranger's shoes. That stranger is the character you play in the game. In philosophical terms, you have to be a phenomenologist. Phenomenology is the philosophy of sensuality and experience. Among its many contributions to our understanding of reality, phenomenology explores the ways in which beings—human beings, animals, perhaps even plants and stones—construct worlds.

These worlds come in two different flavors, roughly speaking. The first flavor has to do with practicality. The second flavor has to do with aesthetic feeling. D&D contains both types of world. The game is about constructing and then mapping and exploring a coherent world complete with tools such as weapons for accomplishing practical aims, such as gaining experience (which helps a player character to advance) or getting treasure. Yet the game also includes countless opportunities for redundant features of the world, features whose only purpose is to delight and disturb.

Aspects of the World

Traditionally, philosophers think of phenomenology as giving reasons for separating humans from other entities as somehow unique in their apprehension of the world as such. And as part of this tradition, philosophers have often imagined this apprehension to carve out differences between various categories, such as:

Foreground and background

Worlds and horizons

Distant and near

Tool and broken tool

Authentic and inauthentic

Human and nonhuman

Presence and absence

Before I have ideas, before I process thoughts, before I generate concepts, I am "in" some world that is more or less explicit to my attention, but which is definitely implicit to my being. In phenomenology, world doesn't mean *planet*. This phenomenological world is profoundly inescapable, unlike the terrestrial globe on which you are reading these words. If you accelerate beyond a certain limit, you will exit Earth's gravitational field. But no amount of acceleration will allow you to leave the phenomenological world.

Early in the twentieth century the German biologist Jakob von Uexküll conducted highly original studies of animal "worlds." Bees, for instance, or ticks, inhabit a totally different environment than humans, according to Uexküll. Martin Heidegger famously remarked that animals are "poor in world," that they lack the ability to see reality as a world, like humans do. This anthropocentrism accords with Lacan and his disciples such as Slavoj Žižek, who argue that humans alone are capable of sticking out like sore thumbs from their "life-world." Against this, some philosophers have asserted that non-humans also have worlds. Still others have argued for a more radical view, namely, that no lifeform, not humans, not bees, have anything like a world. In this sense, humans are like non-humans because *no one* has a world!

How does D&D help us to think about this philosophical debate? For a start, D&D seems to be very much about worlds and "worlding," the processes of creating and experiencing worlds. Aside from engaging in combat, the most basic operation of a D&D player is to map the world in which she finds herself. This spatial mapping is part of a more Heideggerian "worlding" in which player characters generate a sense of care and concern for the entities with which they coexist, fictional as they are: fellow party members, magical treasure, strange monsters.

Such worlds aren't simply boxes for living in, but are themselves alive. The player characters find themselves surrounded by all kinds of equipment that sometimes functions, sometimes fails: tools such as weapons and armor predominate. Things seem to appear and disappear according to whether they are dislocated or dislocating, or whether they simply function. This means that the sense of "world" is always going to be a play between bland inertia and uncanny aliveness. You play D&D precisely to experience the uncanny aspect of *world*. Take this typical description of an encounter from a commercially released "Dungeon Module." The referee (Dungeon Master) is supposed to read such a description to the players:

> You see a small cavern which is overgrown with fungi, very much like the larger chamber to the south. What appears to be another of the huge, pale crickets has just exited from the area, disappearing to the east. Upon looking around, you notice that it has been feeding near the middle of the south wall, and, in the spot it has cleared of fungus, something odd can be seen. There appears to be a mummified body wedged into a cranny at the back of the alcove-like area. Bright metal glints from it. (*The Lost Caverns of Tsojcanth*, p. 15)

The striking strangeness of the description confronts the players at once. Whose is that mummified body? Is the bright metal gold, or not? What to make of the strange fungal and insect life? Before the characters encounter this part of the caverns they are exploring, they are supposed to search through the wilderness, in which they may (or not, according to a roll of the dice) encounter a hermit. This hermit will trade for food a piece of paper, a page from a survivor's journal:

> *The small cave was the secret, for in back, hidden by* (here the text is blurred beyond any reading) . . . *and we descended. There was no certain path, so we* (smudged) . . . *and this is told of above, for it is where Yaim and Brelid met their end. Our persistence paid. The right way was beyond and narrow, so* (writing covered with dark stain) . . . *—eam lies straight pas—* (more stains) . . . *—pe the span swiftly to plunge to doom where the wat—* (here smudges and stains obliterate several lines) . . . *They were right. It is more dismal here than above. Only the two of us su-* (blotch) . . . *We pray that the lucky* (smudge) *is true, for we are now going to attempt entry fo—* (large rusty smears have wiped out the next words) . . . *of no help. I managed to escape. Why did we* (here the remaining few words are smeared and unreadable, save for the last word) . . . *beautiful.* (p. 7)

The party of characters is supposed to figure out how to proceed. But they're also confronted with a haunting strangeness, and this is very much part of the game. Part of this strangeness is the allusiveness that a fantasy role-playing game can draw on. In particular, this damaged text alludes to the journal kept by the dwarves in the Mines of Moria in Tolkien's *Lord of the Rings*. Like those Mines, as the hermit reveals, the caverns are rumored to be a "nexus of planes, and many odd monsters now inhabit" them (p. 7). The caverns are not only strange in themselves, but act as gateways to other non-material planes of existence, where, for instance, demons reside. The very opacity of the writing, the blurring and staining, some of it the "rusty smears" of blood, is what contributes powerfully to the sense of being in a world, that is, a place full of strange pathways trodden by others, of strange meanings inscribed by strangers. The last word, "beautiful," marks this. The paper, the story, the traces of conflict and loss, are powerfully *alluring*, drawing the players into the world. Worlds are not transparent.

The sense of *world*, then, is like resting on a stone only to find that it's part of a ring of standing stones. There is a combination of mystery and earthiness in D&D that evokes the double-sided quality of *world*. This alluring mystery is the very dimension in which causality happens, if we accept the view that action is the result of what Graham Harman calls *allure*. That final word of the journal makes us wonder: how beautiful? For whom? Might there be something of value there? Where is "there"? The trouble with the aesthetic dimension is that it is where the lies live, including the Cretan ones: "What constitutes pretense is that, in the end, you don't know whether it's pretense or not" (Lacan, *Le Seminaire*, p. 48).

Objects appear to have their own vitality, particularly in the case of special objects: a piece of treasure to be found on a quest, perhaps a magical one. A magic item, for instance, such as a sword found in some frost giant's castle, beckons with the thought of strangers who have handled it and the giants who slew them. As Heidegger remarks about a boat: "The boat anchored at the shore refers in its being-in-itself to an acquaintance who undertakes his voyages with it, but as a 'boat strange to us', it also points to others."

It is the arising feeling of *world* that Heidegger settles on, as does D&D: "The others who are 'encountered' in the context of useful things in the surrounding world at hand are not somehow added on in thought to an initially merely objectively present thing, but these 'things' are encountered from the world in which they are at hand for the others" (*Being and Time*, p. 111). It is fundamentally this coexistence, and the feeling of coexistence, that makes D&D a special game. The technical aspects of the game seem to sink from view, and a distinctive tonality arises, like the sound of a certain piece of music. The world is nothing other than coexistence with strangers.

The very fictionality and displacement of the role-playing game as a game seem only to enhance this world-like quality. But perhaps the DIY quality of D&D also militates against these worlds having a fundamental coherence. You can see so easily around the back of the stage, as it were. This ambiguity is illuminating. So a study of D&D will definitely help us to get clear about what worlds mean in philosophy.

Sincerities

There is a phenomenon that the phenomenologist Ortega y Gasset calls *ingenuousness*, but which we could also, following Graham Harman, call sincerity. Sincerity means that you are irreducibly glued to your "intentional objects" (Husserl), your experiences, or, in the words of Buckaroo Banzai, the 1980s cult film character, "Wherever you go, there you are." For instance, if you try to maintain a critical distance towards an experience you are having—there you are, distancing yourself. You just can't jump outside your phenomenological skin.

The D&D fan will know what I mean if she or he only considers the reverence with which the Player's Handbook, Monster Manual and the gem dice are handled. These supposed metalanguages (they help to define what the game is) are treated with care and respect—they even tell us to do so themselves, in various places. The ten-year-old me savored readily and distinguished the smell and feel of these different objects, let alone what they were saying. They themselves constituted part of the D&D world, as did the Games Workshop (for this UK-born player), located at 1 Dalling Road in Hammersmith, London, where you could buy the paraphernalia. Long after I stopped playing a friend of mine took me to dinner, via a train station that happened to be just next to the store in question (Stamford Brook on the London Underground). We descended a staircase and exited to the street, and there we were. It was an uncanny sense of what Heidegger calls "nearness" that assailed me as I realized where I was standing. In this sense, I am still inside the world of D&D.

Now some forms of hermeneutics and postmodern theory think they have mastered the truth of this phrase, by claiming that it means that there is no top-level explanatory discourse that can account for everything, just a mélange of micro-narratives to choose from. This means that hermeneutics (such as deconstruction) didn't take phenomenology seriously enough. For sincerity has nothing to do with the lack of a mode of thinking that will act as a key to all others. Sincerity means that *my being ontologically precedes any idea about it I have whatsoever*. So that even if we're imagining ourselves as ironical postmodern free-players, there we are, imagining that.

Now this doesn't have to mean, as many ecological critics have taken it to mean, that we're embedded in some kind of lush lifeworld that gives meaning to our lives. For this too is uncannily similar to the postmodern idea (like it or not) that *world* is about *meaning*. What postmodernism and its mortal enemy, ecological criticism share, ironically, is that we can see clearly what the world is and that it "means something" for humans (even if this is a lack of meaning).

What phenomenology is really saying is that entities such as humans (and teacups, lions and dungeon modules) find themselves on the inside of some other entity (or "object" in the lingo) whose essence is real yet radically unknowable. The viscous, sticky quality of sincerity means that we are on the inside of another entity, like dreams unable to touch the inside surface of the skull in which they happen. Our experiences stick to us like bacteria in our stomachs or DNA in our cells—we can't imagine existing without them. They are immanent, they fill up every nook and cranny of our being like the filling of a marshmallow.

D&D allows players to study and to handle different forms of sincerity. There's Elvish sincerity, Orcish sincerity, the sincerity of Paladins and the sincerity of Rangers (these are characters and monsters in the game). There's the sincerity of Druids and the sincerity of Clerics. Magic Users, another character class, have Magic User sincerity: they have Magic User strength (or lack thereof) and Magic User spells and Magic User ways of talking and moving. Different characters, different monsters, have different environments, different physical and experiential "worlds."

Only consider the sincerity of the Illusionist player character. Such a character is fascinating from this point of view, since she or he is able to create deceptive illusions that appear real to those easily influenced by such things—and if the spell is powerful enough, that includes a host of beings. These spells are graded in seven levels of intensity, all the way up to "Alter Reality," which does pretty much what you would expect. The spells descend through "Permanent Illusion," which generates illusions that seem real to the sense of touch, smell, sight and sound; to lesser spells that create walls of fog, or hypnotic hallucinations (*Advanced Dungeons and Dragons Players' Handbook*, pp. 94–100). These are illusions that have causal effects on others, not simply eye candy (or any other kind of candy) for sheer aesthetic amusement. Indeed, the *Player's Handbook* suggests that Illusionists may in many circumstances be "more potent" than regular magicians. The Illusionist character is a recursive feature of D&D, which wholly depends upon the play of illusion and the willing suspension of disbelief, and at the same time an uncanny recognition that this is indeed a game.

No wonder, then, that different types of alignment (codes of ethical and moral conduct) imply different worlds beyond the physical everyday of the "Prime Material." The world of demons, for instance, is the world of Chaotic Evil. The world of devils is the world of Lawful Evil. The various gods of the religions that D&D cheerfully allows to co-exist inhabit these realms. The bizarre frog-like Slaads inhabit the anarchic world of Chaotic Neutral. The gods of Lovecraft's Cthulhu exist in their non-Euclidean city. And so on.

Worlds versus Objects

This isn't just a case of fantasy versus reality. On that score, the boot might even be on the other foot. Have you ever seen matter? Sure, you've seen patterns of electrons in a cloud diffusion chamber. You've seen iron filings spreading out around a magnet. You've seen pictures of wave packets. But have you ever seen matter? Do electrons even encounter matter? Sure, they bombard one another in particle accelerators, but they don't bombard "matter." Wherever you look, there is form: with all due respect to Mr. Spock, you have never seen "pure matter without form." Imagining that worlds transcend matter—that they are a about form and disposition and alignment—so that the Prime Material is only one realm among many is an Aristotelian insight. This is not a materialist vision of "matter" floating in a void.

Wherever a player character looks, there are worlds. There's no letup in the "wherever you go, there you are" of sincerity when a character travels between these worlds. The Astral Plane is a connective tissue that bonds the worlds together in a plenum that can be accessed by magic and paranormal powers ("psionics"). A Druid can walk through trees as if they were soft air, or transport herself or himself via plants. A Druid can talk with nonhuman lifeforms. An Illusionist can generate seemingly real worlds, just like a Dungeon Master. There are elemental planes of water, air, fire, and earth. In terms of traditional phenomenology these worlds constitute backgrounds against which meaningful action can take place.

Even for an Illusionist, the whole point of D&D is to explore sincerity, all the way to the end, which is when your character dies. This is why D&D is associated with nerdish fascination, rather than cynical cool. The great innovation of games such as D&D is that they allow players to handle sincerities at will, to turn them around in their hands like snow globes and watch the flakes falling inside, differently, onto different scenes. The sincerities are the worlds of D&D, and to be capable of such handling they must be (at least partly) open worlds. And the sincerities can coexist side by side, or even inside one another, so that we can encounter paladins in a Norse landscape, or Greek mythological beings in a Tolkienesque world, or vice versa.

Romantic Worlds

Sincerities are fundamentally open, because we can never get to the bottom of them. Who knows exactly what a Druidic way of walking is? Yet there you are, a Druid, walking. Who knows if you even make it explicit to yourself or to your fellow players? Your Druid character continues to walk through the forest. There is a mystery and an opacity in sincerity. This is why a narrative form is so conducive to exploring it, and a particular narrative form at that. D&D is about narratives, and narratives are about Romantic art (with a capital R). In this kind of narrative, the protagonist explores a world: this is done explicitly in D&D through mapping terrain, and less explicitly by evocations of milieu in the atmospherics of dungeon mastering (refereeing), the various companion items in the commercially available D&D modules such as *The World of Greyhawk*, and a culture of gamers who share stories about their games in specialist publications such as *Dragon* and *White Dwarf*, and now online.

Why Romantic? *Romantic* comes from the French *roman*, meaning story. The Romantic sees the world as story-shaped: life is an adventure, a quest. This story shape has to do with the vicarious consumption of an identity—playing a role, imagining what it would be like to be someone, putting yourself in someone's shoes. Romantic narrative, in other words, is a kind of virtual reality without computing hardware. A game version of the kind of late-Romantic versions of this narrative—Tolkien's stories spring most obviously to mind—only enhances the vicarious quality of consuming the other's identity. This is because things become so much more intimate and personal when you play them rather than simply reading about them. It's also because the game structure is open-ended—you need never reach a conclusion or cycle around in a development section. You can always be at the beginning, which is the best place to be in a Romantic story. Look at how Wordsworth tells the story of the French Revolution: "Bliss was it in that dawn to be alive, / But to be young was very heaven!" (*The Prelude*).

Tolkien's refashioning of Celtic and Norse mythology, Old English epic and so on is Romantic, precisely insofar as it allows the reader to inhabit a vicarious identity, participating in a fantasy world that layers multiple traditions to create something new. Tolkien systematically created believable lifeworlds for his stories before he wrote a single episode, by constructing languages such as Elvish. Words contain archaeological evidence of the philosophy and ideology of the social contexts in which they are used.

D&D's exhaustive, inclusive approach to the kinds of being who can be player characters and non-player characters (NPCs) invites a kind of super-Tolkienesque imagination: from Tolkien's unique overlapping of myths and languages, to a potentially infinite space of similar overlappings. Alongside Tolkienesque Nordic mythology, some obvious realms present themselves: orientalist (and just plain Eastern) worlds; pirates (the TSR *Slave Lords* series is a straightforward example); Gothic horror (*The Tomb of Horrors*, a host of undead monsters).

D&D assumes a gigantic, continental-scale milieu—Gygax's World of Greyhawk is only the commercial one but really the template is Tolkien's painstaking imagining of Middle-earth. Beyond this, there are oceans. Beyond these, there may be other worlds, either on the players' plane of existence (the "Prime Material") or in other realms on the Astral Plane. Gods inhabit this beyond—as many or as few as the players desire, furnished in the first instance by the *Deities and Demigods* volume. Beyond this, as several commercial dungeon modules make plain, there are intersecting times and places, such as sci-fi aliens (*The Barrier Peaks*), Latin American cultures, and so on.

Forms of Play

D&D allows its players to imagine multiple characters that inhabit discrete, specific worlds based on their species, ethnicity, profession, languages and physical makeup. Each character class is a genre, that is, a horizon of expectation (in Hans Robert Jauss's terminology)—that is, an imaginative configuration space in which all kinds of actions, speech and thought are permissible and impossible. Players are encouraged to imagine the sort of thing that their characters do, think and say: this imaginative identification immediately places them in a world.

Worlds depend upon all kinds of aesthetic mood lighting and special effects, such as the background–foreground distinction. Players are encouraged to project imaginatively, filling in less detailed parts of the D&D world. This only serves to enhance its vividness. In this way a back-and-forth oscillation between nearness and distance is established. Players know their identities, and a little bit of their history. They know their colleagues. They know the immediate milieu they are in (a commercially available "Dungeon Module" or a hand-crafted campaign). But there are constant encouragements to think beyond the immediate terrain and beyond the exigencies of eating, sleeping and slaying orcs.

Yet the worlds that players and DM can assemble can be disassembled and examined from different angles. Unlike the world of a novel, in which the narrator controls our access and the kinds of readerly experience we have there, the worlds of D&D supply a strange mixture of *Gesamtkunstwerk*—Wagner's idea of a seamless "total work of art"—and constructivism—the avantgarde approach of dissolving the spell of aesthetic realism.

D&D creates DIY totalities can be put together and taken apart. It's as if D&D speculatively combines these approaches into a package that neither would have liked very much, though ironically for the same reason: the worlds of D&D aren't integrated enough. D&D doesn't have the veneer of respectable shock, nor does it have the sheen of the total work of art. Just think of the varied ways of illustrating D&D in the official products: Sutherland's and Trampier's drawing styles, not to mention Errol Otus, are profoundly different. No problem, because we're dealing with a playful modularity. For a D&D fan, seeing how it works is part of the fun.

D&D is thus part of the long history of realism, which can be seen as the ongoing encapsulation of one mode by another mode. First epistolary novels, made of letters between the characters, string together those moments in drama in which characters read letters. Then fictional devices such as early realism (Jane Austen for instance) encapsulate the epistolary form, so that isolated letters appear in a wider sea of narration. Realism rapidly develops ways of encapsulating the direct speech of characters so that the narrator can control what some narrative theories call focalization, the sensation that we are inside one or more character's heads. Focalization is achieved through the simple technological leap of dropping the "tagging" of indirect speech, so that instead of "Kermit woke at 4 A.M. He thought that it was going to be a good day," we read, "Kermit woke at 4 A.M. It was going to be a good day."

Thus realism progresses into naturalism, in which the narrator almost entirely stops holding our hand and guiding us through the narrative world. In the meantime, Tolkien and others start to encapsulate diverse Norse and Celtic myths within the realist mode, giving rise to fantasy adventure stories. Roleplaying games encapsulate Tolkien, so that there is no one single world with one single guide (the narrator), but a multitude of worlds that can be explored and dismantled at will.

The long history of realism is the long history of the inclusion of the narrator in the act of "reading," which must now be defined within the broader configuration space of play. First the reader gets to read over the shoulder of characters reading one another's letters. Then the reader gets to follow a kind of "blank" in the text, a moving target like a cursor—focalization, moving from inside one character's head to the inside of another's. (Austen begins this further empowerment of the reader.) Then realist narrators such as Dickens begin to move the reader around the narrative world like tour guides. Naturalist narrators stop holding the reader's hand and permit her to wander in and out of focalization as if at will—a powerful special effect that renders a feeling of freedom and verisimilitude. Truly the reader herself provides the realness—

a fantastically elegant economy: all the writer has to do is drop the "tagging" of indirect speech. The narrative *I* is encapsulated in a larger configuration space that imagines the reader participating—albeit in a rather passive way—in the co-creation of the story. The dropping of the indirect speech "tag" forces the reader to project into the narrative, to put herself in the shoes of the "speaker" (a term used roughly to describe speech and feeling and thought).

What happens in the move from realism to naturalism is a refinement. What happens in the move from narrative fiction to role-playing games is a drastic jump. Suddenly, the encapsulation swallows the whole configuration space in which realism plays out, turning it into just one element of a higher dimensional configuration space. Narrative is something the DM performs, sometimes, but it isn't everything. Thus the notion of "world" becomes less authoritarian, more participatory, where before gaming the history of realism had been one of increasingly subtle kinds of control of the reader.

Willing Disbelief

D&D is a game in which pieces of story, and the worlds they evoke, are allowed to co-exist within a wider configuration space that allows for sudden dislocations and jumps. Unlike most post-Romantic-period philosophy, then, D&D is a both–and form that allows equally for totalizing worlds and complete demystification, sometimes at one and the same time. Just consider what happens during a "melée round" in which player characters fight monsters.

These rounds are totally arbitrary, allowing each party (players and DM-controlled monsters) a chance to attack and defend. No realistic world would operate like that. Yet this arbitrariness is accepted, indeed it's a central feature of the game, since slaying monsters is the most important way to gain Experience Points and advance one's character to the next level. What happens in the micro-mechanics of the game, then, is not so much a willing suspension of disbelief, allowing oneself to be immersed in something one knows is a fiction, but the precise opposite. What happens is a *willing disbelief*, that punctures the Romantic narrative continuity of world building to get on with the serious business of earning Experience

Points. A kind of fetishistic humor operates here: we know this is clunky, but this is how we have to proceed. Otherwise it really would just be a novel and we would be passive recipients of a master narrative. In evoking worlds and simultaneously allowing them to be changed, added, sorted, punctured and ruptured at every turn, D&D makes us think about the manifold, overlapping and confusing—not to say oppressive and wonderful—worlds that we humans regularly inhabit.

13
A Role of the Dice

LEVI BRYANT

Dungeons and Dragons discloses a world populated by active substances divided between their virtual proper being and their local manifestations. A substance consists of any individual entity such as enchanted swords, white dragons, humans, and torches used to light one's way in a dungeon.

The virtual proper being of a substance consists of its powers or the actions of which it is capable. For example, an enchanted sword has the capacity or power to cut. These powers are referred to as *affects*, where affects are understood as capacities to affect and be affected. An elf's capacity to see in the dark is a capacity to be affected. Such affects are passive insofar as they are defined by our ability to be affected by other things.

An enchanted sword's capacity to cut and parry blows is, by contrast, an active affect insofar as it is a capacity to act on other things. Local manifestations, by contrast, refer to the *qualities* and *acts* a substance actualizes in acting. The color of a finely wrought elven stein is not a quality that the stein *has*, but is rather the actualization of the stein's powers of color, an event or happening, produced as a result of the stein's relationship to *different* lighting conditions. In candlelight the stein is a deep, dark blue that flickers and dances. In sunlight the stein is a brilliant blue. In darkness the stein is black. Qualities are not possessions of objects, but rather actions on the part of substances.

Gods, characters, monsters, equipment, natural entities like rocks, and magical items are all active substances. How are substances individuated? The question of individuation raises the issue of what constitutes an entity. The question of individuation asks, *When* is a substance? It's not a question of how *we* *identify* substances, but rather a question of what makes a substance an individual. In other words, when is a substance a genuine individual thing such as an ogre, rather than a *plurality* of individual things such as a set of ogres that happen to be enjoying grog at a particular tavern?

Are substances necessarily *simple* entities that cannot be divided any further like atoms as conceived by the Greek philosopher Democritus? For Democritus and his followers such as Lucretius, atoms were the only true substances because they were thought to be indivisible, while *combinations* of atoms were rejected as true substances because they could be broken apart or divided. Are more complex aggregate entities like carrion crawlers and enchanted cloaks individual substances or are they mere aggregates because they are made up of simpler, indivisible parts? If substances need not be simple or indivisible to be individuals, if they can be aggregates, then is a blind man with a cane one or two entities?

Often entities do not act alone, but rather act in and through *alliances* with *other* entities. Much of what we do and think is deeply reliant on our relations to entities independent of us. Compare the difference between a person solving a complex mathematical equation such as solving for x in the equation $4x + 274 = 488$ in their *head* alone versus the person solving the equation using pencil and paper. Our tendency is to hold that mind and the cognitive activities of mind take place strictly *inside* of our heads, and that objects such as pen and paper are strictly external to our minds.

However, as we reflect on examples such as solving a complex mathematical equation, we find that while there are some of us that can solve these equations solely in our heads, many of us can only do so with great effort and time or not at all. The pencil and paper are not merely optional prostheses for these sorts of cognitive activities, but are indispensable elements of these cognitive activities. If solving such equations in my head alone is so difficult, then this is because I must remember the equation and each step of the equation that I have completed while simultaneously carrying out operations of subtraction and division.

By contrast, the paper upon which I solve the equation *remembers* previous steps of the solution for me, allowing me to momentarily forget them so as to attend to the step I'm currently working on. Not only this, the very *script* I use to solve the equation makes a profound difference in the mathematical operations of which I'm capable. There are forms of mathematical reasoning that are only possible, for example, with *arabic* numerals. Imagine trying to solve the above equation with *roman* numerals!

This simple example of mathematical reasoning suggests that the mind is not what is restricted to what takes place "*inside* the head," but is rather *extended* out into the world, such that mind is a circuit, an interplay, and interactive relationship between brain, body, and other substances in the world. I'm not saying that entities such as pencil and paper are *mental* entities, so that if brains did not exist they would not exist. What I'm saying is that these entities are integral elements of the thought process, not merely secondary props, that they are part of where thought itself takes place.

While there would be no thought without my brain, nonetheless, in solving the mathematical equation, my thought is literally taking place right there on the paper. This thesis was first proposed by Andy Clark and David Chalmers in 1998 as "the extended mind hypothesis." Cognitive scientists and philosophers of mind, they argue, have too long sought to understand mind based strictly on what goes on inside of their heads. This, they contend, has led to difficulties.

Clark maintains that mind should not be understood as what takes place inside the head but as an interactive relationship between brains, bodies, and entities in the world. As Clark puts it in *Supersizing the Mind*, "once we put our bioprejudices aside," then we see that physical objects are "a functional part of an extended cognitive machine."

> Such body- and world-involving cycles are best understood . . . as quite literally extending the machinery of mind out into the world—as building extended cognitive circuits that are themselves the minimal material bases for important aspects of human thought and reason. (p. xxvi)

The "bioprejudices" that Clark here refers to consist of seeing mind as bound within the limits of the skin and the soul, refusing to see the substances we engage with as elements in the thought process. It's not the boundaries of the body that individuate minds, but rather minds are a feedback circuit between the body and the substances the body engages with. And so the blind man by himself and the blind man with his walking stick are two distinct minds, just as the halfling thief with a cloak of invisibility and the halfling thief without such a cloak are two distinct entities. In each case, the capacities, powers, or abilities of the entities in question differ.

Substances are individuated not by their *qualities*, but 1. by their history, and 2. by their powers or abilities. The qualities of an object are variable and are a function of the powers of that substance. The skin of a warrior is now tan, now pale, depending on how much time he has been spending in the light and dungeons, yet the warrior, despite these variations, remains *that* warrior. As the warrior gains experience points he also gains new skills or powers, yet he nonetheless remains *that* warrior because his development is continuous with the past in which he lacked those powers.

Extensions, Assemblages, and Alliances

If substances are individuated not by their qualities but by the volcanic powers that populate them, then if a relation between two or more entities generates new powers that are not to be found among any of their elements alone, wherever new powers emerge as a result of these relations, wherever there are alliances between entities, we are looking at a distinct substance. The person who has a smart phone is quite literally a different type of mind than the person without a smart phone. There are things of which I am capable with my smart phone that I am not capable of without.

In *Dungeons and Dragons*, monsters attack the party together, the party works collaboratively searching dungeons and fighting monsters. In these instances, the monsters and the party become collective entities or war machines pitted against one another. The difference between a set of ogres that *happen* to be drinking mead together at the same tavern and a *band* of ogres is that the former do not form an assemblage, an alliance, whereas the latter are a well co-ordinated war machine whose actions depend on one another and result from one another in the common task of defeating the party.

However there are the less obvious alliances that characters have with their equipment and magical items. Michael Moorcock's Elric of Melniboné is different with and without his sword Stormbringer. Without Stormbringer, Elric is sickly and weak due to his albinism and is quickly fatigued if he does not continuously take drugs and magical potions. With Stormbringer, Elric is fed by the souls of those he slays, and filled with strength and energy. The sorcerer Raistlin Majere depicted in the *Dragonlance* novels written by Margaret Weiss and Tracy Hickman is different with and without his Staff of Magius. With the staff he is able to melt locks, open doors, and illuminate rooms. Without it he is not.

The French sociologist Bruno Latour writes that, according to materialists, "the good citizen is *transformed* by carrying the gun. A good citizen who, without a gun, might simply be angry may become a criminal if he gets his hands on a gun—as if the gun had the power to change Dr. Jekyll into Mr. Hyde." When active substances enter into relations with one another they generate *new* powers or affects capable of acting in ways not possible for either of them alone.

Canadian media theorist Marshall McLuhan famously said that a medium is an extension of man. A medium is any object that extends the powers of a humanoid. So, television extends the eyes, cars and airplanes extend the feet, the phone extends the ears, the stick a chimpanzee uses to capture insects in a rotting log extends its fingers, and so on. However, media do not merely extend powers or affects of entities in such a way that those powers remain as they were before, but rather they transform the very nature of those powers. The warrior's sword extends his teeth, hands, and nails, but the cutting power of the sword turns a humanoid with a sword into an entirely different being, now lethal to all sorts of beings within the vicinity of his weapon.

Where McLuhan argues that a medium is any object that extends man, and where Clark sees circuits between humans and objects like swords as distinct *minds*, this idea should be broadened to argue that a medium is any object that extends another *object*, whether that object is human or nonhuman, living or non-living. Wind is a medium that extends grains of sand in a sandstorm. Street lamps extend the world of insects. Humans are mediums for cultural memes that get replicated throughout society. Container ships extended cane toads from South America to Australia.

Humans extend technologies to the same degree that technologies extend humans insofar as in using technologies humans find they must embroil themselves in all sorts of other technologies to function. Human transit systems extend bacterial diseases across the planet, providing them with opportunities to replicate and undergo natural selection in unheard of ways. As Kevin Kelly observes, technologies are actually assemblages or networks of technologies that lead the users of the technology to extend these networks even where it is not their intention.

My television requires not only the television set itself, but electricity, cable, an internet connection, so that using my television I unwittingly extend this tangle of wires, radio singles, cable boxes, fiber optic cables, and all the rest in ways that are not my intention. In cases such as this, is the television an extension of my affects such as the capacity to see and hear, or am I, as it were, a part of the reproductive organs of this technological network, extending this mesh of wires, fiber optic cables, and so on throughout the world like the creep of kudzu in Virginia?

The catch is that in extending another object the object that is extended not only has its powers enhanced, but rather its very being, as Latour claims, is *transformed*. This is why constellations of active substances should not simply be talked about in terms of *use*, but in terms of *alliances*. In using something I merely embody my aim or goal in that tool. The tool I use is reduced to the purpose or aim that I give to it.

When I enter into an alliance, by contrast, my aims and goals are often modified and transformed as I must negotiate with the aims of those others in the alliance. This regularly happens in the case of technologies. In owning a car it was not my intention to have to regularly fill it with gas, get maintenance checks, or attend college meetings miles away, yet with owning a car these become necessary responsibilities and it becomes reasonable for the college to ask me to attend such meetings. In owning a smart phone it was not my intention to text throughout the day, to be available to my colleagues wherever I am, and to constantly respond to emails, yet I now find that my smart phone draws me to these activities and even transforms them into *responsibilities* as others come to expect us to be "plugged in" in this way. How often do we today hear students complain about professors who do not immediately respond to email?

Elric of Melniboné's sword Stormbringer is not merely an instrument that he uses for his ends, but rather fills him with a thirst for souls against which he must perpetually struggle. Just as the heroin addict complains that he has become a slave to this substance, so that all activities of his life are organized around getting and injecting heroin, Elric's life increasingly comes to be at the behest of his demonic sword.

Blogging and writing articles have very different structures by virtue of differences in technology. Articles are slowly paced, taking a great deal of time to appear, even longer to hear responses from people beyond the editors, and tend to work in the medium of writing alone. Blogs, by contrast, are multi-modal at the level of perception, deploying image, text, song, and video, and are pervaded by hyperlinks creating labyrinths for readers to follow. The time of the blog is lightning quick, generating very quick reader responses and therefore leading to condensation of arguments and a quick evolution and devo-lution of thought. As a consequence, one's process of thought and argumentation becomes different.

In *Laws of Media*, Marshall and Eric McLuhan, following Eric Havelock, argue that the shift from oral culture to pho-netic writing fundamentally changes the nature of our minds. With writing, the argument runs, complex mathematical thought becomes possible because paper can preserve complex chains of reasoning, allow us to see relations that would be invisible in thought alone due to the simultaneous juxtaposi-tion of numbers and figures on paper, allow for abstract philo-sophical thought, the formalization of law due to paper's ability to preserve prescriptions, and leads to a new experience of space, and so on.

Paper and writing change the very nature of our thought so that minds that exist only in an oral framework and minds in a written framework think very differently. Here the technolo-gies and tools we use are not things we merely impose *our* intentions and aims upon, they are not merely *records* of thought that would have taken place anyway in the absence of paper and writing, but rather they transform the very nature of our intentionality, thought, and aims. This is why our relations to other entities deserve to be understood as alliances and why these alliances ought to be understood as generative of new entities.

Everywhere in *Dungeons and Dragons* we see an attentiveness to the manner in which alliances are generative of new entities. Nude characters have their powers like strength, dexterity, and constitution, they have their resistances, they have their hit points tracking how much damage they can endure, and they have their skills and magical powers, yet they nonetheless remain ordinary humanoids. Yet when these humanoids enter into alliances with their equipment and magical items they become true war machines. A warrior in his armor undergoes a "becoming-turtle" that enhances his defensive powers, allowing him to ward off blows from other creatures. Yet, depending on the armor he also pays a price in mobility, having to adjust his movement to the type of armor he has. A warrior in plate armor will be encumbered in ways that one in leather armor is not. The weapons that the character uses will all have their own powers, advantages and disadvantages, and will be capable of dealing such and such an amount of damage.

The profound alliances we conclude with enchanted items change us, just as we become something akin to "prosthetic gods" with our technologies, as Freud put it in *Civilization and Its Discontents*. Enchanted swords increase the damage the warrior is able to deal with her blows. They will sometimes enhance the powers of the warrior, giving her greater strength or dexterity. Magical potions will give their users the power to fly, to see in the dark, or to breath fire. Certain cloaks, robes, and rings will grant their user powers of invisibility, resistance to the chilling breath of frost dragons and other creatures of Lovecraftian arctic worlds.

With alliances among substances it becomes possible not only for certain powers to activate themselves in ways that they otherwise would not, but there is also an emergence of new powers and entities through the coupling of entities together in assemblages. Entities can posses powers without exercising them. The sword that lies on the ground is unable to exercise its powers of cutting. The warrior without his sword is unable to actualize the powers of his muscles in that unique fashion that takes place when using a sword. Yet when substances enter into assemblages with one another, new constellations of powers emerge and therefore new entities. The priest with a mace and without a mace are two different entities. With the mace the priest becomes a poetic athlete of blunt force trauma, a force to be reckoned with. Without the mace the priest prays.

A Throw of the Dice and Local Manifestations

The question remains as to how substances actualize their powers in local manifestations. Recall that affect—which here is synonymous with power—consists, on the one hand, of the ability to act and be acted upon, while on the other hand, it consists of an "idea" or quality that accompanies acting and being acted upon. When sixty-year-old Patricia Gallant swam the English channel on August 21st and 22nd, she not only exercised her body's power of swimming in that way unique to swimming, these active affects on the part of the body were, no doubt, accompanied by "ideas". These ideas consisted of the joy of using her body, the fatigue that accompanied her action, the excitement of nearing the completion of her goal. When my four-year-old daughter eats blueberries, she is not merely acted upon by the blueberries, but this state of being acted upon is accompanied by an experience of intense alimentary pleasure.

Let us broaden this idea of "ideas" accompanying actions and being acted upon to include any local manifestation. A feeling, a thought, a sensation, an emotion are all local manifestations of particular types of substances—aardvarks, humans, tardigrades, cane toads, blue dragons, hobgoblins, orcs, dragonflies, and so forth—undergo through actions and being acted upon. The color of my blue stein wrought by elves will no less be an "idea", a local manifestation, accompanying the stein's being acted upon by wavelengths of light.

Here the point is *not* that nonhuman, non-living entities are *conscious* or think, but rather that ideas are but one type of intentional actualization among many others. The particular way in which a plant or tree grows, the way its branches or limbs reach out when growing in an area heavily populated by others trees will also be an "idea" or local manifestation arising through a combination of the tree's acts in growing and how it is acted upon by other trees and plants blocking its access to sunlight. The configuration of the tree's branches will mark the petrified, yet still living, history of the tree's "decisions" in response to these other factors. The way in which molten lava crystallizes upon the land of a Hawaiian island will be a local manifestation of how acts on the part of lava and how it is acted upon by air and the local environment interact with one another as the highly viscous lava unique to this region flows. The pattern it takes on will be the result of a combination of the viscosity of the lava, the terrain of the land, air temperatures, humidity, trees and houses in its path, and so on.

Yet how is it that substances produce their "ideas" or local manifestations? By what processes do substances produce their intentional states or actualizations? Sometimes local manifestations will result from acts of will on the part of the humanoid, monster, or god. At other times an entity will be acted upon by others, leading to the actualization of a quality such as a rock being heated and thereby changing its color. Yet in all these cases, there will be multiple mediations among affects of acting and being acted upon and the encounters between entities that incubate local manifestations. The qualitative manifestations that are produced will be pervaded by *chance*. The encounters between entities are not determined *a priori*, and from this it follows that the substances that populate the universe are not related *internally* and that not *all* things are related to all other things.

As every starving person knows, we are often unrelated to vital things that we need such as food. Rather, relations between active substances are external, variable, and pervaded by chance. Likewise, even among those entities that act according to their own will or initiative, the actualizations they produce are variable and often acts are undertaken in alliance with a variety of different substances. How, then, are encounters produced and what determines the particular form a local manifestation takes?

Dungeons and Dragons is famous for its dice. Seven in all, they come in beautiful crystalline shapes, often wrought like fine gems, and consist of four-sided, six-sided, eight-, twelve-, ten-sided, and "one hundred"-sided dice. Presiding over each moment, encounter, and action in the game, the events that transpire in this alternative world are everywhere ramified by chance, creating a strange combination of freedom and necessity, choice and constraint, that allows the game to evolve and develop in ways that neither the dungeon master who presides over the game nor the players can anticipate.

The dice will determine the aleatory encounters that take place between the characters, non-player characters, and monsters, the way in which different active substances are brought into imbroglios with one another, and will determine the precise qualities local manifestations take. The paradox will thus be that it is *chance* that generates *necessity*. The way the dice come up when thrown will generate the parameters of the necessities, the networks of relations, and the circumstances to which the players and monsters must respond.

At the level of encounters, the dice will generate fields of relations between different active substances. The Dungeon Master throws the dice. Will a pack of giant rats appear? Perhaps a hoard of pigmy imps will flood in from an unnoticed hallway. Or perhaps it will be oozing green slimes, filled with poison or emitting deadly gases. Maybe there will be a trap. Or again perhaps there will be some unnoticed treasure.

Fate rains down from the dice, generating circumstance to which all involved must respond. It determines the parameters, the necessity, with which the characters must contend like surfers having to respond to subtle variations in waves to remain upright. The Dungeon Master's throw of the dice thus generates a *regime of attraction*. A regime of attraction is a network of relations between active substances, an "ecological situation", to which all the entities involved must respond and react. If these regimes are regimes of *attraction*, then this is because they call to the participants, in much the same way Alfonso Lingis describes the world calling for appropriate responses from us in *The Imperative*, demanding a response.

The Dungeon Master throws the dice and they come up null. The characters proceed as before, oblivious to the potential fate they just escaped. The dice are thrown again and there is a trap in the vicinity. Now the dice must be thrown again. Will the halfling thief or elven ranger in the party detect the trap? No, it is sprung. Another throw of the dice. Will they resist the poison on the tips of the daggers flying at them? Chance ramifies itself again. There is an encounter. With what? The dice rattle across the table. Wraiths drift up from behind abandoned casks. Will they save against the frosty powers of the undead?

A throw of the dice draws active substances together in circumstances or regimes of attraction, yet from the standpoint of questions about local manifestation, the truly interesting events occur when the characters and monsters strive to act. Local manifestations are manifestations because they are actualizations of a quality and are local because the way the quality manifests or embodies itself in a state can be *variable* and is dependent on local conditions. On the planet Earth, tendrils of fire lick up towards the sky striving to escape their terrestrial prison. In outer space, fire flows in waves like water with smooth rounded surfaces, spreading everywhere. This is because of the different regimes of attraction pertaining to the fire's relationship to gravity generated by the planet Earth or the absence of such bodies.

When my blue stein is seen in candlelight it is a deep, rich blue. In sunlight it is a bright, radiant blue. My skin contracts and tightens in the cold such that the rings on my finger become loose, while it becomes swollen and flushed in the dismal Texas heat of August. The local relations among entities determine the type of qualities the entity actualizes in local manifestations.

Everywhere *Dungeons and Dragons* is cognizant of this *variability* in the way in which qualities and events manifest themselves in local manifestations. Chance is ramified even at the heart of action borne out of will. The warrior swings his sword seeking to slay the lich. Will he hit the lich? If he does, how much damage will he do? The lich grasps the warriors sword and cold spectral power begins to dance up the blade. Will the warrior save against the powers of the undead? Will damage be done to him? And how much?

In all of these cases, there must be a roll of the dice. Powers and energy fluctuate as the characters and monsters endure wounds and exert themselves. Skills and abilities are suspended as magicians, monsters, and the undead wield sorcery, deploy the powers of the gods, and unleash their spectral forces upon the world. Through the throw of the dice the actions characters and monsters attempt to execute are never pure exercises of will, but rather they are always ramified with chance such that what is willed and the outcome of willing produce variable qualities or local manifestations.

A Flat Ontology

The universe of *Dungeons and Dragons* is flat. To be sure, this universe, like our own, contains all sorts of spherical active substances such as planets, moons, and stars. No, the flatness of this universe lies in the egalitarian affirmation of a universe composed entirely of active substances, all contributing their differences modifying the actions and local manifestions of other entities, where the living and the non-living, humanoids of all kinds and other creatures, the undead, equipment, and gods are equally actors and powers tracing their course throughout the world. Some of these entities are, of course, more interesting and complicated than others, and some have greater degrees of self-agency than others, yet all are powers and forces to be reckoned with.

This universe teaches us of a world that is everywhere pervaded by chance and will, where all entities are pursuing their own aims and fomenting their own plots. The humanoids are not sovereigns that preside over everything else, giving all other things form and meaning, but are themselves transformed by the entities they encounter and the things they enter into alliances with. As such, it is a multi-cultural and multi-material universe in which entities exist in collectives of a variety of different species and non-living artifacts, perpetually facing questions of how these collectives are to be formed. Most importantly, it teaches us of a world where entities or substances can never be reduced to their actual qualities, but where objects always harbor hidden potentials behind their current qualities, awaiting the circumstances under which these powers might unleash surprising qualities upon the world.

If we squint a bit, it's not too difficult to discern our own world behind the veneer of this fantastic world. Like the universe of *Dungeons and Dragons*, the substances of our universe harbor all sorts of hidden powers whose capacity to produce qualities can only be discovered by varying their local circumstances. Like the universe of this game, we live in our universe in collectives composed not just of humans, but of animals, different groups, ethnicities, religions, asteroids, viruses, institutions, floods, technologies and many things besides that we must navigate.

Like *Dungeons and Dragons*, our universe is everywhere ramified by chance, bringing about surprising encounters and relations that we can never fully anticipate. Is it a surprise that so many players of this game go on to become engineers, chemists, physicists, and biologists? For what is it that scientists and engineers explore if not the furtive powers of substances when related in aleatory encounters?

14
The Secret Lives of Elven Paladins

MONICA EVANS

Here's a quick and easy way to test the patience of your friends: tell them, in great detail, about your latest *Dungeons and Dragons* campaign. If they aren't familiar with the game, see how long they'll listen to you talk about dice, stats, and multi-classing before they ask for a translation.

If your friends are D&D players, on the other hand, see how long it takes before they interrupt your brilliant exploits with their favorite monologue about this dwarven cleric they used to play who was agoraphobic, or that amazing time their gnome wizard ran out on an arranged marriage, got chased by an extra-planar lawyer, and had to come up with twenty-seven thousand, six hundred and thirty gold pieces and a live goat in less than seven days.

As human beings, we're necessarily interested in ourselves. We spend a great deal of time and energy on fundamental questions of our identity, such as: Who am I? Who should I be? What's my place in the world? One of the most seductive things about *Dungeons and Dragons* is that the game lets us answer those fundamental questions as many times as we want, and in as many different ways as we can—limited only by our imagination, the rules of the system, and the tolerance of our Dungeon Master. The power of games, both digital and tabletop, is that they let us walk for a time in someone else's shoes. Games in which we create our own, individual character let us take one step farther: we can try on new faces and new identities, play with personalities and character traits that are different than our own, and, when the game is over, go back to being ourselves with a little more understanding of what it might be like to be someone else.

When it comes to *Dungeons and Dragons* characters, however, the line between your friend and that agoraphobic dwarven cleric isn't as clear-cut as it might first appear. We can learn a great deal about ourselves by examining the way we play *Dungeons and Dragons*, from the first time we roll up a character to our latest tales of high adventure, and from the things we suspected but never knew about ourselves to the things we had no idea we were giving away.

Me, Myself, and Ioun, God of Knowledge

In traditional philosophy of identity, the core questions are often more abstract than the very personal "Who am I?" In particular, philosophers of identity study questions of relationships: for example, What is a thing's relationship to itself? If a thing changes over time, is it still the same thing? Is the acorn, for example, the same as the oak tree, or as the eventual oak table; is the rotten apple the same as the apple seed?

One of the most famous questions comes from Plutarch and is often posed as the "Ship of Theseus" paradox, namely: if you build a ship, and over time you replace the wood, the sails, the ropes, and eventually every original part, is it still the same ship? Additionally, if you save the original pieces of the ship as you replace them, and use them to build a second ship: which one is the original ship? These questions often attempt to express whether the history of a thing or the current physical composition of a thing is more important.

In *Dungeons and Dragons*, one might be tempted to pursue similar thought experiments: for example, does a character who has been rolled up but never played in a campaign exist? If I play an identical level-one human rogue in two separate campaigns, what relationship do they have with each other when they are both level ten? What happens to the identity of a single character that is played in succession by two or more players? If I recreate my favorite character from an Advanced Second Edition campaign with the Fourth Edition rules, or with the digital *Neverwinter Nights* system, how is that character the same or different than the original?

To explore any of these questions, we must begin by examining the fundamental relationship between characters and players, which has been most thoroughly explored in game studies.

Game studies is still a new field, one that has roots in both traditional academics and the continuously evolving games industry. Game studies is also a multi-disciplinary field—game studies scholars come from backgrounds as varied as computer science, psychology, linguistics, drama, world literature, anthropology, educational technology, new media studies, and philosophy. Some of the major research questions in game studies deal with games as cultural artifacts, technological systems, as a medium for artistic expression or social change, or as tools for communication and socialization. Games studies scholars are also interested in the ways that games affect us as individuals, cultures, and societies, which often includes an examination of how players and their characters interact.

There are a number of theories that describe the player-character relationship. One of the best-known was proposed by James Paul Gee. In *What Videogames Have to Teach Us About Learning and Literacy,* Gee describes three kinds of identities that players experience simultaneously while playing games: a virtual identity, or the player's identity as a character in the game world; a real-world identity, or the identity of the player playing a game; and a projective identity, or the way in which the player actively creates the game character through playing the game, including the player's wants and aspirations for that character (pp. 54–56).

In *Dungeons and Dragons* terms, we might express Gee's three identities in this way: Wil Wheaton, for example, plays a *Dungeons and Dragons* character named Aeofel. His virtual identity is the character of Aeofel himself, or Wil Wheaton as *Aeofel*: an eladrin (or high elf) servant of the goddess Melora and an Isolating Avenger, a type of divine, monastic warrior. His real-world identity is Wil Wheaton, or *Wil Wheaton* as Aeofel: a white, thirty-nine-year-old American male, actor, writer, and geek celebrity. His projective identity is in the way that Wil plays Aeofel, or Wil Wheaton *as* Aeofel. This includes Wil's performance as Aeofel in real time within the constraints of the game system, and includes Wil's desires and aspirations for Aeofel, such as his need to successfully integrate into the questionable adventuring company "Acquisitions Incorporated" while remaining true to his goddess and his own principles.

Another theory of identity is best explained by game designer Matthias Worch in his 2011 GDC presentation, "The Identity Bubble." Worch begins by quoting Gary Fine's *Shared Fantasy*, in which the table-top role-player's identity is again described in three parts: the fictional character embodied by the player, or "I am Ulgar the dwarf"; the player acting within and exploring the framework of the rules, or "I am rolling a natural twenty"; and the person with real-world needs that are pushed aside during the game but not forgotten, or "I need to feed the cat at six o'clock." Worch builds on this definition by introducing the concept of double-consciousness: that embodying these identities simultaneously is understandably difficult, and can cause a number of issues for the person playing the game, especially when it comes to the player's immersion in the game world. Worch then describes the "identity bubble," a hypothetical space in which all three identities—character, player, and person—exist in close proximity to one another. If one of the identities drifts too far away from the others, the bubble pops and immersion in the game is broken.

In digital games, keeping the identity bubble intact is up to designers like Worch: for example, characters like *Uncharted's* Nathan Drake or *Portal's* Chell must be designed so that their story-based wants and needs are in sync with the player's game-based wants and needs. In table-top games, and particularly in *Dungeons and Dragons*, the identity bubble is more clearly the responsibility of both the Dungeon Master and the players. For players, it often comes down to management of "meta-gaming," or keeping the player's knowledge separate from the character's knowledge. There's a difference between a group of players rolling dice, consulting the *Player's Handbook*, calculating damage and movement speeds, and dealing with each other's personalities; and a group of characters going on adventures, fighting monsters, solving problems, and dealing with each other's personalities. These two fictions—the game rules and the story of the player characters—must exist simultaneously and in harmony, and no single player can make that happen. Only a group of players and a Dungeon Master working together can keep the game engaging, coherent, and ongoing, without letting it break down or destroying any player's immersion in the game world. This group dynamic is one of the reasons *Dungeons and Dragons* is often referred to as a shared fiction or shared fantasy.

When a player's motivation is out of sync with his character, keeping the game coherent can depend a great deal on the individual player. Let's return for a moment to Wil Wheaton and Aeofel. During one of his adventures, Aeofel met an unfortunate end, one that could have been avoided by the player being "smart", but one that would have been completely out of character for Aeofel. In Wheaton's words:

> I can already hear the cries from other members of the gaming tribe: 'Never split the party you dumbass!' Normally, I'd agree completely, but here is where actual role-playing sort of lead [sic] to . . . unforeseen consequences. Allow me to explain: Aeofel is an Isolating Avenger. He is, in normal language, a zealot. Where a Paladin brings comfort to the afflicted, the Avenger brings great vengeance and furious anger to those who caused the affliction.
>
> So, if I'd been metagaming, if I'd mixed player knowledge with character knowledge, Aeofel never would have chased after Leer. . . . I wouldn't have split the party. But Aeofel had sworn an Oath of Enmity on Leer. He had Leer on the run. Leer was *bloodied and had offended Melora.* That alone was enough to get Aeofel to go after him, but if there was any doubt, Aeofel had been implored by [his friend] Binwin to "get him." Binwin was the only Dwarf in the 'verse who Aeofel actually liked, the only Dwarf in the 'verse who could actually be a friend to Aeofel, and Aeofel was intensely loyal to those who were close to him. . . . So when you add all that up, Aeofel had no choice but to chase Leer down, and end up in that acid pit.

Wheaton's description fits perfectly into Gee's definition of projective identity. The player Wil wanted the character Aeofel to live by certain principles, regardless of consequences, and though it cost Aeofel his life it left him with a history and identity that was exactly what Wheaton intended. It also fits with Worch's "identity bubble," but with the added notion that the player Wil was aware that choosing these actions for the character Aeofel would likely cause game-based problems for the other players in the group, but would support the shared narrative fiction they were creating around their characters.

Wheaton made a choice: to play Aeofel in a way that was consistent with the character he had already created, regardless of whether it was a poor gaming decision. This brings us to one of the most fascinating things about *Dungeons and Dragons*: that the relationship a player has with his character is more akin to the relationship a writer has with fiction than with most kinds of digital game characters; and that, even though it is a game, playing *Dungeons and Dragons* isn't always about winning.

Backstabbing Your Best Friends

In any discussion about identity and games, it's worth taking a moment to look at game designer Richard Bartle's four player types, which were defined as a response to the question, "Why do players play?" Bartle's player types were created with digital MUDs (multi-user dungeons) in mind, and are most often used when discussing identity in MMORPGs (massively multiplayer online role-playing games) such as *World of Warcraft* or *Dungeons and Dragons Online*, but are equally applicable to tabletop games. These four player types are:

- *Achievers:* Players who enjoy focusing on the rules of the game, and who like doing things that achieve defined goals within the game.

- *Socializers:* Players who enjoy interacting with people, particularly through the medium of the game.

- *Explorers:* Players who enjoy exploring the game world, discovering new things, and increasing their knowledge about how that world works.

- *Killers:* Players who want to dominate other players—most commonly by attacking, killing, or otherwise making life difficult for others, but also through less overt actions, such as politicking, rumor-mongering, or guilt-trips. (*Designing Virtual Worlds*, p. 130)

While some players fall most clearly into one of the categories above, nearly all players exhibit aspects of three or four of these types to varying degrees. In MUDs and MMORPGs, hundreds or thousands of players can inhabit the same space, and players can find other players like themselves relatively easily—in fact, many digital games encourage this through designated server types or in-game friend- or guild-finding systems. Players are also relatively anonymous online, and can choose to keep part or all of their real-world identity private. *Dungeons and Dragons*, on the other hand, involves a much smaller group of players interacting in much closer quarters, with their real-life identities obvious to the other players, and with a Dungeon Master rather than a computer arbiting the world. While groups of player-killers or socializers can find each other online and pursue similar goals with a minimum of fuss, consider how difficult it is for a Dungeon Master and a group of players when one person wants to "win" the adventure as quickly and efficiently as possible, one person wants to wander around the countryside and see as much of the world as possible, one person wants to make friends with all of the NPCs in town, and one person keeps slipping the Dungeon Master notes about how his character is preparing to stab the other three in the back.

Granted, most *Dungeons and Dragons* groups are made up of friends, or at least of people that knew each other in real life prior to the game, so they might have closer play styles than a collection of complete strangers. But even among a group of all explorers or all achievers, there are still many opportunities for friction between players. Once again, we come back to the idea of *Dungeons and Dragons* as a shared fiction as well as a game, in which all players must be invested in creating a shared experience. Regardless of individual motivations, players and their Dungeon Master must create a social contract between themselves to keep the game experience going smoothly, or at least interesting.

Bartle says that "the celebration of identity is the fundamental, critical, absolutely core point of virtual worlds. Everything that players do ultimately concerns the development of their own identity: who they are. It's why achievers achieve, explorers explore, socializers socialize, and killers creep up from nowhere and batter you with a stick" (p. 159). We might say that the fundamental, critical core point of *Dungeons and Dragons* is exploring who you are, or who you might be, with other people as opposed to by yourself.

Trying Legolas on for Size

Discussions of identity in games often focus on identity play: for example, why men play female characters, or whether players naturally create avatars that physically resemble themselves. With *Dungeons and Dragons*, these questions are tempered by the huge amount of control players have over the creation of their character. Unlike digital games, in which choosing to play a paladin might mean that your character must also be male, black, and bald (as in *Diablo II*, in which the appearance of a character is completely determined by that character's class and abilities), the rules for character creation in *Dungeons and Dragons* are very nearly guidelines. In short, you can create an overpowered elven paladin in the Advanced Second Edition rule set, even though the *Player's Handbook* says you can't, if your Dungeon Master will allow it.

If *Dungeons and Dragons* is a shared fiction, then it is implied that the players and the Dungeon Master are collaborative authors of that fiction, along with the original creators of the game. Creating a *Dungeons and Dragons* character does have constraints: some based on the rules, some dependent on the desires and intentions of the Dungeon Master, and some dependent on the player's ability to play that character in a particular way. But players are effectively free to write their character in any way they want, as long as that character fits within a certain campaign—much as an author creates a character to fit within a certain fictional world. Likewise, a player with a sympathetic Dungeon Master might arrange for a campaign to be created around a specific character, in the way an author might create a world for a particular character to inhabit.

This level of narrative freedom might relate to the fact that *Dungeons and Dragons* has its origin in two places. The rules, mechanics, and systems of the game are most heavily inspired by traditional wargaming, but the content comes from the classics of fantasy literature. The basic classes and races, such as wizard, ranger, elf, dwarf, and halfling, are most clearly inspired by Tolkien's *Lord of the Rings* series, but many other major authors influenced the design of the game, including Robert E. Howard, Michael Moorcock, L. Sprague de Camp, A. Merritt, Bram Stoker, and Roger Zelazny. Gary Gygax himself credits Jack Vance's *Tales of the Dying Earth* series with heavily informing the design of the magic system and the thief character class, as well as contributing specific spells and magic items, including "Evard's Black Tentacles" and Ioun Stones. *Dungeons and Dragons* was created by people who read and loved fantasy, and who understood good storytelling. The stereotypical *Dungeons and Dragons* player is someone who loves fantasy worlds and good stories, but who also has the deep creative impulse necessary for role-playing—in fact, exactly the sort of person who might like to see what it would feel like to be Aragorn, Elric, Van Helsing, or Cugel the Clever.

That said, most of us aren't Tolkien, Michael Moorcock, Bram Stoker, or Jack Vance—meaning that, despite our creative impulses, we aren't necessarily very good writers. This contrast between our desire to tell stories and our ability to actually tell them gives rise to a wealth of other stereotypes about *Dungeons and Dragons* players, including the too-perfect-to-be-true "Mary Sue" character, or the forty-five-page cliché-ridden backstory for a thinly-veiled copy of Legolas. Thankfully, *Dungeons and Dragons* doesn't require us to be good writers, only good players. A player's narrative investment is not in creating characters and stories that will withstand critical reception, but in creating something meaningful because it's personal, and because it's experienced and enjoyed by the other members of their gaming group.

Unlike characters in fantasy literature, *Dungeons and Dragons* characters are not only written: they are performed. As the game goes on, each character changes, gains a history, and becomes more complex based on both the choices the player makes and the way the player chooses to embody the character, especially in the words that they say. We differentiate between things we say "in character" or "in-game" with things we say "out of character" or "out of game," and some Dungeon Masters can be very finicky about the two—to the point that some choose to consider every word that a person says during play as being "in character," which can lead to remarkably awkward situations.

There's also the question of whether "personality will out"; that is, whether a player can truly play a character that has a significantly different personality than their own. Given that playing a *Dungeons and Dragons* character requires a performance, this question becomes extremely interesting when, for example, a fundamentally good person attempts to play a chaotic evil warlord, but simply can't bring himself to murder a bunch of innocent townsfolk; or when a naturally shy person decides to play a gregarious, charismatic bard and constantly hesitates to draw attention to herself in crowds of NPCs. Anecdotally, I have seen this question reversed with a player who used his character as a mouthpiece to say things out loud that he felt he couldn't say in real life, banking on the fact that he could always say, when pushed, "That's not me; that's just my character." This player's situation brings to mind the aphorism, often misattributed to Plato, that you can learn more about a person in an hour of play than in a year of conversation.

Lastly, the creation of a *Dungeons and Dragons* character also has a survival component, as the player must keep their character alive among the dangers and trials of the game world.

Players must balance their desire to create an interesting, challenging, and ultimately meaningful character in narrative terms with their desire to keep that character alive and playable, desires which are both informed by the player's understanding of the game rules. Keeping a character's personality balanced with their survivability can be a challenge, particularly when one begins to eclipse the other.

I Twink Therefore I Am

Let's look more closely at player knowledge versus character knowledge: the idea that players often know things that their character couldn't possible know, and must at times actively ignore or refuse to use that knowledge. Consider a veteran D&D player whose latest character, a level-five wizard, is confronted by a bulette. The player, either from a previous encounter with a different character or by having read the *Monstrous Manual*, likely knows that the bulette is a type of heavily-armored "land shark" that tunnels through the ground, can leap ten feet, has prodigiously destructive stomach acid, and tracks its prey through seismic vibrations. The level-five wizard, on the other hand, knows only that a huge armored thing with teeth is charging toward him. Given that the wizard's life is on the line, how much of the player's knowledge about bulettes is fair for the character to use?

There are some mechanical ways to resolve these issues. The player might be allowed to make a knowledge-nature check to see if the wizard can dredge up a passing memory about bulettes; or, if he has memorized the spell and has enough time, he can cast Fox's Cunning on himself to improve his intelligence and attempt to make an intuitive leap about the monster. In general, resolving player knowledge with character knowledge is left up to each group of players and their Dungeon Master, and the way in which each individual player deals with the issue can tell us a great deal about their identity, particularly in terms of their investment in both their character and the game.

Unlike many other games, in which the goal is often—or at the very least includes—winning the game, in *Dungeons and Dragons* the goal is often to make the most interesting thing happen, something that the players and Dungeon Master are all responsible for and attempt together. Players have multiple goals, both as a group and individually. A human druid might join a party of adventurers tasked with finding a pair of missing children in a forest, but have an individual goal of discovering why the creatures in that forest have been acting strangely, a mechanical goal of gaining another level so he can access the "Call Lightning" spell, and a character goal of overcoming his racism against the two dwarves in the party. Achieving any of these goals, with the possible exception of finding the missing children, cannot be said to have caused the player to win the game, and often lead to new goals.

It can also be more interesting to lose. Sometimes the best, most memorable stories are the ones in which the players fail, and losing can be more fun than winning—particularly when that failure is gloriously, irrevocably spectacular, such as burning down the entire village you were meant to save with one disastrously bad roll on an extremely ill-advised use of a fireball spell. Consider also that games are often fun because they are challenging. A level-twenty character that only ever fights level-two monsters is boring to play. A party of level-five characters that must find a clever way to overcome a level-twelve monster, which is numerically impossible in straight combat, can make for a memorable campaign.

This is true not just in play, but in character creation as well. One of the most interesting characters I have seen played was a barbarian named Dak, whose intelligence score was a devastatingly low seven. Dak's player chose to keep the seven for two reasons: one, because he had rolled it and felt it was fair; and two, because he thought it would be interesting to play a character that started with a severe gameplay disadvantage.

The difficulty with playing Dak is that his player had to balance player and character knowledge with nearly every decision he made. For Dak to be successful, he would not only have to survive the campaign, but his player would need to make his performance of Dak overt enough to be meaningful but controlled enough not to be annoying. As an example: Dak confronted every problem by screaming his own name and charging into battle, with monsters as well as shopkeepers, government officials, chickens, trees, and occasionally his own reflection. When timed right, this could be hilarious, but would also disrupt other player's plans and often threw the campaign into chaos.

Creating Dak as a character took a great deal more than an intelligence of seven: it required Dak's player to understand good storytelling and timing while being aware of the other players' individual goals and emotional states, as well as the probable outcomes for each encounter based on the rules of the game. Dak's player then had to decide whether Dak would follow his usual strategy, or whether he would be distracted by something shiny and let another character take the lead. Dak is an example of a good balance of player-character knowledge, in that the player used his knowledge outside of Dak's limited capacity to make what could have been an extremely frustrating character a success, in terms of his activity in the game world, and an entertaining companion for the other members of the group.

Mixing player and character knowledge can easily go bad, however, particularly when players lose sight of the spirit of the game. One example is the power-playing achiever player who makes overly tactical, number-crunching decisions through her knowledge of the game systems, such as hit points and damage rolls, that her character is ostensibly unaware of, and regardless of the intelligence and personality of her character. Another example is the player who attempts to find loopholes in the system that will allow him to dominate other players. One such player might choose a character with very high charisma, then during play use a skill such as "Bluff" or "Intimidate" to force other players into doing what he wants.

Players like these aren't necessarily playing *Dungeons and Dragons* wrongly or missing the point, but they can make the game frustrating—or worse, no fun—for other players if not corralled. Consider also that there's a difference between "roll playing," or focusing primarily on the rules and mechanics of the game system, and "role-playing," or focusing primarily on the characters and storytelling aspects of the game. Most gaming groups experience a mix of the two, but all ways of playing the game are valid. That said, for gaming groups new to *Dungeons and Dragons*, the final, friendly word is had by the current writers, as quoted in the Fourth Edition Players Handbook:

> But even when your character is defeated, you don't 'lose'. . . . You might fail to complete the adventure, but if you had a good time and you created a story that everyone remembers for a long time, the whole group wins.

I'm Not a Nerd, I'm a Level-Twelve Paladin

As much time as we spend creating, playing, and retelling the stories of our *Dungeons and Dragons* characters, there's something remarkably appealing about defining ourselves in those same terms. We see how much we can carry or lift to calculate our Strength score, compare our IQ test to the range of Intelligence scores, and guess at our Charisma based on our leadership abilities or number and closeness of friends. There are numerous tests online that will examine your skills and life experience to assign you the most appropriate character class, or posit ethical questions to determine whether you might be best described as lawful neutral, neutral evil, or chaotic good. More directly, players can take their campaign away from the gaming table and into real-world settings with live-action role-playing, or larping, further blurring the lines between the fictional world, the game space, and the real.

Now more than ever, we're drawn to game systems as another way to make sense of our real-world experiences. For some, perhaps it's comforting to think that the question "Who am I" might be reducible to numbers and statistics. For others, it may be a way to see what we might have done in Legolas's place, or to wonder whether we would be able to survive in Conan's Cimmeria. For some others, creating a character as similar to themselves as possible might be a way to reduce the gap between their own identity and the identity of their character during play, making for a theoretically smoother play experience. And for others, creating a character based on themselves might be anathema, the exact opposite of the experience they intend to have in this and other game worlds.

That seemingly strange desire to define ourselves in game terms throws a light on the core question of player-character identity: that when we create characters, we are creating extensions of ourselves. Our identity while playing *Dungeons and Dragons* isn't a set value, but a spectrum: we move through layers of identity as character, person, and player as we experience the game. That fundamental question of "Who am I?" isn't set aside during a campaign, but is informed by our experiences in that shared, social fantasy, and perhaps reflected on with a little more knowledge than we had before.

So the next time someone asks you about *Dungeons and Dragons*, tell them you're participating in a complex form of identity play that involves the creation of a shared fiction and centers on the relationship between multiple player and character identities. They should be more than happy to hear what happened to your gnome wizard after he showed up with twenty-seven thousand, six hundred and thirty gold pieces and a live goat.

And the next time your Dungeon Master is foolish enough to let you craft a magic item, tell her you'd like to build a Ship of Theseus—if only to see what she assigns you as a modifier to the difficulty roll.

III

Epic Tier

Leveling Up

15

What *Dungeons and Dragons* Is and Why We Do It

CARL EHRETT AND SARAH WORTH

In *Bill and Ted's Bogus Journey*, the 1991 follow-up to the classic *Bill and Ted's Excellent Adventure*, Bill and Ted (spoiler alert) die. Death is not the end of their story, for they have the opportunity to challenge Death to a game, on which the fate of their souls will hang; win, and they may return to life. Death even allows them to choose the game. They choose first Battleship, then Clue, then an electric football game (Death loses each game, but unfairly keeps demanding a rematch). After a particularly humiliating loss at Twister, Death relents and lets them go.

They could have chosen any game they liked. But could they have chosen *Dungeons and Dragons*? This would raise all sorts of troubling questions—who would DM? What would count as winning, and what would count as losing? Could Death avoid these headaches by insisting that D&D is not really a game at all?

Well, what *is* a game? What *makes* something a game? Once we have a solid grasp of what exactly D&D is, this can help us to understand the answer to a mystery: why do we play D&D? Contrary to what inflammatory culture warriors sometimes claim, players of D&D do know that the D&D world is not real. So how can something we know is not real be so engrossing? Philosophers call this the "paradox of fiction."

Family Connections

Philosophy has been very much occupied with finding definitions for our concepts. In Plato's dialogue, *Euthyphro*, he por-

195

trays his teacher Socrates engaging in conversation with a man named Euthyphro who believes that he understands piety. Socrates flatters Euthyphro by asking him to share this wisdom and explain what piety is. One explanation after another is easily knocked down by Socrates, and it becomes clear that Euthyphro actually has no understanding to share.

Euthyphro's first attempt is to provide an example—namely, his own conduct is pious. Socrates rejects this answer—an example is not a definition, he reminds Euthyphro. What we want is to understand the common thread running through all pious acts—the thing that makes them all pious.

Likewise for games, there are many different sorts of things that fall under our single concept of a game. So, to really analyze our concept of a game, we need to figure out what is the common thread uniting all those sorts of activities—what's common to solitaire, soccer, and Super Mario Brothers. Once we've defined our concept of a game by locating that common thread, we can check whether D&D meets that definition. Only then can we look further to try to understand the real ways in which we engage in this so-called "game" of D&D.

Not so fast! There are reasons to be skeptical about the plan as laid out above. On the sidelines, Ludwig Wittgenstein is frantically waving his arms at us to stop us from heading down what he would say is a hopeless dead end of philosophizing that has trapped unwary thinkers for millennia. Wittgenstein upended the model of what understanding a concept consists in (finding the one thread) and he specifically used the concept of a game to do so. Wittgenstein says:

> Consider for example the proceedings that we call "games". I mean board-games, card-games, ball-games, Olympic games, and so on. What is common to them all? —Don't say: "There *must* be something common, or they would not be called 'games'" —but *look and see* whether there is anything common to all. —For if you look at them you will not see something that is common to *all*, but similarities, relationships, and a whole series of them at that. To repeat: don't think, but look! —Look for example at board-games, with their multifarious relationships. Now pass to card-games; here you find many correspondences with the first group, but many common features drop out, and others appear. When we pass next to ball-games, much that is common is retained, but much is lost. —Are they all 'amusing'? Compare

chess with noughts and crosses [tic tac toe]. Or is there always winning and losing, or competition between players? Think of patience. In ball-games there is winning and losing; but when a child throws his ball at the wall and catches it again, this feature has disappeared. Look at the parts played by skill and luck; and at the difference between skill in chess and skill in tennis. Think now of games like ring-a-ring-a-roses; here is the element of amusement, but how many other characteristic features have disappeared! And we can go through the many, many other groups of games in the same way; can see how similarities crop up and disappear.

And the result of this examination is: we see a complicated network of similarities overlapping and criss-crossing: sometimes overall similarities, sometimes similarities of detail. (*Philosophical Investigations*, p. 27)

Wittgenstein rejects the central guiding idea of the time-honored model of conceptual analysis. Worse, he rejects Plato (which for a philosopher is sheer blasphemy)! He instead suggests that with games, as with many of our concepts, there simply is *no common thread* that runs through all things united under that concept. To illustrate this idea, Wittgenstein uses the notion of *family resemblances*: what unites all games is not some one feature or set of features that they all share, but is more like "the various resemblances between members of a family: build, features, color of eyes, gait, temperament, etc., etc. overlap and criss-cross in the same way. –And I shall say: 'games' form a family" (p. 28).

This notion of family resemblance may be somewhat misleading. In the case of actual families, there really is some hidden fact about the members that makes them all part of the same family. That is, your brother isn't part of your family just because he shares your nose and chin—it's not those resemblances that make you siblings, it's the fact that you share the same parents. But in the case of games, Wittgenstein is suggesting, the resemblances *just are* what makes solitaire and soccer both games.

The Family of Games

But this is puzzling. Does solitaire really resemble soccer more than it resembles, for example, performing magic tricks with cards? If being a game is a matter of resembling other games, then shouldn't we expect card tricks to count as games, since they are after all so much more similar to solitaire than soccer is? If so, that's a problem, since magic tricks are not games. And how exactly do solitaire and soccer resemble one another anyway?

According to Wittgenstein's view, the answers to these three questions might well be: no, no, and in no interesting way whatsoever. Consider a large family—say, the Do'Urden family—who tend to resemble one another in all the ways Wittgenstein listed above. We might then say of someone that she has the Do'Urden look. But notice that one person might have the Do'Urden look purely by virtue of facial features other than eye color, and another person might have the Do'Urden look in virtue of body shape, gait, and eye color. There is *no single feature* that these two people share—no interesting sense in which *these* two people resemble one another. But they each still have the Do'Urden look; they each have different parts of that family resemblance. And likewise, solitaire may have little or nothing in common with soccer, and yet share the family resemblance of games.

So what features are part of this family resemblance? Wittgenstein identified a few for us already: being amusing, winning and losing, competition between players, patience, a balance of skill and luck. In addition, we might say the use of strategy is a feature of games, as is being constituted by rules; part of what it means to play chess is that two people are moving their pieces in accord with the rules of chess. But rather than just treat the above features as a uniform list of equally important criteria of gamehood, we might plausibly say that some features are more important gamelike features than others. By analogy, maybe the Do'Urden look is *mostly* defined by a sharp chin and a piercing eyes, even if there are other, less important features of the look. It's possible to have the Do'Urden look if you lack the chin, but it's harder in that case than if you just lack the cheekbones. In the case of games, being amusing would seem not to be a very central feature of games; plenty of games aren't really amusing. Strategy games like chess don't seem to be very amusing; neither do most sports. By contrast, winning and losing seems to be a more central feature of games. There are games that lack it (for example, a children's game of tag) but they seem a rarity. Likewise, the feature of being governed by rules seems to be a more central feature of games. So having either or both of these features would be especially important for the question of whether D&D is a game.

D&D has some of the features listed so far, but lacks others. It's amusing sometimes, but not always; some players prefer their adventures to be deeply serious affairs. Competition amongst players is also sometimes part of D&D, but usually not. D&D definitely requires patience and includes a balance of skill and luck and the use of strategy. But what about those two more important features? If D&D lacks both of them, its status as a game will be dubious. And in fact it seems to us that D&D does not involve winning and losing—at least not in any straightforward sense.

Even the death of your character doesn't seem to be a clear case of losing. Not only is resurrection possible, but even a final death for a character can be a good outcome. Consider one player whose character completes all her objectives in a riveting and interesting campaign, dying an honorable death in doing so; and consider another player whose character stays alive by always playing it safe, and whose adventures are boring and lifeless. Does the first player "lose" and the second player "win"? To say that the first player loses is to suppose that staying alive is the point of the game, as capturing the king is the point of chess; and to give such a central role to staying alive is neither part of the rules of D&D, nor a good description of what is most important to players of D&D.

So no, winning and losing is at best only loosely a part of D&D. This means that the other important feature—being rule-governed—becomes especially important. How does D&D fare here?

Rules, Rules, Rules!

Surely, D&D passes here with flying colors! It's hard to imagine that there are more than a handful of human activities more rule-governed than D&D (the US tax code perhaps?)! It's so rule-governed that even advanced players with years of experience often haven't learned all the rules. But a puzzle is lurking here, because role-play*ers very commonly break or bend* *rules of D&D.* Not only do players adopt house rules that add to or even contradict the official rules, but many groups adhere to the unofficial "rule 0": that the DM has the power to alter or suspend rules at will.

So here's the puzzle: it seems that, with D&D as with other games, like chess, the rules *just are* the game. To be playing chess just is to be moving pieces around in accord with the rules of the game. If two people are just pushing chess-pieces around a board willy-nilly, trying to make nice patterns, then they are not playing chess—even if their activity *looks* like a game of chess. So if the rules are the game and someone is not following the rules, then they aren't playing the game. And this would mean that in fact almost no one ever plays D&D! Not only do DMs and players often consciously break or bend the official rules, they also often do so without knowing it—and at least in earlier versions of the game, the rules are inconsistent, which makes it impossible to obey all the rules.

When some small violations of a game's rules happen, it seems people can still be playing that game; but when the violations are big enough or of a particular sort, then they aren't playing the game anymore. What we want here, then, is an understanding of where that line gets drawn. Wittgenstein has a suggestion for this problem too: what matters is whether or not the rule violation undermines the *purpose* of the game. So if that's right, then when players violate the rules, they are still playing D&D if those rule violations do not undermine the purpose of D&D. And this relationship between a game and its purpose might even help solve the puzzle of whether D&D is a game or a story. Rather than just say "it's both", we can be more specific: maybe D&D is a game the primary purpose of which is to create a story. This would make for a good resolution of the rule-breaking puzzle, because it is *precisely* when rule-breaking helps tell a better story that DMs seem most willing to do it. If a freak accident (say, a series of ridiculously bad rolls) kills a PC, and the death would make a senseless and unsatisfying end to an otherwise thrilling and interesting campaign, this seems to be precisely when a DM is most likely to bend the rules so that a wound becomes less mortal, or a cleric happens to walk by, willing to offer healing. This would also help to flesh out the idea that being a skillful DM requires knowing when to bend the rules—we can now more specifically say that being a skillful DM requires knowing when bending the rules *helps to craft a better story*. The rules are there to help facilitate a bit of group storytelling; but slavish obedience to those rules might undermine that very purpose of group storytelling. A good DM knows how to sail those tricky waters.

Why Do We Respond to Things when We Know They Aren't Real?

There are many games a major purpose of which is to be a test of strategy; many games the purpose of which is to test various sorts of athletic ability; many games the purpose of which is pure amusement. It's easy to see why we'd be interested in playing such games—we want to see who is the better strategist, or we simply want to exercise our strategic abilities, and likewise for athletic abilities. Amusement is pleasurable for its own sake, and so it is its own reward, whereas strategy and athleticism have real-world applications; they are valuable outside of games. So it's no surprise to see that we're interested in games that have strategy, amusement or athleticism as a primary goal or purpose.

But storytelling? Why are we interested in that? Fictional storytelling seems specifically *not* to be an activity with real-world applicability—after all, it's fictional! So why do we do it? Well, we do it because it's fun, and more importantly, it's good for us in a way most players don't even really acknowledge. Being fictional is significantly different from being a story. Being fictional means it isn't literally true. No one would argue with us if we suggest that the worlds that D&D campaigns create don't really exist. Thus they are fictional. But storytelling isn't just about what isn't true. Storytelling is intentionally crafting a story out of possibly unrelated events. Stories, by definition, include multiple events and implicit causation and timelines between those events. As players have a hand in creating the storyline of a D&D game, they are doing important cognitive work in terms of understanding their own causation-making strategies of how they organize and make sense of their own real worlds, and the real events in their own lives.

But the storytelling that takes place in the game of D&D is endlessly fascinating to us, and perhaps one of the most salient features of the game. We might say that it is the thing that makes it a great game *and* a great thing to get really into—a great use of our time. We believe that the two most practical of all philosophical questions are always "What is it?" and "What do we do with it?" So now that we know sort of what D&D is (game or story or both) we can move on to the "What do we do with it"? question. More than just what do we do with it (let's play the game and get on with it!) what we want to examine here is how we really get involved in the game. We might even go so far as to suggest that we get *emotionally engaged* in the game. But how can we become emotionally engaged or emotionally invested in something fictional (although we all know we do it)?

Philosophers like Colin Radford have come up with this puzzle or paradox about engaging with fiction that they call the paradox of fiction. It goes basically like this:

1. I don't have real reactions to things I know aren't true or aren't really happening (for instance, I don't get *really* excited if I only *pretend* that I have won the lottery).

2. I know fictional characters and the events in their lives aren't really happening (because they are fictional!).

3. I have real reactions to fictional characters (we cry at movies and even get scared sometimes).

All three of these statements seem to be obviously true, but being put together like this in a paradox we know that they can't all be true at the same time. One of them has to go. One of them has to be false. But which one?

The easy answer (and a good philosopher will never take the easy answer) is just that it is part of life that we have emotional responses to fictional events—let's get back to the game. This is known as the "Who cares?" response, but it doesn't really address the problem.

Another easy and wrong answer is that we engage in a "willing suspension of disbelief." This is a nice attempt by Samuel Taylor Coleridge to come up with an explanation of why we seem to get so involved in fiction, but it really just does not cut it as a way out of this paradox. One can no more "willingly" or knowingly change one's beliefs about an event than one can willingly believe that it is snowing outside when it is not. We do not just change or suspend our beliefs, and we certainly don't do it willingly when we read novels, go to movies, or play D&D. This is what we will call the "dismissive" response to the paradox.

Make-Believing in Fictional Worlds

The response that we think actually has some teeth is one that was proposed by Kendall Walton in his book *Mimesis as Make-Believe*. He suggests something like this: children get involved in games of make-believe psychologically and physically. They set up rules ("Let's play a game of 'bears'—yes—and this stump will be a bear, and you will be the bad guy and I will be the good guy—don't let the bear get you—and the steps over there will be base"; or, "As your paladin pursues the warlock toward her castle, an owlbear emerges ten paces ahead of you from the trees beside the path").

And then you run around within the fictional world that you've set up. Sometimes rules remain from game to game, and sometimes they change as players change, as frustrations come up ("I don't want that stump to be a bear if that means I am already out!" or, "*Another* owlbear? How convenient!"), and as random circumstances come up as they often do with children.

As adults, we drop the physical part of the game (unless you're a LARPer) and keep up the same kinds of interactions psychologically. But as Walton explains, in the fictional worlds there are things that can be said to be *true* in the fictional world ("it is true that the miniature on the table is an owlbear" and "it is true that I fear the miniature"). So the way he resolves the paradox is basically to deny the first premise of the above paradox—that we DO in fact have real emotional responses to things we know aren't really happening. He changes it around to say that we have real responses to things that are "true in the fiction." He calls these responses "quasi" responses. We think "quasi" is a bit of a misleading word since it implies something a bit less than "real" but Walton intends for it to describe emotions that are truly genuine, physiologically felt, and very real. They just aren't the exact same reactions as they would be if we were in a "real" situation. That is, if we say that we fear something in a movie, it's true that we're genuinely moved, and the emotion is physiologically felt, it just isn't the *same* fear we would feel if we were *really* being chased by an owlbear. So we have genuine, real emotional responses to things that happen in our fictional worlds. This is also known as "pretense theory." So far so good.

Walton calls "props" the things in our fictional worlds that stand for one thing or another—the stump as a bear, or the miniature as an owlbear. The props prescribe some specific imagining and they help to allow fictional truths to exist in what can become a fictional world. So props allow us to have certain kinds of imaginings within a prescribed fictional world. Walton came up with this theory in order to explain the kinds of imaginings and emotional engagement that we have with the representational arts—painting, sculpture, some music, narratives, and theater. "Fictional," according to Walton, means the same as "true in the fictional world." What that allows us to do is talk about true statements within a fictional world, and to explain the kinds of emotional and imaginative engagement that we have as well.

Immersion and Interaction in D&D Worlds

Walton's theory seems to be a philosophical account of the "representational arts." Why are we talking about it here in this book then? Well, it seems to us that Walton's theory is a natural explanation of the ways in which we get involved in the game world of D&D.

We wouldn't go so far as to call D&D one of the traditional representational arts like painting and sculpture, but we would say that it is representational (it has props!) and there is certainly a game world that generates fictional truths. So here is *our* solution to a puzzle posed by Adam Brackin in Chapter 18 of this volume. Fictions (stories) generate game worlds and game worlds generate fictional worlds—they can't be separated! And, people get imaginatively and emotionally wrapped up in it as much if not more than any novel as far as we have seen. And this leads us to our point. D&D is an *experience* ("game" now seems too trite and ""fiction" too pedestrian—it is a whole psychologically engulfing experience) the intensity of which can be accounted for well by Walton's theory.

When you read a novel, say, you sit quietly engaging in your own little fictional world of the book. It's a solitary experience of just you, the book, and the fictional world. But D&D offers you a truly different kind of fictional world—one that is potentially even more engaging, and even more gratifying. D&D offers you the ability to be your own protagonist, to interact with other protagonists, and to have a bit of control over what kind of narrative develops (the DM has ultimate control, but we like to think even in D&D we have some say in our own destinies). D&D also offers you the possibility of campaigns that go on for days, weeks and even months. Thus the "fictional world" set up by each campaign has the potential to become very real as each character becomes more and more ingrained in the fictional world. And just as in real life, the more a fictional world is talked about, navigated, and conquered, the more real it become to each of the players.

So, what is D&D? It's a game, and it's a story, but it's a very unusual case of each. Unlike most games, D&D has the telling of a story as a primary purpose; and the story that is D&D has a very different kind of hold on us than most kinds of story. D&D is interactive storytelling in a way that even video games can only begin to emulate. D&D role-players shape the world they inhabit in a more thorough way than you do in other sorts of fiction. D&D allows players to cross the threshold from third person to first person, from persona play to *role-play*, and from observer of a fiction to participant in that fiction. If Walton's right about why we care about fiction and are impacted by fiction, then it's easy to see why D&D should be an especially compelling variety of fiction; this transition from observer to participant allows for a kind of immersion in and engagement with the fictional world that neither other kinds of games nor other kinds of stories can offer.

16

Why *Dungeons and Dragons* Is Art

PETE WOLFENDALE AND TIM FRANKLIN

Before there were Role-playing Games, there was *Dungeons and Dragons*.

When, in 1974, Dave Arneson and Gary Gygax published *Dungeons and Dragons: Rules for Fantastic Medieval Wargames Campaigns Playable with Paper and Pencil and Miniature Figures* in a print run of one thousand copies at GenCon (now known as *Original Dungeons and Dragons*), there was no terminology to describe the type of game they had created.

You can feel the anxiety that must have caused in the game's ponderous subtitle. For those of us who came to the RPG hobby after the 1970s, it's hard to imagine a world without a plethora of different RPG options to cater for every taste; a variety of genres, a range of complexities, differences in tone and style, multitudes of fantastic worlds to explore and dozens of different game systems to facilitate that exploration. But once upon a time, D&D was a unique mutant: a miniature wargame that didn't use armies, or terrain, and needed five people to play at a time—four people to play as heroes, and one person to play as the world.

The rules for *Dungeons and Dragons* evolved from Gary Gygax's miniature wargame *Chainmail*, published by Tactical Studies Rules. In the 1970s miniature wargaming was a niche and fairly nerdy hobby, even more so than today (if you can credit that). Most wargaming was historical, using armies of lead soldiers to simulate battles from history, or to create historically believable match-ups. In the era before Games

Workshop, *Chainmail*, with its rules for spells and monsters, was an oddity, though with the huge popularity of *The Lord of the Rings* at the time it was perhaps an inevitable oddity. So there's something quirky: *Chainmail* required that the game-players threw out any idea they were re-enacting a battle. Obviously, since the battle *could never have happened*. So whatever stories the little lead soldiers would tell around the little lead fireside, they would be completely new. The rules of *Chainmail* would *simulate* the workings of reality to determine the outcome of the battle—and the ending of a story which had never before been told.

When Dave Arneson got his hands on Gygax's rules, the oddity of *Chainmail* was transformed again, into an aberration. In *Chainmail*, one lead soldier represented twenty men— a rather considerate abstraction, given the limited bank balance of your average wargamer. But Arneson tilted the other way. With the friends he was playing with, each figure stood for just one man—or, since this was a fantasy game featuring miniature knights and wizards, one hero. And each player had only one figure to play with. Crucially for the history of RPGs, it blurred the lines between the hero represented by the figure, the figure itself, and the person playing with that figure. One player, one figure, one hero—one *character*.

But the character wasn't Arneson's only innovation. The word "campaign" as used in wargaming comes from its equivalent in military terminology: a series of linked battles. In wargaming, if the player stands for anything in relation to their army, it's either the army's general, or perhaps the spirit of the nation riding behind the army, directing the actions of the little lead men as they go about their deadly business. In a campaign the player maintains that role between games, carrying the same flag through a series of battles.

When Arneson was running a campaign for his friends, he was acting as arbitrator and also scenario designer, and they were acting not as the spirit of a nation, but as individual characters. The players carried their heroes from one game to the next. The characters gained histories. The characters gained stories. And so too did the world through which they were adventuring. He may not have meant to when he started tinkering with *Chainmail*, but Arneson invented the first ever wholly original RPG *campaign setting*: a fantastical world which existed purely so that people who weren't its author could tell stories in it.

The parts themselves were not revolutionary. They were not even new. Humans have used figurines in games to represent people since before Chess. They have played roles on the stage (or around the campfire) for centuries, and have been improvising for as long as there have been children. They have modeled real-world probabilities using randomizers (dice, usually) at least since H.G. Wells's *Little Wars*. They have imagined fantastical worlds since they first saw the stars, spoken about them since they had voices, and written about them since Gilgamesh.

But it was the combination of the parts—the rules of simulation with the narrative continuity of campaigning and the blurring between player, character and figurine—that created something entirely new, in the worlds of game-playing and of story-making, something that was in its own way brilliantly revolutionary. If you want to learn about Role-playing Games as a distinct artistic medium, look to *Dungeons and Dragons*. Putting it another way, if we want to understand the *aesthetics* of role-playing, this is the place to start.

Roll to Detect Traps

Let's take a typical D&D session. Abel, Beccy, and Charlie are gathered around Dominic's dinner table. Dominic is the dungeon master. There are stacks of paper all over the place, with maps, crude doodles and tactical diagrams. Dominic is rifling through a stack of notes he made earlier, looking for the list of treasure hidden in a room the players have just raided. Beccy and Charlie are pretending to be a Dwarf Fighter and an Elf Wizard respectively, arguing whether they should press deeper into the dungeon or return to town with the dire news of a troglodyte uprising. Charlie is rifling through a setting book and eating left-over pizza. There are loads of dice, everywhere. What, if anything, is *artistic* about that? Sure, everyone's enjoying themselves, but is anyone having what might be called an *aesthetic* experience?

The parts that make up a game, session, or campaign of D&D are extremely varied, ranging from the content of a published D&D book to the performances of the players and the dungeon master. Each of those elements might be artistic in its own right. D&D is made up of lots of components which can be artistic, at least under some circumstances.

Let's take the campaign setting book that Charlie was reading (he won't mind, he doesn't exist). Inside the book are stories, maps, the history of an imagined world, descriptions of the people and creatures that would live there if it was real. It's heavily illustrated. It's pretty much a travel guide to a place that doesn't exist, mixed together with a bunch of tables of numbers and game rules. The tables and rules give you a system to work out what would happen if you took an imaginary holiday there. So D&D involves pictures and stories, both of which may be artistic to some degree.

Then there are the performances being given by Beccy and Charlie. There's art in a good theatrical performance, bringing out the internal motivations of a character by exploring their physicality and speech. Improvisation is an art form, found in the Italian theater tradition *Commedia del Arte* and the TV show *Whose Line Is It Anyway?*, and, unless Beccy or Charlie have prepared a speech in advance, they'll both be ad-libbing like crazy. A game of D&D will involve plenty of improvisational performances, though you might not call a D&D session improvisational theatre, since it is rarely performed for an audience except the players.

On top of this, the session as a whole has a narrative of its own, which feeds in to the wider narrative of the campaign that Dominic has put together. It's a narrative that shifts as the players take unexpected decisions, which means Dominic doesn't have the final say about what will happen in the story he has invented, but some pretty cool stuff can emerge from that unpredictability; RA Salvatore's tale of *Wubba Wubba* is a fantastic example.[1] D&D can resemble a collective act of uncontrolled myth-making.

But we've got to be careful here. It's deceptively easy to say that *D&D* is artistic because it's like something else. Picking out a bunch of artistic things that can be part of a D&D session won't tell us what it is about D&D that gives it a *unique* aes-

---

[1] At time of writing, http://youtu.be/PzpgAQpcp8o will take you to a video of this hilarious tale. If the link is dead, google Wubba Wubba. We suspect the tale will live forever.

thetic character. Staring at the oil-painted backdrop on a theater set and studying the intricate period costume won't clue you in about Shakespeare. In picking out these various things D&D has in common with other art forms we're catching elements of the role-playing experience, but it's the peculiar way these elements are brought together that makes it an artistic medium in its own right.

Another problem with a "sum of its parts" argument is that most of the aesthetic elements that go to make up a D&D game are, in and of themselves, middling at best. The performances of a D&D player might be passable, but they're rarely inspired. The art in a D&D book is frequently awesome (Fourth Edition raise your head), but rarely has any dimensions beyond that. The stories in most D&D setting books are second-generation rip-offs from Tolkien and Robert E. Howard. The stories that you create around a D&D table with your fellow players don't always bear recitation: "Beccy cast Force Cage on the troglodyte Arachnomancer, and the Arachnomancer tried to Summon Swarm—except the spiders all appeared inside the cage and she was like 'Agh no, no, spiders, no, eating my face, eating my face, fail!' It was totally epic." Epic perhaps, but rarely as exhilarating to hear as to experience.

Why should we think that D&D has anything distinctly artistic about it at all then? There's a bunch of things we enjoy about it that aren't straightforwardly aesthetic at all. It's a *social activity* where we get to spend time with our friends, and all kinds of fun follows from that on its own: good banter, friendly rivalries, and running jokes. It's also a *game*, and this means it provides all sorts of possibilities for success and failure: scouring dungeons for treasure, saving towns and villages from despotic overlords, and plain old leveling up. But D&D has got more to it than this; something that makes it a completely different experience than playing *Monopoly* (or even, dare we say it, *World of Warcraft*) with a bunch of friends. It *is* about working with (and sometimes against) your fellow players to overcome a series of challenges, but it's not *just* this.

There's a special spark that comes alive when you're playing a really good game of D&D. It's not just that the game is fun (although a really good game of D&D is always fun.) It's something that only really exists in the moment that you're playing; although hearing a great campaign outline or reading a fantastic source book will give you a tingle down the spine, a feeling that something brilliant is waiting to happen and you can almost guess the shape it will take. Whatever it is, it's close to what we feel when we encounter a great piece of art. It may come about as a result of the interaction of the different elements that make up a D&D session, but it's both more than them and fundamentally different from them. Whatever it is, this peculiar aesthetic experience is something that came into its own with *Dungeons and Dragons*.

Experience Points

That's all very well for what the aesthetic experience of role-playing isn't. In that case, what is it? To get a grip on this we have to get a bit more more general: what is an aesthetic experience, full stop?

The most famous answer to this question comes from Immanuel Kant. In his *Critique of the Power of Judgment*, Kant came up with a theory that explains what is special about the pleasurable, exhilarating, maybe even terrifying experiences you get when you encounter great works of art—the shiver down your spine when you're listening to *Mars, Bringer of War*—that separates them from run-of-the-mill, everyday pleasure and amusement you get from, say, a youtube video of a kitten falling off a chair.

Crucial to Kant's theory is an understanding of what's going on in your mind when you have these different kinds of experiences. Some things just push your buttons. The kitten video hits a big red button in your brain marked 'cute response'. You enjoy it in pretty much the same way that you enjoy a really tasty meal—you chew, you swallow, but the pleasure is a more or less *passive* response to what you experience. The aesthetic experience of art is more *active* than that. It kicks your brain into gear and forces it to make sense of what you're experiencing. Kant thinks that the feeling of pleasure is a *result* of this *cognitive* activity, rather than something added on top of it.

This is only part of the story though. Doing a crossword puzzle can be both fun and a good bit of mental exercise, but that doesn't make it art. Keeping track of all the robots, collapsing buildings, and explosions filling the screen when watching the latest *Transformers* movie is harder than following the otherwise complex camerawork of *Citizen Kane*, but that doesn't necessarily make it more enjoyable, or more artistic (or even, artistic at all . . .). A D&D combat can be a lot like both: trying to remember who's keeping the arachnomancer busy, who's taking care of which of her spidery minions, and working out how best to deploy your resources (feats, spells, artifacts, and the like) to save the day. Yet some D&D combats are awful grinds, others are just a bit of fun, and some reach beyond this to become downright spectacular, in a way that makes a crossword look mechanical and a Michael Bay movie look frivolous. If we're going to say anything interesting about what makes these moments border on art, then we need to figure out what's special about the cognitive activity art encourages.

Suppose you're mulling over a famous painting in the National Gallery in London, something with lots of fat naked people in it (they've got whole wings of the stuff!) The aesthetic experience you're having involves contemplating it in an active way. There's one way your mind is active, all the time, whenever you're experiencing stuff. Your mind is continually *recognizing* the properties of things. When you look at the painting, you recognize the brush-stroke pattern. Maybe you recognize the particular paints that have been used, or the wood the frame's made out of. That doesn't make for much of an experience—you can, and do, recognize all those same things whenever you see a painted wooden chair. But there are a couple of ways that recognizing the way a thing is does give us a more interesting experience, though not an aesthetic one.

If we *desire* something, we'll be satisfied when we recognize that it's come about. If I want my chair yellow, I'll be satisfied if it's yellow, and pissed if it's purple. If I think that a chair should be good at supporting my bulk (if I think that durable ass-support is the chair's function), I'll be appreciative when I recognize a sturdy hardwood chair, and derisive of a chair made out of balsawood; not because I need to sit down, but because seeing something that is fit for its purpose can be pleasurable in itself.

But back at the National Gallery, what do you honestly *want* a painting of three fat naked people to be like? What kind of *function* do you think it should have? The cool thing about the aesthetic experience is that it can come out of things which a. we don't necessarily want to be a certain way, and b. are utterly pointless. Trying to explain why things that are useless and sometimes even unpleasant can be so enthralling is why we invented aesthetics in the first place. The experience we have when we encounter art isn't concerned with the function or desirability of whatever causes it. As Kant puts it, aesthetic experience is disinterested.

Kant's original idea is that the pleasure we feel in aesthetic experience comes from the *process* of cognition, rather than from its *result*. In other words, it's not *what* we understand the object of our experience to be, but *how* we go about understanding it that's important.

Imagine that you're walking along a badly lit street in thick fog. Something appears on the edge of your field of vision. It might be a person—it looks like a person. Or maybe two. Maybe it's one person and a dog—but who would walk a dog this late at night? Whoever it is (or they are), they're wearing something yellow. Maybe it's a woman in a dress (a dress, in this weather?), or maybe it's a policeman in a fluorescent jacket. You're not sure. You continue to run through possibilities, imagining different scenarios, trying to detect patterns in the fog, and comparing these to what you know about dogs, dresses, policemen, and everything else.

Normally you'll come to some conclusion about what this indistinct shape is. Either you walk closer and get a better view, or you come up with a plausible hypothesis, or you give up and go home for a cup of tea. What happens if you don't, though? What happens if you simply get caught up in the process of imagining and understanding? This is what Kant thinks happens when we experience the *beauty* of a moment. The cognitive processes that normally let us make sense of things go into a short-circuit, analyzing and re-analyzing, testing theories, making mad new combinations, and generally experimenting with their own awesome capacity to apply different models to the things around us. Kant calls this a state of *free play*.

What goes on in free play differs between types of aesthetic experience. Listening to a good piece of classical music stimulates your ability to trace intricate patterns in sound, pulling out interlocking melodies, counterpoints, and repeating themes. Quality theater plays on your capacity to track social relationships, finding juicy subtexts in dialogue, picking out the complex interactions of plot and metaphor, and concocting dozens of shifting maps that pin those different elements one to another in constantly varying ways. On top of this, no two art works of the same type ever stimulate your cognitive processes in exactly the same way. A *Midsummer Night's Dream* and *Waiting for Godot* fire up some of the same machinery in your mind, but the raw materials they feed in are really different.

So, aesthetic experiences are caused by all kinds of cognitive free play. But why does any of this feel good? Where does the pleasure come from?

Seeing that something fulfils its function is satisfying to us. It's a pleasure to see a damn fine bowie knife, not because we plan to skin a deer carcass, but because it's fine to see something that is so perfectly itself. Anything that has a function could, in principal, be a source of satisfaction and pleasure for us, if we get evidence that the thing is well made for its function. Despite his claim that aesthetic experience is disinterested, Kant does think that something like this happens when our minds enter free play. The difference is that it's not the *object* of experience that fulfils the function, but the cognitive abilities of the *subject* who experiences it. We enjoy free play because it demonstrates our mind's ability to do what it's supposed to do. What is it supposed to do, you ask? It's supposed to build *worlds*.

As we said earlier, our mind is always recognizing the way the things around it are, categorizing and cataloguing the various things we encounter in experience. There's more going on here though. It's not just a matter of making sense of the *particular* things we encounter in experience—a book here, a fridge over there, a bunch of cars going by outside—as if we were making a list of the furniture of the universe. We also have to relate these different encounters in various ways, drawing intuitive and conceptual connections between our experiences, picking out relevant similarities and differences, revealing the *general* patterns that underlie them. This is what it is for our minds to create a world. They take the disparate bits of information provided by experience and use them to build a single picture of how things are, making sense of everything *as a whole*.

Kant thinks that we're always *reflecting* on our experience in this way, even if we're not always aware of it. The reason this doesn't produce the pleasure we get in the experience of the beautiful is that we're too focused upon making sense of the *things* we're experiencing to notice what we're *doing* in making sense of them. It's only when the process of understanding stops aiming at anything in particular and instead starts roaming wildly—experimenting with new patterns and combinations of ideas—that we have a chance to experience it on its own terms.

What we encounter in this moment of creative free play is our own ability to make the sorts of connections needed to make sense of the world as a whole. We experience the sheer *power* of our own mind, and it feels good. This experience differs depending on which of our cognitive abilities get stimulated, but regardless of whether we feel the range of our capacity to sense emotions in the face of Da Vinci's *Mona Lisa*, or our power to grasp the abstract ideas at play in Asimov's *Foundation*, it gives us pleasure to feel the reach of our own intelligence.

Now, we don't need to agree that this is all there is to art. We also don't need to use the word 'beauty' to describe what it is about art that causes aesthetic experiences. We don't necessarily want to say that a great piece of art is beautiful, even if it has an important effect upon us, as the word has a number of common meanings that can lead discussions astray, so we'll stick to talking about 'artistic' and 'aesthetic' things. This works well for talking about the aesthetics of RPG campaigns. Most players wouldn't call a D&D campaign beautiful, no matter how good it was, and even if they're certain that it's more than *simply* enjoyable. Despite this, Kant's account of aesthetic experience captures something very important, and it will help us explain why there is something very special indeed about the aesthetic of RPGs.

Saving the World

So, as Kant sees it, an aesthetic experience is caused by the disinterested free play of our mental faculties. The cognitive processes that enable us to make sense of things stop aiming at a fixed goal and start experimenting wildly. This lets us take pleasure in our own sheer capacity to understand the world. We've also seen that the specific character of the aesthetic experience depends both on *which* faculties are involved, and *how* they are involved: painting is different to poetry, and Rimbaud is different from Rilke. So if role-playing is aesthetic, we can explain the unique character of the role-playing experience by finding the distinctive ways in which it deploys our cognitive abilities.

We want to suggest that the way role-playing games *simulate* worlds generates a unique aesthetic experience. It's the peculiar way a game of *D&D* takes our capacity to create a picture of *the real world* and uses it to build a picture of *a fictional world* that makes it different from other forms of art.

RPGs don't have a monopoly on fictional worlds. Novels, movies, and plays all weave fictional worlds around us using various devices, and the aesthetic experiences they engender stem in part from our sense of experiencing another world. How does the simulation of a world in a role-playing game differ from one we find in a book, movie, or play?

The most obvious difference is that role-playing is *interactive* in a way that reading a book, watching a film, or attending a play (usually) isn't. Rather than simply *immersing* ourselves in the world as it is revealed to us through a prescribed experience, when we role-play we take a hand in *creating* the story ourselves, and thus in building the world it implies. In this respect, tabletop RPGs like D&D are far more similar to video games like *Fallout*, *Elder Scrolls*, or (again) *World of Warcraft*. (Not really surprising when you think how many videogame developers cite First Edition D&D as a major life experience.) These all have worlds which are revealed through interaction, and which are responsive to players' actions, to a greater or lesser extent.

But when it comes to interactivity tabletop RPGs (and to a lesser extent live action RPGs) win hands down against even the most interactive of available video games[2]. The Games Master (or Dungeon Master) can mediate between the rules, the setting, and the players' imaginations to an unlimited degree, whereas for any videogame there will always be some limits—limits to the plausibility of cause and effect, limits to

---

[2] We're not trying to start a fight. Computer games do very many other things extremely well. They can throw bucketloads of dice far faster than even the best dungeon master, for example.

geography, limits to emotional realism, limits to your possible actions, and so on. In a pen and paper RPG it is always possible to burrow deeper, provided the players and DM are up for it. In a pen and paper RPG players are *directly* engaged in drawing the boundaries of the game world, rather than just uncovering them. Hand in hand with this, role-playing involves a lot more imagination than computer gaming. If you want to see a towering citadel of glass in your game of D&D, it's you who has to imagine it.

If it's the fact that RPGs allow us to simulate worlds in an interactive fashion that distinguishes the experience of role-playing from the experience of *reading* a novel, what distinguishes it from the experience of *writing* one? If you want to create a world, why not just cut out the middle man and *design* it directly? You can even do this collaboratively with your friends, dreaming up a setting, characters, and narrative arcs without having to play it out with dice and character sheets.

We won't claim that there's nothing aesthetic about the act of composing a work of art, or dreaming up a fictional world in the process, but we think it's different from the peculiar aesthetics of role-playing. Compare the experience of the DM with that of the players. The DM's experience is closer to that of an author: they design (or at least curate) a campaign setting, they outline each game session's plot, and they act as the ultimate arbiter of the consequences of the characters' actions. But it's not the finished story at the end of a campaign that makes running a game enjoyable. Rather, it's the way the story shapes *itself* in front of your eyes, the way it runs away from you, flips off in unexpected directions and suddenly revolves around seemingly superfluous details, none of which you could ever have expected in advance. Who knew that instead of handing over the holy relic the party would blackmail the corrupt cleric who hired them to steal it? Or that the local Lord's taste in prostitutes would turn out to be so important?

The DM *guides* the creation of a story, setting constraints, negotiating options, and ruling on outcomes, but the *process* of creation is bigger than him. The contribution of the players and the rules they play with is indispensable to flesh out the game world and create the story that unfolds within it. It is the *collaboration* of the DM, the players, and the rules that means things happen that no one could plan in advance.

Although the aesthetic experience of *running* a game is certainly different from that of *playing* it, it's the way the collaborative process of simulating a world extends beyond the expectations of everyone involved that characterizes both. We'll call this the *depth* of a game world. We experience this depth when we see the *consequences* of our choices spiral out of our control, producing interesting and unforeseen results, suggesting new and exciting ways in which the world can be filled in.

This often happens in cases of both great success *and* great failure, such as when, in a climactic battle with a giant spider demon, the wily sorcerer is able to use *Polymorph Other* to turn it into a small purple platypus, because the DM unwittingly picked the only high-level monster without magic resistance; or when trying to scam some gold between dungeons, the hapless rogue fumbles his *Bluff* check and gets the whole party locked up by the town guard, turning the rest of the session into an elaborate prison break. It also happens when the players' actions throw up unusual situations that encourage creative improvisation on the part of themselves and the DM, such as gatecrashing a half-orc wedding (what will the vows be?) or converting a church of halflings to the god of thieves (just how much chaos will ensue?). It's these experiences of depth that make RPGs a truly unique artform.

Deep in the Dungeons

How does this fit into the Kantian story we've been telling? What does the experience of depth have to do with cognitive free play?

When you admire a painting, your mind freely experiments with different ways of making sense of it. Although we can influence each other's understanding of artworks by talking about them, the free experimentation here is a largely *personal* matter. It's something that goes on in your mind and no-one else's. The artwork is also *independent* of this free experimentation. The painting is neither produced nor changed by the way you experience it. What's special about the experience of role-playing is that neither of these things is true of it: the story is *collectively produced* by the process of experimentation. This isn't to say that we fuse into some sort of weird hive mind when we role-play together, or that the choices another player makes are somehow dependent on what you think about them. Rather, we're claiming that the free play we experience when we role-play *just is* the process of collaboratively generating a fictional world.

But hold on a minute. Earlier we said that when our minds enter a state of free play, they stop trying to reach a *finished* understanding of what they're experiencing. Yet in D&D it seems as if that's exactly what we're trying to do. We're focused on uncovering as much of the world as we can, and *pinning it down* so that we can achieve our various goals. We want to know what nefarious plans the corrupt cleric has for the holy relic we've stolen, so we can thwart them, or just how the Lord is protected when he visits his favorite brothel, so we can exploit his vices. Our success or failure often depends on how good a picture we've built up of the parts of the world we're dealing with.

Yet we don't need to constantly reinterpret *everything* in order to be in a state of free play. This is clear from the way we enjoy novels, films, and other forms of art based on simulated worlds. For us to be drawn into the fictional world in a way that encourages us to play with various ideas and associations, we need a relatively fixed understanding of what we're playing around with. What's important is that we have the resources to keep on interpreting (and creating, in the case of RPGs) different features of the fictional world so we get a good mental workout. The story has to keep unfolding in an interesting way.

What about disinterestedness then? Just like any other story, the tale we tell when we're role-playing isn't *for* anything, but aren't we implying that the *purpose* of role-playing just is to make a good story? Well, yes and no. As we've already pointed out, a role-playing game is not just a group exercise in world building. It's a *game* in which we face various challenges and strive to achieve new goals: getting enough experience points to level up, stuffing our characters' swag bag with loot, and thwarting the villain's plan to destroy the world. It's a *social activity* in which we aim to have fun: one-upping our friends, playing pranks on NPCs, and cracking some good jokes. And it's also about *playing a role*: trying to keep our decisions in line with our characters' personality and history.

The elven ranger will give up anything to find the man who killed her brother, while the dwarven warrior would rather cut off his own nose than sell his father's ax, even if he needs the money to achieve his (or his player's) goals. Although most good role-players will make the odd decision to keep the story interesting—to further the plot, speed through an otherwise boring encounter, or to keep the party together—this probably isn't the main goal that they have in mind when they're gaming.

All this means that we always have a whole bunch of in-character and out-of-character goals that exist in tension with the task of producing a good story (as well as with each other). This draws our attention away from the overarching narrative and our role in making it. Most of our in-game choices are made as if we don't have any part in *designing* the world of the game, or the story that takes place within it, and this contributes to the experience of depth. It keeps the interplay between the players, rules, source material and DM that generates the world genuinely *free*, stopping our collaborative world-building from aiming at some fixed thing. It also gives this world a kind of *autonomy* from us, letting us experience the world as if it is unfolding *itself*, even though all its elements are contributed by us. It allows us to see the choices we make as spontaneously coming together to form a coherent picture of a world which is full of potential *surprises*, even though it doesn't exist.

This autonomy is enhanced by the *rule frameworks* that constrain our choices and inform us of unexpected consequences, and by the use of dice and other *randomizers* that inject small amounts of chaos directly into the world: all the parts that come to D&D from its heritage as a simulation-style game. So, while the players' interests are important to the experience of role-playing, it's not because the players collectively plan their actions to ensure the game satisfies them, but because the more or less messy interaction of their goals helps *embed* the players in the game world.

We're now left with the big question: why do we enjoy the experience of depth? Why do we get such a kick out of projecting ourselves into imaginary worlds that seem to unroll before us, playing the part of heroes in tales that zigzag in unpredictable directions? Or simply: why is role-playing aesthetically pleasurable?

The short answer is that, just as we enjoy admiring an Old Master's landscape, listening to Beethoven's Ninth, or reading *A Hero of Our Time,* the depth of a *fictional* world displays the ability of our minds to effectively build a unified picture of the *real* world, and this is pleasurable because it demonstrates our minds as fit for purpose. The long answer goes on to tell us how role-playing does this differently from painting, music, or literature, because it highlights different *aspects* of our world-building ability. Painting and music tend to stimulate cognitive abilities that let us make sense of *specific parts* of the world, tracing *patterns* in our sensations and *associations* between our concepts. These are only *means* in relation to the *end* of understanding the world as a *unified whole.* In contrast, the simulations involved in literature and RPGs evoke our capacity to pull all this together into a single consistent picture, *imagining* whole sections of the world and *reasoning* about how they relate to each other. They demonstrate the power of our minds to fulfill their world-building function holistically.

But the pleasure we get from role-playing isn't the same as the pleasure we get from reading (or even writing) a story. This is because the experience of depth reflects another dimension of the process of making sense of the world: it's *dynamic.* The real world is real because it *resists* our attempts to understand it. It can always throw something up that forces us to rethink how we look at it. The models we build of it are often incomplete and frequently just wrong. This means that we must constantly *revise* our picture of the world: filling in specific details, tweaking general principles, and resolving inconsistencies. It's this back and forth that makes the process of understanding the world a dynamic one. The fictional worlds we encounter in novels, movies, and similar artforms activate our capacity to construct a picture of the real world, but only role-playing mimics the *friction* we encounter in bumping up against an autonomous reality. Role-playing presents us with our own power not just to construct a consistent world, but to do so in response to external constraints. The experience of depth is pleasurable because it demonstrates our ability to cope with the *reality* of the world. Deliciously ironic for a medium occasionally accused of escapism.

Back to Reality

As the first, indisputable role-playing game, *Dungeons and Dragons* brought this bold new aesthetic into the world.

Since its inception, D&D has gone through numerous editions, and spawned an industry of imitators, variants and blatant ripoffs. These have tilted the balance that D&D established between playing a game, playing a character, telling a story and experiencing a world: becoming more simulationist (*GURPS*) or more easy-going (*Storyteller*); more closely tied to a single character's emotional experience (*Call of Cthulhu*) or abstracted towards politics (*Reign, Vampire: The Masquerade*); more game-like (D&D Fourth Edition) or more narrative focused (*Polaris: Chivalric Tragedy at Utmost North, Dogs in the Vineyard*); establishing greater synergy between rules and theme (*Unknown Armies*) or making generic rules systems for any type of game (*GURPS, FATE, FUDGE, ORE, BRP, Hero System, OGL*).

D&D (and modern retro-clones such as *Castles and Crusades* and *Labyrinth Lord*) strikes an excellent balance, particularly for the artform's first attempt. We don't want to suggest that D&D is the greatest RPG ever made; nor that it will be the most aesthetically invigorating game that you could play. But it has a few things going for it.

We've spoken about the need for in-game goals to promote disinterestedness. The adventure focus of D&D on heroes killing monsters, finding loot and saving the world is a dependable, bread-and-butter goal, which most players will follow of their own accord. When it comes to in-character goals, the archetypal fantasy characters enforced by the class and race system ensure that even the hammiest actor can easily slip into a role. As for giving cues for a narrative for the DM to develop, the heroic quests for magical macguffins that D&D suggests are a dependable staple.

The fantasy setting is also a strength. A fictional world needn't be like ours to be coherent, and the *depth* of a world isn't the same as its *realism*. Many game settings (such as in the *World of Darkness, Call of Cthulhu* or *Unknown Armies* RPGs) use the real world as a basis from which to extrapolate, and that can be a great boon for fixing down certain points of agreement to make play and simulation easier (not to mention being useful for lazy DMs like the authors). But the aesthetic experience of a successful, believable but fundamentally *unrealistic* world can take things to a new level, as we experience our mind's incredible flexibility in creating coherent worlds out of disparate or absurd parts.

There's more to be said about the distinctive aesthetics of role-playing. The debate about the significance of and tension between the *game* part and the *role-playing* part of role-playing games may benefit from this aesthetic model. We can add a new concept to our aesthetic toolbox for discussions of art objects: the 'RPG aesthetic', as real and valid and unique an aesthetic as can be found in cinema, theatre, painting, sculpture, music, dance, literature and more. Likewise, RPG creators may do well to bear it in mind when they make their games. How will they affect the RPG aesthetic of their game by striking away from the template established by Gygax and Arneson?

And if nothing else, we would suggest you get out your dice, call up some good friends, get round the table, and have a profound moment of aesthetic bliss as you unconsciously recognize your own innate ability to weave worlds out of nothing more solid than play acting, rolling dice, making jokes, eating pizza, getting tea stains on your character sheet, arguing with the DM, storming into dungeons, and of course, hunting down dragons.

17
The Rules of Imagination

CHRIS BATEMAN

Gary Gygax is reputed to have once remarked to one of his colleagues that if the players ever discovered they didn't need any rules they'd be out of a job. Fortunately for everyone working in tabletop role-playing games, this secret has remained in plain view and thus no-one has ever suspected how spectacularly apposite Gygax's claim might be.

However, I maintain that the rules of *Dungeons and Dragons* and other RPGs remain central to the experience of role-playing. Even in the case of games that minimize this element (such as Erick Wujcik's *Amber Diceless Roleplaying Game*) or seem to eliminate it entirely (as in freeform role-play) there's always something that can be called 'rules'. What's more, these rules always function primarily as a means of prescribing what's to be imagined, and only secondarily in the normative sense of regulating conduct.

This may seem like a strange claim—if we think of a rule like Saving Throws in *Dungeons and Dragons*, which states that players must roll above a target number to avoid or end a particular fate, we'd have to recognize that although players could alter or ignore this rule, few if any players would accept such a change as part of the normal play of *Dungeons and Dragons*. Sure, these kinds of rules do regulate play, but this is somewhat beside the point. What's important about a rule like the Saving Throw, the check against THAC0 or anything else you'd care to think of in the vast canon of tabletop role-playing is not that it is a normative rule but that it asks that players *imagine specific things*. The Saving Throw presents that moment of dramatic tension when a hero might live or die, while the roll associated with THAC0 represents the excitement of an attempted strike—will the blow land, or merely glance off?

These examples of the imaginative consequences of rules depend upon die rolls for their meaning, but there are many that do not. Experience points in class and level systems of the kind initiated by D&D, for instance, represent the growing knowledge and capabilities of their characters. Kevin Siembieda, the lead designer of the *Palladium Fantasy Role-playing Game*, a derivative but well-regarded class-and-level game inspired by D&D, once wrote a passionate defense of the decision to base their "Megaversal" role-playing system around an experience point system. His argument ran along the following lines: how often, when watching an adventure story, does the hero almost fail but then just manage to succeed because their years of experience taught them just the right thing to do in that circumstance?

The reason I can claim that this imaginative or *representational* aspect is more important to tabletop role-playing games than the regulative element is because no-one comes to a role-playing session to enforce the mechanics. People don't enjoy making sure no one bends the rules of the Saving Throw, but they do enjoy coming together to enter into a fictional world. True, there are 'rules laywers' (as Gary Alan Fine observed in 1983) who will pick into the letter of the rules of the game to find advantage, but even they are seeking advantage *within the representation the rules provide*. The fun of being a rules lawyer is gaining advantage, and that advantage is gained within the fictional world of the game.

Prop Theory and Fictional Worlds

Kendall Walton first began to explore the roots of what was to become his make-believe theory of representation in a paper from 1978. Walton realized that when considering what happens in the world of a novel, painting, or film, what we say is 'true' within this specific context is what we also say is *fictional*. Thus, since it's true in Fritz Leiber's Hugo and Nebula winning novella 'Ill Met in Lankhmar' that Fafhrd is a seven foot tall barbarian and the Gray Mouser is a small mercurial thief we can say that "it is fictional that Fafhrd is a barbarian" and "it is fictional that the Gray Mouser is a thief".

Furthermore, Walton allows that fictional propositions also occur with games of make-believe, staying: "If it is 'true in a game of make-believe' that Johnnie is a pirate, then fictionally Johnnie is a pirate." These kinds of fictional truths can then be grouped together into *fictional worlds*—such as that of Nehwon, where the Fafhrd and Gray Mouser stories take place, or that of René Magritte's painting *The Treachery of Images* in which it is fictional that there is a pipe, and it is also fictional that under the pipe appears the sentence "Ceci n'est pas une pipe" ("This is not a pipe"). The point of Magritte's marvelously wry painting is that even though we cannot help but see the painting as a pipe, it is no such thing—it is merely fictional that it is a pipe, which is to say, it is only in the fictional world of Magritte's painting that there is a pipe.

Walton's masterstroke was to recognize that there were no substantial differences between Johnnie's game of pirates, Leiber's game of barbarians and thieves, and Magritte's game of something that is not a pipe. All these games of make-believe are phenomenologically equivalent, and thus Walton is able to say that whenever we participate in the experience that accompanies a work of art, we take part in a game of make-believe. He called this the *make-believe theory of representation*, and developed it in detail over the next twelve years and beyond.

Central to Walton's make-believe theory is the idea of a *prop*, which is something that prescribes specific imaginings, and for this reason I call Walton's theory prop theory. Magritte's painting prescribes that we imagine a pipe (and also, it paradoxically prescribes we imagine that what we are imagining is not a pipe). Leiber's novella prescribes that we imagine a seven-foot-tall barbarian and a wily thief. In Johnnie's game of pirates, there may also be some ad hoc props—for instance, he may grab a broom and imagine that it is a cutlass. The broom is thus an ad hoc prop that prescribes that anyone participating in Johnnie's game of pirates imagines that the broom is a sword. The connection with tabletop role-playing games is obvious. The fictional worlds of RPGs are of the same nature as the fictional worlds of other representations.

However, the kind of props that prescribe imagining the fictional worlds of role-playing games are actually quite different from those that prescribe specific imaginings in the case of paintings or written stories. There are clear parallels, but also unique differences.

The Dungeon Master's Word Is Law

In Walton's theory, there are two principal kinds of representations—firstly, *depictions*—such as paintings, sculptures and photographs—which are sensory in nature. Secondly, verbal representations (or *narrations*)—such as poems, novels, and song lyrics. It's clear that the lion's share of the work of representation in a tabletop role-playing game is being done by these latter kind of props, namely the sentences uttered by the players.

What the Dungeon Master does (and what, in general, every Games Master must do) is not so much like the role of a sporting referee as it first appears. The DM effectively allocates *authority* to the statements and propositions that are submitted to the game by the players. In prop theory, the reason that particular representations can be interpreted in specific ways lies in the idea that there are certain culturally authorized principles at work in the context of any artwork. In a game of *Dungeons and Dragons* the authority rests almost entirely with the DM.

If a player says "I open the large iron chest" their making this statement *does not* prescribe that all the players imagine that this has happened—it's only when the DM acknowledges this (perhaps by saying "As you open the chest . . .") that the player's statement becomes an authorized part of the game of make-believe all the players are participating in.

The Dungeon Master's word is law when it comes to the contents of the fictional world of any given game of D&D. If the DM says you can't do something, you can't do it. He or she has "absolute power". Even the rule books, which seem to have a fair share of authority, can be overruled by the DM, especially if so doing makes for a better experience. This is the secret that all great DMs must keep to themselves: they are covertly working *on behalf of the enjoyment of the players.* Far from being neutral, a great DM is committed to the satisfaction of their players—in whatever that might mean—up to and including in some cases covertly cheating to make the game more fun.

Dice of Destiny

Rolling dice isn't an essential part of role-playing—*Amber* and freeform games do without, for instance—but it is an important aspect of the enjoyment of the hobby for many people. When I first started studying how and why people play games, I was surprised by just how attached role-players were to their dice, with many people expressing disappointment that the eclectic mix of tetrahedral (D4), cubic (D6), octahedral (D8), pentagonal trapezohedral (D10), dodecahedral (D12) and isosa-hedral (D20) dice were being systematically trimmed down in most of the role-playing games market to just the D6, D10 and the D20. Ken St. Andre, who in 1975 created the second commercial role-playing game, *Tunnels and Trolls*, designed his game to use only six-sided dice because at the time polyhedral dice were an exotic commodity and hard to come by—D&D had required custom molds for the original dice that came in its boxed sets. But in the years since, every hobby game store now stocks a vast panoply of multi-sided dice, and for many players there is an esoteric appeal to rolling odd shaped objects that runs counter to the current trend in simplification.

In talking about the role of dice as a prop, therefore, we recognize that part of the appeal of the polyhedral dice is precisely their exoticism. If you are imagining that you're a wizard who brews potions for sale in a pan-dimensional bazaar, it helps to set the mood that the objects you are physically handling are equally peculiar. The ancient Greek philosophers were not the only people to be fascinated by what are even now termed the Platonic solids! In the modern market for role-playing games, however, *Dungeons and Dragons* is unusual in maintaining its commitment to the full array of dice. In so doing, it may have helped secure its appeal with its core audience, those quirky and unusual teenagers who come to D&D precisely for the escapism from the humdrum regularity of the everyday world.

However, the role of the dice as a prop goes further than the aesthetics of their form. There is an appeal to dice-rolling which goes far beyond role-playing, and indeed goes back deep into the history of our species. There's a deep rooted psychological connection to the dice roll for the vast majority of people, such that you almost can't help but feel a sense of *ownership* over the outcome of a die roll, even if you intellectually know that it's a random process that you can't influence. Computer games are inferior to tabletop games in at least this respect: a rolled die offers a sense of connection to the outcome that a button press can never quite manage. As Roger Caillois wrote in 1958, gambling with dice "reveals the favor of destiny;" the player cannot affect the outcome with their skill or intelligence, all they can do is "await, in hope and trembling, the cast of the die."

What *Dungeons and Dragons* did with dice, which was utterly revolutionary, was capture the same intensity of experience that a die roll can offer in gambling by connecting the outcome of a roll with a *narrative* consequence. Dice had already been used to produce representational outcomes for some time—*Kriegspeil* (literally "Wargame") had been used for training Prussian army officers as far back as 1812, using dice to simulate battle, and Avalon Hill had been publishing wargames since Charles S. Robert's *Tactics* in 1954. But all these games, while providing an indispensible background to the arrival of D&D, had placed the player at a point of narrative distance from the events. Players were generals, in command of forces, of something similar, invested in the outcome because of a powerful desire to be victorious over the other players. D&D made it personal. By giving players individual characters, the outcome of die rolls were suddenly transformed in their narrative implications and intensity.

Other board games had already given the player control of a single character. This explicitly happens in *Cluedo* (*Clue* in the United States). But this conceit was never really carried through to the extent that was possible in the role-playing game. Sure, I might imagine that I am Miss Scarlet, but my only investment in the outcome of the die roll is whether or not I can make it to the Library this turn or next turn. Conversely, in *Dungeons and Dragons* it was quite literally a matter of life or death (well, *fictional* life and death): if I fail my Saving Throw against Petrification or Polymorph, I *could be* (fictionally) *turned to stone*! It works without the dice, sure, you can still enter the fictional world of a role-playing game using just words. But the dice simulate the intensity of feelings that are interjected into the narrative being developed—and this is an essential part of the appeal of *Dungeons and Dragons* and other dice-based role-playing games.

Another aspect of the intensity of narrative experience involved in the use of dice in tabletop role-playing games is the concept of a *critical hit* or a *fumble*. The notion of a 'critical hit' can be traced back to the incredible (but commercially unsuccessful) *Empire of the Petal Throne* role-playing game, published by TSR in 1975 just one year after D&D. As well as a campaign setting of unparalleled detail and quality, the game also had the first rule for what was termed a 'lucky hit'—a 20 on a D20 caused double damage; a second throw of 19 or 20 resulted in a killing blow. By modeling not just success or failure, but also allowing for extremes of outcome, critical and fumbles intensified the experience of die rolling—creating magical moments of triumph when the die just happen to roll the number you needed to save you and your friends from certain death. It's another reminder of just how important dice can be to the uniquely immersive experience of role-playing games.

The Class Struggle

At first glance, the trend in recent years has been away from the use of classes in tabletop RPGs. Role-players curmudgeonly grumble about being made to pick a class, complaining that it is not realistic to tramline career choices in this way. Such people often feel, as I once did, that they're fully justified in their calls for the abolition of the class system, and that skill-based systems are superior in every way. But they're mistaken.

To understand the argument in favor of class systems, it's important to recognize something that is not often discussed in the context of role-playing games, despite its self-evidence: role-players are imaginative people. Use whatever psychometric measure you wish, you will find that whatever measurement is correlated with the powers of imagination scores more highly among role-players than among anyone else. In fact, imagination is a strict requirement for playing a role-playing game for quite obvious reasons: while just about anyone can suspend belief while watching a movie, it takes a different kind of person to suspend belief when developing a verbal narrative sat around a table with other people. Many people just aren't up to this task. Similarly, not everyone is capable of enjoying books because it requires a certain degree of imagination to conjure up the mental imagery that the sentences prescribe that readers imagine.

Once it's accepted that it takes something special—imagination—to be able to play a role-playing game, it quickly becomes apparent that the less imagination is required, the more people are able to play. Those role-players who favor skill-based systems are often those who enjoy actual role-play—getting into the drama of character dynamics and interrelation. But *Dungeons and Dragons* doesn't just (or even primarily) attract players interested in this kind of participatory story-telling. Some just want to imagine they are a powerful warrior who can biff dragons on the head with a sword, or want to accumulate treasure and experience so that they can become a more powerful warrior who can biff bigger dragons on the head with an even bigger sword.

When dealing with someone who's imaginative enough to play a role-playing game, but not so imaginative as to be interested in participation in an evolving dramatic narrative, classes have an absolutely unbeatable advantage in terms of accessibility. The *Dungeons and Dragons* basic set (which was originally marketed in parallel to the more rules-heavy *Advanced Dungeons and Dragons*) offered players simple choices about *who they could become*: Fighter, Magic User, Cleric or Thief, as a human, and Dwarf, Elf or Halfling, for those who favored something more exotic. Similarly clear lines are offered to players joining a modern videogame such as *World of Warcraft*, which clearly owes an immeasurable debt to *Dungeons and Dragons*. Each class is a prop that prescribes the player imagine what kind of hero they become. The clear definition inherent in these classes is precisely the point of appeal for many players, and of course, precisely the point of objection for more imaginative players who do not want to be constrained in their choices.

A related issue is the complexity of the character generation process. A complex system, like the one in Marc Miller's seminal *Traveller* science fiction role-playing game, has great appeal to certain players, but that intricacy can be off-putting to many other players. Skill-based systems (like *Traveller* or *Call of Cthulhu*) appeal to players more tolerant of complexity, and more gifted with imagination, who can craft a character that interests them out of the raw materials of the rules. But this does not describe everyone. Many players need a little help, and character classes provide this.

Even when class is not explicit, the same kind of channeled props to assist player imagination can often be found. The original *World of Darkness* game, *Vampire: The Masquerade*, doesn't seem to offer classes, but it *does* support player imagination with two vital props: the fact that every player's character will be a vampire, and the highly significant choice of clan, since the nuances of the clan definitions in this game provide the same essential support as class in this game and its descendents.

Class offers a simple and comprehensible access point for new players coming to a game, making their initial choices manageable and, like the cover of a modern fantasy novel, making a promise as to what their fictional adventures to come will offer them. Even role-playing games that don't use class often have class-like elements lurking under the hood. Like it or not, the class system is here to stay.

You Are Your Numbers

Class may set the scene for a character, but the prop that really prescribes everything that is imagined about any given hero is the *character sheet*. This humble piece of paper, perhaps neatly laid out with elaborately decorated boxes for writing in attributes, or perhaps just a hand-written page, is crucial to the experience of tabletop role-playing games, and indeed to the computer role-playing games that directly descend from them. The numbers that appear on this sheet (as well as certain important words like 'class', discussed above, and 'alignment', which I discussed in Chapter 4) are precisely the prop which prescribes we imagine the particularities of any character.

The idea of abstracting properties into numbers was already an important aspect of the game mechanics of wargames and the like when *Dungeons and Dragons* came into being, but the kinds of properties abstracted in these games had all been focused on the elements of warfare, such as movement speed, range of attack, damage caused, and so forth. With D&D came a whole new set of abstractions, ones suited to describe not a military unit but an individual hero. The choices Gygax and Arneson made for the game have continued to influence role-playing games—both digital and paper—ever since.

What's particularly interesting about them is the way they seem to move beyond purely combative concerns.

True, Strength, as a measure of physical power, and Constitution, as a measure of endurance, are still largely tied to the notion of combat—but then battle is an important part of the game. The implicit message of the title "Dungeons and Dragons" is that the players are going to be assaulting the former in order to slay the latter, not painting dungeons in order to get a letter of recommendation from a local dragon. Dexterity too has something of this leaning, in that it speaks of speed of reactions and manual skills, but with the addition of the Thief class in the first D&D supplement, *Greyhawk*, Dexterity was to take on more of a role-playing meaning as the attribute that prescribed players imagined a superior skill at picking locks and balancing on tightropes.

Intelligence, Wisdom, and Charisma, however, are abstractions that would be almost unthinkable in a game simulating, say, panzer warfare in World War II. These are not about strict battle capabilities (although of course D&D makes Intelligence and Wisdom grant spell bonuses that *do* give benefits in combat), but are about how the character relates to the world. The distinction between Intelligence and Wisdom has been a long held point of contention among role-players. Ken St. Andre was perhaps the first to complain that he couldn't see the difference between the two, and replaced Wisdom with Luck in *Tunnels and Trolls* (in a not-unrelated decision, St. Andre also ditched Clerics later stating "religion was not very important in my life, so why should it clutter up my game?"). However, Gygax always defended the separation between the two attributes. In the original *Dungeon Masters Guide* he wrote what has become the classic definition of that distinction, namely that Intelligence is knowing that smoking is dangerous to your health, while Wisdom is actually quitting once you find that out.

Charisma, the most unique of the classic D&D attributes, was perhaps the first attempt at quantifying interpersonal relations in a game. The idea behind the attribute was that it would reflect how other people and monsters would react to you, and thus a charismatic hero might be able to avoid combat where a less charming adventurer might be knee deep in blood without noticing that they could have avoided the fight. In practice, most *Dungeons and Dragons* adventurers were keen to get straight into combat all the time, since they wanted experience points so that they could level up and become more powerful, making Charisma something of a damp squib. Nonetheless, there have been many players for whom it has been a point of pride that their character had a high Charisma attribute – and many others for whom having a *low* Charisma has been a point of pride. In this way, Charisma was as vital a prop in prescribing how players imagine their characters as any other attribute.

It's worth remarking on the unsuccessful attempt to differentiate Charisma from appearance, which it was never expressly intended to represent. The publication of *Unearthed Arcana* in 1985, a hardback supplement for AD&D that collected material from numerous RPG magazines along with some new experimental rules, introduced the never-popular attribute of Comeliness to provide this distinction. Gygax (in *Dragon* #67) stated that he disliked 'Beauty' as a term seeing it as "too specific, as it calls to mind a positive state of good looks." But his choice of such an unfamiliar and awkward word as 'Comeliness' may have blocked acceptance of this attribute. That said, it probably didn't help that in the fictional worlds of most players' games, Charisma—no matter what it said in the rule books—was already a representation of attractiveness.

There are many other numerical abstractions at use in many other games, such as the Basic Role-playing system's approach of representing character proficiencies in terms of skills which are scored with a percentage value, representing an absolute chance of success that could be rolled against using percentile dice. However, regardless of the kind of numerical abstraction at work, the basic principle remains the same as the attributes in *Dungeons and Dragons*: numbers can be used to 'score' the characters capabilities. In terms of prop theory, each attribute, skill or what-have-you serves as a prop prescribing the players imagine not only the relative capabilities of their characters within the fictional world, but also coupling with the dice to determine the actual chances of success in various situations.

Numeric representation is a powerful aspect of the way role-playing games capture and maintain the attention of their players, and this is never more true than with the central

advancement mechanic in class and level systems such as
D&D: experience points. This mechanic is also a powerful functional element of the play of games, because by holding out a
goal state ("the next level") to be attained, role-playing games
—and even more so computer role-playing games—create
highly compulsive circumstances, encouraging players to keep
going, keep earning more points, keep getting more powerful.

It is impossible to underestimate how important this has been
in the modern history of games. The videogames industry in the
early twenty-first century has exported experience points (often
in the form of graphical bars) into almost every genre, and
secured greater commercial success almost every time it has done
so. As a game designer myself, I am highly conflicted about this
development, but now is not the time to explore the moral implications of these game mechanics. For good or ill, the addictive
pursuit of points for advancement is critical to the commercial
fortunes of the current videogame industry, and this is yet
another element that traces its origins to *Dungeons and Dragons*.

Modules, Maps, and Models

The history of *Dungeons and Dragons* has been inextricably
linked to its modules, the pamphlet-sized booklets which
describe dungeons, wildernesses and other adventure possibilities. This may seem strange—can't Dungeon Masters make up
their own adventures? Certainly they might, but many don't.
Whether from lack of time or lack of imagination, D&D players
have always wanted to buy modules to specify the framework
of their stories—which is just as well for TSR, since sales of
modules had been one of their key sources of income when they
were an independent company. The role of such modules as
props is fairly apparent: they prescribe a fictional world for a
specific adventure (part of a fictional world, from a certain perspective, but from Walton's theory it is in effect an entire fictional world just as much).

Within each module, however, a specific kind of depiction
serves a crucial role: the map. It is the maps which prescribe
imaginings concerning the geographic and spatial arrange-
ment of the fictional world, and part of the fun of reading a
module is looking at the maps and beginning to imagine, even
before the game begins, the shape of the fictional world. That

world is already in (fictional) existence when the map is used as a prop for a game of make-believe that takes place solely in the Dungeon Master's imagination, long before the players sit down to begin their adventure for (fictional) real.

Once the players are assembled, another kind of depictive prop can serve a crucial role: the model (traditionally, the lead miniature figurine). In the early days, such things were a desirable luxury, but far from essential, but later editions of *Dungeons and Dragons* have made the use of models—and with it, tiles or map sheets—absolutely *de rigueur*. One can be cynical and say this is simply to sell more lead miniatures, and no doubt there is a commercial motive of this kind. But it is also for the same reason that *Dungeons and Dragons* benefits from having specified classes—as a prop for the imagination. Players with less imagination can see what is going on in the game if it appears before them in miniature, and this opens up the game to a far wider audience and may have helped the venerable tabletop game remain somewhat competitive with its explicitly depicted videogame descendents.

The Climactic Finale

I started this chapter with the story of Gary Gygax joking that if the players ever discovered they didn't need rules, the makers of RPGs would be out of a job. But the only way that the rule-makers can be put out of a job is if the players themselves become rule-makers. So this would be more a case of stealing game design jobs than it would be of putting all game designers out of work. This is good news for me, since I am one of those intrepid individuals who began by realizing I didn't need Mr. Gygax and his fellows to make the rules for me, and ended up making the rules for other players to play by. It transpires there is a genuine craft behind creating good rules for role-play, and indeed for all kinds of play, and not everyone can do it well.

It's reported that Gary Gygax once asked that people send to him anyone who claimed that their role-playing was an art form of any kind so that he could stick a pin in their head and deflate it. Gygax claimed that you can play a game artfully, but that doesn't make the game (nor its play) art. True enough—the artfulness of play is not enough in itself to make a game into art. What makes a game and its play into art is the recognition that all artworks—paintings, sculptures, films, novels, symphonies, and even tabletop role-playing games like *Dungeons and Dragons*—are at their heart games of make-believe. Now it may be true, as Lawrence Schick remarked in his exhaustive guide, *Heroic Worlds*, that "most role-playing is oriented toward acting out adolescent power fantasies", but as he says "What of it? The same can be said of fiction and film. Real artistry is rare in every art form."

Chaosium's Greg Stafford once said: "Role-playing games are a new form of art, as legitimate as sculpture, drama, or prose fiction." Schick lent his support to this claim, calling role-playing "a new approach to storytelling, a new and separate form of fictive art". Walton's prop theory is a philosophical foundation that takes these claims from being tentative assertions of opinion and elevates them to the point that they must be taken seriously. All games are art, and especially tabletop role-playing games. If it were not for *Dungeons and Dragons* we couldn't even begin to guess what the digital games industry would have been like, since the history and development of the videogame form owes an epic debt to D&D, as does every other RPG system in existence. Games are art, and role-playing games are the purest form of those games of make-believe that are not just experienced, but lived.

18

You Got Your Gameplay in My Role-Play!

ADAM BRACKIN

"Role-play" can be a strange and sometimes confusing word. It conjures up images of video games to some, and images of character sheets to others. Some see miniature figures on a one-inch grid or scattered among elaborate tiny scenery of varying quality. Others imagine a table cluttered only with pizza boxes, cola cans, and the beady eyes of a game master peeking over the top of his mysterious DM screen as his tale told only in words begins to unfold. Is role-play a story game or a story with rules? Something else entirely, perhaps?

It's obvious that the term "role-play" is "role" and "play" stuck together, but what's less obvious is the underlying oxymoron created by combining those particular two words. Usually role-play refers to a role-playing game or "RPG," and so "role" in this context is referring to a character—or more accurately, to various RPG characters acted out through an interactive story created through the second part—"play." For role-play also implies that there is a game to be played, a set of gameplay rules to be followed, and in an RPG it's especially likely there will be some form of combat to be fought in glorious pursuit of some noble and epic quest. So is it "the game" or "the story" that makes it all worthwhile?

Believe it or not, this duality is at the heart an old (and often childish) debate over which is more important. In order to understand how these two tricky fundamentals of role-play and gameplay work together, we first have to decide if they can even work together at all. The debate has taken on many forms. Are games art? If so, is it because of the visuals, the story, or some combination of both? What's the difference between mature content in books and movies, as against the interactive nature of games? Video games seem to get the worst of the criticism because of the ability to make real-time choices within a highly visual medium, but how is that worse than rolling dice to hack, slash, and pillage, or deciding your character is going have an imaginary one-night stand with the buxom Elvish NPC barkeep if you pass your charisma check? In many ways that's even more intimate, is it not? It's at least more open-ended.

The Great Divide

For decades now the philosophical divide that separates gameplay and story has plagued game designers and academics alike. Eggheads and university professors (such as myself) with too many letters behind their name are usually required to talk about these troublemakers as "Ludology" and "Narratology" since "Ludos" and "Narro" are the Latin words for game and story, which of course reminds people that the debate is really old and therefore must be important. Unfortunately this just has a tendency to further confuse the issue, because whatever you call it, the extent and deeply complex nature of the argument is often overshadowed (and undermined) by mainstream media. We often find them shouting at each other across a chasm of terminology differences that games should "be looked at as games not stories" or vice versa and in effect vilifying both, especially in early game design writings.

The debate has naturally inspired polarized reactions: we either get gameplay models which are infused with minor story elements from action-oriented game designers exemplified in current rules-heavy systems; or else we get rhetorically heavy arguments which disregard the basic rules structures of a game like the ones that can be found in narrative-heavy systems.

In the popular game design fundamentals textbook *Rules of Play* for example, the authors are keen to point out the two theoretical camps but still choose to call the chapter "Games as Narrative Play" anyway, having clearly chosen sides and even going as far as to suggest we see games as "interactive narratives," saying:

> We do not ask, for example, 'Are games stories?' or 'How do we create better narratives?' These kinds of questions focus more generally on the nature of narrative itself, rather than on the role of narrative as experienced through gameplay. . . . it is not a question of *whether* games are narrative, but *how* they are narrative. (*Rules of Play*, p. 378)

Theorists and game designers alike are still seeking a sound testing ground for this cultural battle amongst game design theorists. It's about the only thing most can agree on. Ironically they continue to this day to create very different theories and ways of measuring either the mechanics or the story elements of a game without trying to find a model where the boundaries of the one are not simply defined by the other like some kind of ludo-narratological yin-yang. For example, renowned game designer Chris Crawford writes that games are "a closed formal system that subjectively represents a subset of reality." Similarly, Jasper Juul, an internationally renowned ludologist supposes:

> Using other media as starting points, we may learn many things about the construction of fictive worlds and characters . . . but relying too heavily on existing theories will make us forget what makes games *games*: Such as rules, goals, player activity, the projection of the player's actions into the game world and the way the game defines the possible actions of the player. It is the unique parts that we need to study now. (*Rules of Play*, p. 379)

With an equally polarized but opposite opinion, narratologist Brenda Laurel couldn't disagree more, saying the "game" label is actually quite irrelevant:

> I don't think the interactive game changes the popular understanding of what a story is. In popular culture, people talk about characters and worlds in relatively media-independent ways. In common speech, the name 'story' actually refers to the central bundle of potential created by characters, worlds, situations, histories, and so forth, rather than to a specific instantiation (for example, Star Trek, Care Bears, Myst). (*Rules of Play*, p. 379)

But what if we took a more balanced approach?, you might ask. Game designer Greg Costikyan provides us that in a direct online response to Brenda Laurel's very comment, saying:

> A story is best envisioned as 'beads on a string,' a linear narrative; a
> game is best envisioned as a triangle of possibility, with the initial
> position at one apex, and possible conclusions along the opposite
> side, with myriad, ideally, infinite paths between initial state and out-
> come. To the degree that you try to make a game more like a story by
> imposing arbitrary decision points, you make it less like a game.
> (*Rules of Play*, p. 379)

Even the newcomer RPG-like genre known as "Alternate
Reality Games" is not without its debating factions. Essentially
complicated collaborative scavenger-hunt style stories that
embrace emergent properties and take place both online and in
the real world, ARGs were born out of a climate of interactive
storytelling, but even knowing this, the debate rages on within
the ARGer community over the question of "tinag"—the
mantra of ARG—which stands for "This is NOT a game." Some
say it is a narrative construct similar to the "willing suspension
of disbelief" required by any fiction, while others take the
statement quite literally, eschewing any "game" element that
seems at all contrived in a maverick storytelling genre that has
taken over a decade to even find a proper name for itself (*This
Is Not a Game*, pp. 1–15).

So, what can we hope to do? While there are elements of
truth to all of these positions, it is clear that we all too soon
become tangled in technical definitions and objectifications of
story and game before we can even get started talking about it.
Even the so-called balanced approach seems to identify an
event horizon of sorts where story ends and game begins, and
like oil and water, where one is, the other cannot be. In other
words, instead of trying to understand how role-play and gameplay could possibly exist together, we have tried desperately to
pull them apart, which any seasoned gamer can tell you really
makes no sense at all.

There is a better choice though. It is revealed when focusing
on the nearly invisible space that exists where these other two
supposedly meet, and it also happens to be the most interesting one. What better way is there to find this intersection of
opposites than to look at it through the lens of the oldest and
most iconic pencil and paper tabletop roleplaying game system,
Dungeons and Dragons?

D&D and Duality

One of my favorite illustrations of the fundamental ridiculous-ness of the role-play versus gameplay argument is the 2010 April Fool's Day joke played by Wizards of the Coast via their website, when a new (albeit fake) D&D tome *Roll-Playing for Roleplaying* was announced. The overtly cynical ad for the self-proclaimed "unnecessary game core rules" expansion for the Fourth Edition proudly proclaims:

> Swinging swords and slinging spells in combat with fantastic crea-tures isn't all you'll wanna do in your D&D game. There could be a time when you want your character to do something radical. Maybe you want to have a conversation with an NPC. Perhaps you want to exhibit a quirky trait or mannerism. There could even be an opportu-nity to wear an interesting hat or something. Clearly, you'll need extensive rules, charts, and tables for doing things that are pretty much just creatively describing your actions. That's when you turn to *Roll-Playing for Role-playing*—the most in-depth book of guidelines that will govern everything else your character does. There's never been D&D rules like this before. Mainly 'cause you don't need 'em.

The joke works because it is a scathing reminder of the fact that good role-play is telling the story by doing what your char-acter would do, even if you the player might not do it within the given game mechanics. By using the popular slang homophone *roll*-play, in reference to the act of throwing dice and all the other mechanics based activities and rules that the game requires to function, The D&D publisher's joke is really just reminding us of the difference between "character knowledge" and "player knowledge" known to any RPG gamer who ever sat around a table with their character sheet and dice in front of them, then chose not to use either one for the sake of the story.

There are other reasons why Fourth Edition D&D is an espe-cially ideal way to examine the relationship between role-play and gameplay. This is not only because of the rich history of changes evident in the various versions of the system to its cur-rent version, but also due to the way Fourth Edition's rules treat the philosophical concept of role-play as being secondary to the mechanics of the system. Or does it? While the *Dungeons and Dragons* rule-set has always had a strong mechanics focus, the rich and fantastic history and culture (both fictional and real-world pop culture) behind the system is very story-centered. Additionally, there is a sort of middle "border" region of "scenario" which acts as a third space that exists as a sort of no-man's-land where not just any story, but "the" story—"OUR" story being told right now around a table—can take place. This is a unique form of interactive storytelling created by role-players that tells the people on both sides of the ludology versus narratology argument to shove it, while you and I go play some D&D.

D&D and Gameplay

At its simplest, gameplay (a.k.a. ludology for you Bardic types, and "roll-play" for you Rogues) is about the defined rules, defined elements, and defined goals of the game. Fourth Edition D&D exists within a strong legacy of books and resources built on this idea.

At first it might seem an overwhelmingly impossible task for any latecomer to understand the full richness and context of the system's various editions, expansions, enhancements, worlds and scenarios. In fact it's only through the last decade or so of online social media that we have collectively been able to fully break apart and reorganize this information into manageable and searchable wiki databases for easy comparison and retrieval when needed—often during gameplay itself. This has simply highlighted the differences in various rules and expansions to the point that the mere mention of "Planescape" or "Spelljammer" at the wrong time could start a riot at a game convention. (If you don't know what that means it's okay, just look it up online, I'll wait.) Indeed it would seem that the official errata, variants, unofficial content, mods, and whatever else had existed in uncountable volumes before many younger Fourth Edition players were even born, to an extent that no single mortal could possibly read it all without a highly advanced "time stop" spell, a distinct problem for all of us non-clerics. Yet they continue to publish D&D content! How can this be?

All of this as it turns out, is simply a large part of the marketing strategy of what is being called by some the "reboot" of the D&D pantheon and when taken in context with the recent trend of reboot movies and video games, it is understandable why the system might need to reinvent itself in its fourth (or is that sixth?) incarnation for this younger audience if they have any hope at all of getting into the game. Setting aside the initial criticisms that proved premature (such as the loss of five character classes which appeared in later player handbook volumes) as well as accidental errors later fixed in errata (such as broken math in a number of places in the first printing), the most notable intended changes in the game for Fourth Edition were its highly scrutinized "simplification" of the rules. This includes the rules for character creation, mechanics, and other fundamental gameplay elements.

One major example of these gameplay changes found in the core rule books is the employment of a static defense value, for use when rolling an attack. It's been observed that this mechanic more closely aligns the Fourth Edition to the rules for the Miniatures Game, a logical choice for reciprocity since the high quality minis and maps of that game were designed for use with the RPG. Connected to this, distances previously measured in feet are now measured in five-foot squares; a diagonally adjacent square is considered to be "1 square" away, so that effect areas are generally square rather than circular or cone-shaped. This allows players the freedom to choose a simpler fight mechanic when needed from the minis game; the new standard aligned mechanic from the core book; and now through added content, various advanced methods also are available. For better or for worse, the goal has been consistency and options across the various D&D rules and tools for Fourth Edition – a goal which has been met very well.

Other examples of significant Fourth Edition gameplay changes include a spiritual renaissance of classic "epic level" rules for extension to level thirty including a "paragon path" beginning at level eleven, and "epic destiny" at level twenty-one similar to the way multi-classing is now handled in the highly successful Star Wars "Saga Edition" reboot, also by WotC. In this spirit, D&D Fourth Edition multi-classing has also been reworked and various other character mechanics redone for the purpose of streamlining and un-complicating things that had become muddled during the prior revisions through Edition 3.5.

As a result of all these changes, some players have literally thrown down their shiny new Fourth Edition core books in passionate outrage for the sake of their dog-eared 3.5 with the broken spine and missing pages. As we tiptoe past these friends and smile nervously, we mustn't forget the reason for these changes. Any game requires rules to function, and by consolidating the best—or in some cases most efficient—rules into a new system that maintains the integrity of the old, while revitalizing and encouraging interest in the new, the game system can remain an effective means of gameplay for the current time. Fourth Edition may not be a perfect revision, but there never has been a perfect edition, as tvtropes.com happily points out while using D&D as an example in its exhaustive treatment of the "Dork Age" change-for-change's-sake trope:

> There are valid complaints about each one: First edition had all the flaws that the first edition of anything could be expected to have. AD failed to fix many of them. Second edition was needlessly obtuse and complicated. Third had extreme variation between power levels in classes, as well as some cumbersome skill rules. (You need both to hide and move silently). 4th edition suffers from notoriously poorly written math (−4 to −7 on a roll of 1–20 is a pretty devastating gap written into the core rules), and reverse power creep, as well as feeling a bit too much like a video game. And yet D&D (any edition) is still the best selling Tabletop RPG in print. ("Dork Age")

Let's face it: it's just cool to complain about D&D gameplay changes like it's cool to complain about new *Star Wars* material and the weather. Perhaps this is because unlike many of those eggheads with too many letters behind their name, the average geek on the street can make a lifetime study of RPGs and is still able to complain about them and play them simultaneously.

D&D and Role-Play

Such overwhelming contradictions as those above might seem to deny the essence and root cause of the relationship between the two necessary elements of RPG, making D&D role-play nigh impossible. As I already mentioned, D&D has gotten a rather interesting reputation in some circles for being a strong mechanics game but sorely lacking in role-play opportunities. Sometimes it seems that anyone not criticizing the system's gameplay changes is complaining about D&D's story mechanics (or lack thereof). But this isn't entirely fair on their part. In fact, some would argue (and I'd be one of them) that it's just an excuse for bad role-playing by those who aren't very good at it.

What we're really talking about when we speak of "good" role-playing is a spectrum of story options which allows the players, and especially the dungeon master, to find the balance that's right for a particular group within the rules system of choice used by that group. It's not very epic if your Halfling Rogue gets his face smashed in by a cave troll on the way to destroy his magical ring in the volcano of death, but it's also not very fun if it's not a possibility. Many agree that the mark of a truly great DM is to make the players believe that they are on the verge of death at any moment, but unbeknownst to them they are really quite safe, relatively speaking.

"DM_Samuel," founder and editor of the popular rpDMusings.com website, the DM Roundtable podcast, and contributor to the 4geeks4e D&D Fourth Edition podcast has been playing D&D since his first encounter with the First Edition in 1981. He took up the topic of gameplay versus role-play on 4geeks4e.com recently, saying:

> They designed Fourth Edition so that combat was rules-heavy and you can run the role-playing in any way that you like. It's the 'we'll give you combat rules, it's your responsibility to put the players in situation where they MUST role-play' school of RPG design. And I like it that way—it gives me a lot of freedom to run the game the way I want to. The idea of Skill Challenges largely failed in the beginning (and still does for many groups) because it is an attempt at putting a strict rule-set on role-playing and it just doesn't work that well in many groups. I feel, in many cases, that it puts too many constraints on how I want my players to role-play a situation.

Skill Challenges are one of the major new mechanics of Fourth Edition designed to encourage role-play. It's fair to say that their launch did not go very smoothly, however, as the numbers had to be revised via an errata after the first printing.

Again the tvtropes.com "Dork Age" entry has a perfect example of how forcing story changes down players' throats can go horribly wrong:

> Although not unbearable, Second Edition was arguably the worst time for D&D. The game shifted its demographic from teen/college-age

players to preteens, resulting in a 'dumbed down' feeling. Pressure from moral guardians saw the game drop references to demons and devils (later replacing them with 'tanar'ri' and 'baatezu'). Finally, whenever sales were flagging, they had the policy of just releasing a new campaign setting in a desperate attempt to gain new players, but it just led to a glut of settings with poor sales (not that all these settings didn't have their merits, but today the likes of Spelljammer and Birthright remain very much cult classics). ("Dork Ages")

These Second Edition changes were not gameplay rule adjustments, they were attempted role-play story changes to settings, characters, and scenarios. It's worth noting too that these "teens" and "preteens" who played these famously "worst time" campaigns are now some of the same thirty-something DMs who have thrown down their books in disgust and outrage over the Fourth Edition reboot, which many still play anyway if for no other reason than to have something good to complain about.

The Border Region and Other New Models

So where does the proverbial Yin end and the Yang begin in this story versus game debate? If we chuck away the notion that there is a defined event horizon between gameplay and role-play and instead look for a common no-man's land where the actual interactive story is being told, we can discover some surprising new models. One way to do this is through the lens of video game theory.

Video game designers know that interactivity means something different to the computer role-play (CRPG) video gamer than it does to the tabletop RPG player, largely because the video game environment provides visuals while the tabletop environment relies primarily on the imagination of the players. Not to mention the closed system mechanics that a computer represents. Much debate has been had as to which is better, but regardless, the relationship of game mechanics versus story within a CRPG environment is well worth comparing to tabletop adventures.

Perhaps the most obvious example to look at is D&D Online. According to the DDO wiki, much of the MMORPG's gameplay is based on D&D Edition 3.5 structures, but necessary major changes had to be made. The most obvious is probably developer Turbine's very logical decision to use a real-time computer combat engine over the tabletop RPG's turn-based system. This subsequently caused considerable changes in major aspects of combat, character skills and feats and even the way combat damage is calculated in order to provide a fun and balanced experience for the player along the axis of all the various character choices within the game. Virtual dice are still being "rolled" via random number tables at rates no human could ever accomplish, a fact noted by the heads up display in the game, but the function of the virtual dice—the gameplay elements—are changed.

Another limiting factor in DDO is that the MMORPG is set in the city of Stormreach, an ancient city built ages ago by giants and recently settled by humans. Quests do take players out of the city, but not in the same way that a tabletop player may simply decide to wander out into the "sandbox" of a world and simply explore what might be there, and possibly requiring a DM to do some fast thinking outside of that proverbial box. This is the fundamental difference between any CRPG and a tabletop game. A computer simulation will always be a controlled, enclosed, and constructed environment. This closed-system model by definition denies the player the same types of choice as an open system and also denies the DM the opportunity to spontaneously create a mysterious "something" behind the next tree if the players need (or perhaps deserve) it. We usually call this sort of campaign "on a rail" and this idea has been the guiding comedic principle for popular web comics like *DM of the Rings* and movies like *The Gamers: Dorkness Rising*.

This is really about the quintessential "Turing test" of computer AI, which is a thought experiment meant to illustrate that as of yet, no computer game can simulate human interaction to believable levels. This is because an AI still lacks that thing which fundamentally makes us human: Creativity. Many of the aforementioned eggheads say it never will. MMORPGs like DDO have succeeded to some extent at giving an open-ended experience by reintroducing the human factor into the online play—a nightmare scenario for the ratings board as can be noted by their disclaimer on the box of any given MMO—but even these have built in problems and difficulties in balancing gameplay with believable story, not to mention expecting all players logged into the game to actually role-play their character, while *in* character. This despite the fully realized 3D virtual D&D environment still rarely happens, except in small dedicated groups.

Jenova Chen is a game designer notable for his highly unusual games such as *flOw*, *Flower*, and more recently *Journey*. His research on "flow theory" available at jenovachen.com has been instrumental in designing games which find the zone between frustration and ability for the player by giving them control over the most basic gameplay experience. This ability to adjust the "difficulty level" intuitively and naturally while playing has strong connections to the tabletop RPG experience which has by definition an open-ended capability. Similarly, writer Jeff Howard calls our no man's land area "Quest", declaring: "A quest is a journey across a symbolic, fantastic landscape in which a protagonist or player collects and talks to characters in order to overcome challenges and achieve a meaningful goal."

Worth noting is Howard's mention of the necessary components for quest to occur. Namely some sort of hero in a place where others provide a challenge for said hero—in other words a plot hook story mechanic. He goes on to clarify that quest is a "middle term" in which gaming overlaps with literature, technology with mythology, meaning with action, and yes . . . game overlaps with narrative. The model is not about defining borders (like a yin-yang), but about recognizing shared space as in a Venn diagram.

Consider again the significance of that weird genre known as Alternate Reality Games. According to social media expert and ARG designer Frank Rose, the decade old experiment in collaborative fiction born out of guerilla marketing might never have gotten off the ground if not for a summer camp experience that occurred to experimental game designer and entrepreneur Jordan Weisman during his sixth summer at Camp Shewahmegon when he was just fourteen years old. "That's when the camp's senior counselor brought out a new game he'd just discovered in college. The game was *Dungeons and Dragons*. The year was 1974." Rose is quick to recognize that the old bi-polarizing ideas about gameplay and role-play are finally dying, insisting that "As the once clear delineations between story and game become a blur, game's more addicting aspects are being copied willy-nilly. They turn up in online extensions of *The Office*, they turn up in ad campaigns, they turn up in Facebook."

Game designer, professor, (and quite possibly our future overlord) Jesse Schell shocked and horrified the game design community at the 2010 DICE Summit with his speech about what to expect "beyond Facebook" when he identified the same very real trend of "reality" in marketing and games evident in everything from achievement points to Angus Burgers. He painted a terrifying picture of a world of "Tattoogle Ad-sense" and quantified piano practice "point scholarships" for college, where literally everything has the potential to generate game points, from your breakfast cereal to your shoes, and because these things will also have screens, wi-fi and a brain, the world we live in may soon be one giant game, and our lives the most epic interactive role-playing narrative ever experienced. According to Schell, it's not about whether these things will happen, it's about who will design the gameplay.

If Schell's vision of the future terrifies you, there are more uplifting words of hope to be had from the Institute of the Future's Jane McGonigal, gameplay theorist and creator of numerous "serious ARGs." First revealed to many though her revolutionary TED talk and further explained in *Reality Is Broken*, she identified our border zone as something called "epic win!" stating that every gamer knows the feeling of being right on the edge of "a win that is so fabulous they didn't even know it was possible." Her bold claims that by playing even more games than we do right now, we will soon be able to change the real world, should have a familiar ring to tabletop RPGers. She defines the phenomenon as a combination of "urgent optimism," a tight "social fabric," "blissful productivity," and "epic meaning." With these elements donned like super powers for players, McGonigal states that we can become "super-empowered hopeful individuals" and therefore literally change the world the same way we use them to change fictional landscapes in RPGs of all kinds. If she can pull it off, that's going to be very cool.

So What? Let's Play!

So we can call it "quest" or "flow" or something else but whatever we call it, this no-man's-land between role-play's dualistic natures is the sweet spot "story hack" where technology and mythology meet, where WotC's "roll-play" gives way to "role-play" and dice rolls are fudged and where Jane McGonigal's "epic win" can truly occur.

But so what? It's pretty clear that neither extreme ludology nor narratology accurately describes D&D, and it's actually the fusion of these two things melting together that have made both the game system and any given session successful. But what can we do with this awesome new philosophical approach of unity and balance? The rules are still a part of the game and we don't necessarily want to go messing around with that all the time. What can we do as Dungeon Master to run a better game?

DM_Samuel again has an answer for us. He lays out five simple ways to run a good story-driven game in Fourth Edition which I'll happily summarize for you:

1. **Let the first session be a party building session.** Especially in Fourth Edition, Role-play the histories of the group members, how they met, when, and why with everyone having a final say in the "product."

2. **Run a game with many choices.** Choice is the defining characteristic of interactivity. Just like a non-linear video game, having various encounters ready "just in case" allows the players to do their own thing without derailing a DM driven story.

3. **Let the backgrounds of the PCs heavily influence what happens in the world.** The PCs aren't IN a story, they ARE the story. Again options are the key, but this time in the form of opportunities for "unfinished business" on the part of the characters.

4. **Let the world continue to exist when the PCs aren't there.** Change is the keyword here. When a group returns to a location let there be very real consequences to their prior decisions and actions from the last time they were there. The reactions of the NPCs to the players can then be varied and the PCs get to react to those reactions and once again change the game world.

5. **Each Combat has to meet four strict criteria to happen:** It must be necessary in terms of the story; obviously meaningful to the players—though this meaning may be revealed later; there must be an option available to avoid it—or if it can't be avoided there must be a very good reason why; and if it can't be completed quickly—no more than 45 minutes with a party of 4–5 players—then it better be a very important "boss fight."

So then what's the solution to the old narratology versus ludology argument?

Well, the simplest conclusion is that while various ways of exploring and understanding this middle space between role-play and gameplay have been proposed by forward-thinking gameplay theorists, we gamers decided a while back that it was a stupid argument to begin with and we would rather just go throw some dice to help us tell stories instead.

Newer theories are an indication of the need for a balanced understanding of gameplay and role-play, but theories don't show what gamers already know: RPG has long since proved that you need both role-play and gameplay for the most epic and fun tales. So I say let the game design theorists and eggheads keep their dualistic theories contributing to the great divide. They can roll off their opposed skill checks until eternity—let's you and me go play some D&D! I call dibs on a Half-Orc Warlord with a two-handed ax. (You do have the second handbook update, right?)

19

Justice Is Not Blind, Deaf, or Willing to Share Its Nachos

TIMOTHY CHRISTOPHER

A Zen archer never fires a bow. He simply draws the bow back, aims the arrow at the intended target, and waits for the bow string and arrow to slip between his fingers.

He does not concern himself with releasing the string and arrow. Instead the archer holds them until they slide between and out of the grip of the archer and into the air of their own accord. This is called "letting the arrow fall." Once the arrow has slipped from the bow, the archer can do nothing more to control the flight of the arrow. He can't stop it, and he can't in any way influence its course. The arrow will go where the arrow will go.

If the archer's concentration while holding the bow and aiming the arrow were sufficient, and if his mind was focused, the arrow will go where he wanted it to go, at the moment before the arrow left his hand. The arrow will travel based on the intent of the archer at the time before the arrow took flight. If the archer's intent changes after the arrow is in flight, it does not matter. The arrow will hit what the archer wanted the arrow to hit in the past, not what the archer has just decided the arrow should hit after its departure.

The study of Zen philosophy has been a significant boon to my endeavors as both a game designer and a Dungeon Master. This example demonstrates what it is like to be a dungeon master before and during a game of D&D. Sometimes, as a DM, it feels as if you plan for a specific campaign outcome, only to release the player characters and watch as your campaign dissolves into chaos. It is like aiming a bow at a target, releasing an arrow, and having the arrow careen wildly off course, based on the will of the arrow, not the archer. It is easy, regardless of the hours one puts into planning a campaign, to have the players misunderstand the intent of the DM, or to simply disregard it. The DM must figure out just how much influence he has over the player, and at what points.

A Zen archer knows that the arrow can be influenced only so long as it is in the hand, but once in the air, the arrow will go where the arrow will go. Unlike a Zen archer, the DM has a far more complicated amount of control and influence over the players. Unlike the archer's arrow, the players may resent the control and influence of a DM. With this in mind a Dungeon Master must begin to understand the relationship between DM and players, who controls and influences what and when.

Much of game studies has focused on the relationships between player and the game world. As an example, Richard Bartle postulated four basic player types: the achievers, the socializers, the explorers, and the killers. Each of these player types had a particular facet of game experience that they were focused on, and a particular manner in which they related to the game world and the other gameplayers.

In order to understand the complexities of being a Dungeon Master, you first must realize that the Dungeon Master is the heart of the game world. The DM is responsible for organizing and maintaining the entire game world for the players. In order to achieve this it helps to understand the relationships that the DM has with the game world, and the player characters.

The Dungeon Master must strive to understand how much control and influence he wants or need to have over two things: the game world and the player characters. The game world consists of several things. First, the world consists of the overall rules or system that is being played. This work will focus primarily on *Dungeons and Dragons*, but some other *role-play* systems do require a Dungeon Master, in one form or another.

Second, the game world could include any number of "realms" within the game system. There are numerous realms in *Dungeons and Dragons*, including the Forgotten Realms, Dark Sun, Ravenloft, and Eberron. There are also numerous versions of *Dungeons and Dragons*, ranging from Advanced *Dungeons and Dragons* through *Dungeons and Dragons* 3.5, and on into *Dungeons and Dragons* 4.0. These realms and versions have various takes on the core *Dungeons and Dragons* concept. The choice of game, realm, and version are all made before the game even starts.

Once these have been chosen, there are still numerous ways the DM can influence the game world before the game starts. Some DMs will create custom monsters for their games, rather than pulling a selection from the Monster Manual. Once the game has begun, the amount of specific and direct control a DM has over the game world may vary greatly.

The second thing the Dungeon Master has to decide is whether to control the player characters, and if so to what degree. The player characters (PCs) are the ones that the players will control. A Dungeon Master may limit the players' ability to create PCs based on the selection of realm and rule set. Gnomes, for instance, are a playable race in the 3.5 Forgotten Realms, but not in the 4.0 Eberron realm. Additional playable races are added via various optional player handbooks. The Dungeon Master may also set limits on the available classes for the players. A Dungeon Master may go so far as to give the player pre-rolled characters. These ready-to-play characters may even have a list of goals for each player to try to achieve. Conversely, a particularly liberal DM may allow the player to roll their characters entirely from scratch, and to provide their own backstories and goals for each character.

In order to understand the relationship that the DM and the players have with the game world and the playable characters, I have created a simple graph. This graph consists of two axes. The vertical axis represents an indication of who has the most control of the game world. This can include decisions as broad as which of the possible realms the game will take place in, or more specific decisions that my result in the crafting of a custom realm for the adventure. The further down one moves on this axis, the more the players influence this aspect. Moving toward the top of this axis represents the Dungeon Master having more sway of the game world. The horizontal axis is meant to measure who has the most control over the playable characters. The more the players control the characters, the further to the right on the axis a point would move. The more the Dungeon Master controlled the characters the further to the left the point would move on the line.

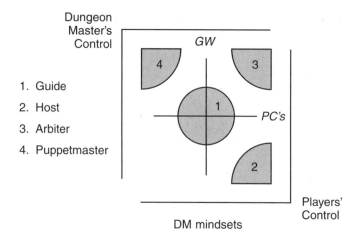

1. Guide
2. Host
3. Arbiter
4. Puppetmaster

DM mindsets

I will look at four archetypal DM mindsets that express some of the extremes that can be experienced by players. These archetypes function as points of reference for DM behavior. In order to better discuss the ways in which a person DMs and their approaches to it, it helps to understand the most extreme outlying cases and what they represent. These archetypes can be likened to the archetypes of the D&D 3.5 alignment chart, in the sense that while it's theoretically possible for a character's alignment to be in the lowermost right point, characters are usually within a range of gray areas. Most DMs, likewise, are a mix of some of these four types.

The Guide

The guide DM is one who will try to share equal parts of influence of both game experience axes with the players. The guide has a moderate amount of control over the game world and the characters; the guide's control is balanced perfectly with the players' control on both axes. The subsequent game would result in a balanced co-authorship of game experience between the DM and the players. This particular mind set can be especially useful when teaching new players about *Dungeons and Dragons*.

The very first pen-and-paper *Dungeons and Dragons* game I ever played was the result of a friend agreeing to teach me the game. He did this by walking me through the character creation rules, and then just asking what I'd like to do. He made up the world around my character as we played, in response to inquiries and requests I had about the game world. He would offer insight my character would never have, but that a new player such as myself woefully lacked. Both the world and my character existed primarily as compromised constructs for the purpose of learning how the game world worked. To this end my friend functioned primarily as a guide to my game experience.

The Host

The least controlling form of the DM is the host. The host exercises little control over the game world and the player characters. This type of DM allows the players to sculpt the world, either through creation of their character backgrounds or through picking or defining the rules of the realm they will be adventuring in. A host DM can result from a number of situations. It could be as a result of a group of people wishing to play, and then selecting a person from the group to DM. This chosen and sometimes reluctant DM exists simply to facilitate the adventures of the other players. It is also possible a person may naturally choose to be this type of DM. This type of DM treats the entire game experience as a co-authorship between the players. Under these circumstances the Dungeon Master exists to keep the world moving for the players. This usually entails rolling all the dice for the NPCs, reminding the players of specific rules, or simply recapping what has happened so far. These forms of games are often less combat-centric, and more about role-playing and world crafting. In effect, the DM is there to help the players craft the story of their characters and the surrounding world.

The Arbiter

The arbiter is a DM who maintains complete control of the game world and game rules, but gives the players as much freedom over their characters' actions as possible. An arbiter carefully and specifically crafts a world with rules and numerous NPC with specific goals or intentions. The players are allowed to create whatever characters they choose and subsequently interact with the world as they see fit. These games can range wildly from sessions of near-complete role-playing, to numerous days of non-stop combat. In the most extreme cases, an arbiter DM can be a force of blind, unfeeling logic.

This DM spends the game ruthlessly and perfectly enforcing the most literal rules of the game world, regardless of the effect on the player characters. This particular form of arbiter can even be considered a surrogate for a computer-controlled game experience. If one were to play a digital adaptation of Dungeon and Dragons, such as Baldur's Gate or Neverwinter Nights, this is the type of game experience one would have. As a person who has studied and worked in traditional game design, I find myself most fitting into this particular mindset.

That is not to say that this type of DM is necessarily unfair. This form of DMing is most akin to traditional game scenario and system design. The arbiter has great control over the game world but little control over the player characters. A person who is skilled at this approach and seeks to be fair will try to create a world such that all of the characters have a fair chance to survive, and numerous interesting means to do so.

The Puppet Master

The puppet master is the kind of DM that exercises the most control over the game world and player characters. In the most extreme cases, this means that the DM has a story they've already decided to tell and they want the PCs to effectively act it out for then. This isn't necessarily a bad thing in that sometimes a player, particularly a *role-play*er, may enjoy the challenge of role-playing a specific character that they've been given. This is akin to an improvisational actor trying to play a particular part. Also, sometimes the players may be happy to be part of a particularly good story, and to see how it unfolds around them. This particular mindset is the reason traditional digital games often succeed by being heavily story-driven.

That said, for some players this can be very frustrating because they have so little control over the game. They may find themselves railroaded by the DM at every major decision point. One of the worst case scenarios for this is when a DM may choose to pit the players against one another.

A possible negative stereotype of the DM is the "God Complex." This is the mindset that the game world is the DM's game world, and the player characters are there to do as they are told. In a particularly negative experience, players may question why they're even playing the game if the DM has the whole thing already written out. This often causes the players to feel as if they are simply "going through the motions." Some may even suggest the DM just write the novel of that particular adventure, rather than creating it as a D&D campaign.

The Host and the Guide

For the host DM, success is often measured entirely by how happy the players are with the experience of the game world and their game characters. This is actually how the DM 3.5 handbook and more recent editions specifically define success. This variant of success is also typically true for the guide DM, the one who more shares influence over game and characters. The big difference between the two is that the guide often has more direct investment in the outcome of the game.

The Arbiter, Slight Return

For the arbiter, there are two particularly common goals for success. The first goal is to get the players interested in the arbiter's carefully crafted game world. The second is a measure of how well the game world functioned in the face of a chaotic, self-driven player group pushing on all the limits of the design, knowingly or unknowingly. This form of success can often be effected by how successfully the arbiter was able to "keep the game on track" without the players realizing they were being kept on rails.

For the most coldly logical arbiters, success is inversely proportional to the number of times the DM had to "improvise" due to unexpected player actions. An especially hostile arbiter may relate success to the number of player deaths during the campaign. The more narratively motivated arbiters would also strive for a game conclusion that was particularly memorable to the players.

The Puppet Master

For the puppet master, success is telling their entire story beginning to end with as much co-operation from the players as possible. For the particularly kind puppet master it also matters that the players enjoy the story that they get to experience. It's possible for the puppet master to use the actions of the players to fill in the blanks for their story, in the sense that the DM knows that they want a prince to save the princess and have them get married, but they can't find a way to do that: so they set up a scenario and let the players figure it out.

Do not fire the arrow that will return upon you.

—Turkish proverb

Understanding these archetypal Dungeon Masters allows us to consciously make decisions about what kind of DM we are or tend to be. Knowing this, we can communicate with our potential players to try to make sure we're in agreement about the kind of relationship those players would prefer to have with the DM. This is the equivalent in D&D to a group of players saying, "We all want to play an evil party." Their shared knowledge of the D&D alignment system gives them all an agreed-upon frame on which to build their characters. If my players are able to sit down and say, "We'd like you to be an arbiter," that tells me exactly what kind of DM approach they prefer that I take. It also means that I can potentially say, "I prefer to be an arbiter" or "I fall between arbiter and puppet master" and in my social circle my friends know who would enjoy playing with me and who wouldn't. Doing this minimizes the potential for friction between the Dungeon Master and players, making it less likely the archer will provoke the arrow.

Unlike the Zen archer, the DM has any number of means to influence the arrow once it is in flight. For the host and the guide, the use of carefully chosen descriptions and game world information can ensure that players are more able to make informed decisions with understandable and reasonable outcomes. For DMs who choose to give the players pre-generated PCs, the use of carefully crafted character backgrounds and motivations can offer much motivation for player characters to behave in a specific manner. The arbiter may often choose to carefully change behind the scene details, allowing the game world to invisibly shift the target into the path of the most erratic players. An especially crafty and experienced DM is like a Zen archer who has the ability to control everything from the direction and intensity of the wind to the strength of the earth's gravity. These abilities may influence a wayward arrow long after it has departed the bow.

20
The Gunpowder Crisis

JASON ROSE

Years ago in one of my *Second Edition Advanced Dungeons and Dragons* campaigns, another player we'll call Logan was playing a dwarf alchemist named Jovan. Jovan loved to perform experiments in-between his adventures, and much of his share of the loot was spent building and maintaining a full magical laboratory. During one game, our party arrived at a small mining village beset upon by hobgoblins. Naturally, the villagers hired our group to clear out their mine so they could get back to work. The Dungeon Master described to us the dark mining tunnels dug through the limestone, the smell of sulfur in the air . . . all well and good.

But then Logan had an idea. He told the Dungeon Master his dwarf wanted to collect some salt peter from the limestone, as well as some of the sulfur that was assaulting our characters' noses. He then mixed the salt peter and sulfur with a bit of charcoal. Some of you might have already figured out what Logan was up to—if you mix charcoal and sulfur with potassium nitrate (also known as salt peter), you get black powder, also known as gunpowder.

Well, our Dungeon Master was in a bit of a jam. On the one hand, there wasn't any in-game reason Logan's dwarf character *shouldn't* be able to mix the readily available ingredients, and it seemed like something his character might do. But on the other hand, he didn't want Jovan to invent gunpowder! Not only would it radically change the medieval fantasy world in which we adventured, but it would also break the gameplay. Hobgoblins with spears aren't as scary when you have a crude

shotgun instead of a sword. Unfortunately, our DM was relatively inexperienced and didn't quite know how to defuse the
situation cleanly (pun intended). He asked Logan to make a
skill check to concoct the mixture, hoping he would fail the roll
and the game could continue, but (of course) Logan rolled an
eighteen. With his huge bonus to alchemy, there was little
doubt that Jovan had succeeded. In the end, the DM had to pull
the "Dungeon Master is always right" card and simply rule that
Logan's dwarf couldn't mix the ingredients together, *just
because*. While this technically preserved the setting and game
balance, it really broke our immersion to be reminded so jar-
ringly of these out-of-game concerns, and Logan felt his character was being artificially limited because the Dungeon
Master was ill-prepared to handle his character's antics. In
other words, our DM's ruling flew in the face of our fun.

Our party finished clearing out the mine, and our campaign
continued, but we felt as if the "gunpowder crisis" (as it came to
be called) had taken a lot of the wind out of our sails. Both Logan
and our DM could have handled the situation better, as we'll see.

Gameplay and Storytelling in D&D

Role-playing games like *Dungeons and Dragons* are "played,"
in several different senses of the word. There is the gaming element—hit points, dice rolls, leveling up once enough experience
points have been accumulated, and so on. The D&D ruleset has
profoundly influenced computer game design. Even looking
beyond the many licensed *Dungeons and Dragons* titles that
have been released through the years—*Baldur's Gate, Icewind
Dale, Planescape: Torment,* and *Neverwinter Nights,* to name
only a few—the game mechanics in *Dungeons and Dragons*
have made their way into everything from first-person action
games to turn-based puzzle games. SquareEnix's venerable
Final Fantasy series of games are called "role-playing games"
because of the many game mechanics they borrow from pen
and paper role-playing games like D&D. Indeed, these "RPG
elements" have become a common sight printed under the list
of features on the back of game cases, usually implemented
with a fair degree of success.

But D&D is also "played" in the sense that a "play" is performed in a theater, or the way a film is "played." This is the

part of the game that causes many new players to hesitate at the game table. While the notion of "gameplay" is fairly familiar to most players, with relatively clear-cut goals and explicit rules for manipulating one's character as a gamepiece, the idea of playing the role of a character can seem daunting to players who have no experience writing or acting on the stage or on the screen.

The limits on how a player interacts with a non-digital imaginary environment take some getting used to for many players. Compare the classic one-inch by one-inch grid, and counting squares based on your character's movement score, to entering the Court of the Elven King to request his aid . . . a challenge far "fuzzier" and less defined than resolving a move action.

Once a player figures out what exactly is expected of them in the storytelling aspect of a role-playing game, the attachment players form to their characters and the adventures they have often become the most memorable and exciting part of the game. Experienced players love swapping stories about their campaigns of old—the ridiculously powerful characters from long-running campaigns, the clever solutions to problems that the Dungeon Master (DM) never saw coming, and that one time everything was on the line and you could only succeed with a natural twenty . . . *and you rolled it!* These are the personalized moments that endear the hobby to so many, and they all draw from some combination of game mechanics and the stories that are told through the game mechanics. And really, it is the (often bizarre) marriage of gameplay and storytelling that makes role-playing games so engaging.

Some campaigns lean heavily on either gameplay or storytelling, but nearly all D&D games give attention to both elements in some capacity. Knowing which side to focus on and when one side should trump the other is a skill role-players learn over time (usually through trial and error, unfortunately).

From Gaming to Metagaming

When philosophers talk about games, they use the word "ludology" to refer to the study of gameplay. The win-lose conditions, the interactions available to players, and the dynamic interplay between the various mechanics of the game system are all part of ludology. Technically, ludology also covers the study of board games and videogames, in addition to "pen and paper" role-playing games like *Dungeons and Dragons*. A huge part of game theory today focuses on the debate between ludologists, who favor an emphasis on the study of rules-based systems, and narratologists, who think games should be thought of first and foremost as extensions of narrative. Narratologists often apply theories of story-based systems to the study of games, arguing that gameplay is a tool used to express a story in a different way—playing the game is fun and engaging, perhaps, but still just a novel means to an end. Much of this debate is found in the field of videogame criticism, but it applies just as much to role-playing games—perhaps more so, since *Dungeons and Dragons* relies more on imagination and player interaction.

Looking though my battered copy of the *Second Edition Advanced Dungeons and Dragons Player's Handbook*, I see the game designers dedicate a chunk of the first chapter to describing what gameplay in a role-playing game actually looks like. The *Player's Handbook* makes an analogy to the ludology of Snakes and Ladders, replacing each element with its equivalent in D&D. The board becomes a "maze" (that is, the dungeon) that only the referee (the Dungeon Master) can look at directly. The snakes and the ladders become hidden doors and passageways. The players tell the group what their characters are doing at a given moment, and the referee controls all the "vampire bats and hobgoblins and zombies and ogres," aggressively shadowing the players as they move their characters through the imaginary maze. And, of course, dice are rolled when conflicts arise between these fictional entities.

As players, the participants in a role-playing game are actors in and co-authors of the story, in addition to their function as game-players. The Dungeon Master functions as chief architect and narrator of the story, but also referees the gameplay and designs the challenges and encounters for the players to play through. It is the DM's job to provide challenging but winnable obstacles for the players to overcome through strategic planning and successful manipulation of the game system. With so many tasks and responsibilities, it can be difficult to maintain a distinction between players and characters, between dice rolls and daring actions, and between the DM's portrayal of non-player characters and the DM's portrayal of the rest of the game universe in which the adventure takes place. What exactly is the relationship between the *Dungeons and Dragons* game system and the stories that are told with it? Part of this ambiguity comes from the fact that "win conditions" in story-based role-playing situations tend to be less explicitly defined than those found in the gaming portion. The "maze" scenario outlined in the example in the *Second Edition Player's Handbook* is pretty straightforward, but success is often more difficult to quantify when the scenarios become more complicated. Dungeon Masters will sometimes include moral dilemmas, like making the players choose between two evils or revealing an unforeseen consequence of the player-characters' earlier adventures. These situations must often be "played" more like a story than a game. Sometimes, the situation is too complex to be summed up by a simple win-condition or lose-condition. These situations are intentionally imprecise and are expected to develop within the make-believe component of the game. "The point of playing is not to win but to have fun and to socialize. . . . Remember, the point of an adventure is not to win but to have fun while working towards a common goal" (p. 11). Clearly, this form of "play" requires a departure from the ludological gameplay found in combat and character progression, as success or failure can fall to the background while the players have fun entertaining each other with role-playing and storytelling.

Even in older editions, the distinction between the ludology of D&D and its capacity for storytelling is difficult to separate completely. We're told that the Snakes and Ladders example

has the essential element that makes a role-playing game: The player is placed in the midst of an unknown or dangerous situation created by a referee and must work his way through it. This is the heart of role-playing. The player adopts the role of a character and then guides that character through an adventure. The player makes decisions, interacts with other characters and players, and, essentially, "pretends" to be his character during the course of the game. (p. 11)

This act of pretending creates an interesting situation where a participant attempts to best the gaming challenges as a player, while simultaneously acting as a character within a story.

While the participant as game-player makes informed strategic decisions based on probability and a quantifiable sense of risk-and-reward, the participant as character-actor also tries to pay heed to his or her character's motivations, interests, and preferences. The contrast between what the player knows and wants and what his character knows and wants is called the metagame, and it has been a concern in role-playing games for a very long time.

Used properly, the metagame can enrich a role-playing game, buffering both the ludology and the narrative. However, problems sometimes arise from the disparity between the more objective, ludological side of the game and the more subjective, narrative side of the game, as we saw in the "gunpowder crisis" example. Logan knew the gameplay benefits of having gunpowder in a world where no one else has it, but while it may have been in-character for his dwarf to try to invent it, he didn't stop to consider the problems it would cause for the storyline the DM had written. Consider the *Second Edition Monstrous Manual* (the book became the *Monster Manual* in the Third Edition). *The Monstrous Manual,* like the *Dungeon Master's Guide,*

> is the province of the DM. This gives complete and detailed information about the monsters, people, and other creatures inhabiting the AD&D world. Some DMs don't mind if players read [the Monstrous Manual], but the game is more fun if players don't know everything about their foes—it heightens the sense of discovery and the danger of the unknown. (p. 8)

This warning against "bad" metagaming seems simple enough—knowing all the strengths and weaknesses of all the enemies in the game is information to which few in-game characters are privy. As *Dungeons and Dragons* evolved through its various incarnations, the game designers wisely tried to rebalance the ludology to allow for these well-informed players without terribly unbalancing the game. Generally speaking, a player knowing the stats of a monster is not as gamebreaking in Fourth Edition as it was in Second Edition, where combat usually involved players frantically testing various attacks on the new monster, trying to suss out its physiology and capabilities. Still, the metagame balance of ludology and storytelling remains a tricky one—when should one side be given priority over the other? How can both sides of the game support and improve each other, and how can players avoid metagame problems in the first place? These questions inevitably arise in nearly every role-playing campaign in some form or another, and each group finds their own equilibrium based on their personal preferences and play style.

Metagaming for Players

A player's knowledge of the real world does not always line up with a character's knowledge of the game-world, as we saw with Logan and his dwarf alchemist. After all, a core component of role-playing games is that players roll dice to simulate their characters' actions. Consider, however, that the characters in-game do not consider their actions "random." If a player makes an attack roll and rolls a natural one, his character's attack misses or is parried, but his character is unaware of the dice roll influencing the result of his attack. To the character in the story, the enemy was able to avoid being wounded. Using the metagame to keep the distinction between gameplay and role-playing clear makes both aspects of the game run more smoothly and helps everyone at the table productively contribute to the game. Logan's first mistake was allowing his character to know what he knows, but of course his dwarf *wouldn't* know to mix salt peter, sulfur, and charcoal together in the first place. That was out-of-game knowledge that Logan was using to confer an in-game advantage.

Metagaming for DMs

Because some instances of metagaming are obviously problematic, metagaming is often misunderstood as something to avoid completely. It's true that reckless metagaming will lead to a number of gameplay and story-related issues, but by better understanding the metagame, players and DMs alike can use it to actively enhance all aspects of the game. For example, proper metagaming helps everyone at the table to easily distinguish between in-character and out-of-character comments. My character probably shouldn't comment on the pizza my gaming group had delivered.

Sometimes it's best to subvert the ludology for the sake of the narrative. For instance, there are rare times when a DM will fudge a roll behind his screen (that is, ignore the number rolled in favor of another) in the interest of keeping the players engaged and having fun. It actually happens more than you'd think, and with good reason! If a single bad roll kills some or all of the player-characters, chances are the event will ignite frustration and a sense of loss of control in the players.

This is the second solution we could have used to defuse the gunpowder crisis—had the DM rolled the alchemy check for Logan's character behind his DM screen, he could have fudged the roll and told Logan he had failed the check, even if he had actually rolled high. In this case, the illusion of chance allows the players to remain immersed in the game while allowing the DM to keep gunpowder out of the game setting. The DM's decision has to occur in the metagame, as the characters in the game world are unaware of their role in the players' story. The decision to fudge a roll comes from the DM's concern for his players as people, not merely as characters in a story or merely players in a game. Fudging rolls too often can quickly sour a game, but when the metagame is utilized correctly, it becomes a very helpful tool for distinguishing between game mechanics and storytelling mechanics.

Group Metagaming

In the same way, the ludology can be used to help support the story. Consider that, during character creation, rolling low ability scores can be a drag since they mean one's character will generally be less effective during the game. Instead, as the 2nd edition Player's Handbook suggests, players and DMs alike can make use of low ability scores to actually inform the role-playing if the low scores are taken as cues to the character's flaws.

Don't give up on a character just because he has a low score. Instead, view it as an opportunity to role-play, to create a unique and entertaining personality in the game. Not only will you have fun creating that personality, but other players and the DM will have fun reacting to him.

This is another great example of how the metagame can add fun and excitement to a role-playing game, turning something that is strictly bad for the ludology into something interesting to flavor role-playing. Again, applying this method to our gunpowder crisis, we can see that the DM could have imposed game limitations on the dwarf's use of black powder—since no one has discovered gunpowder in our game world, Logan's character would have no idea how much powder he should use, or how to construct a gun or cannon that won't shatter after one use. And, of course, he would have terrible aim, since no one in the game world has had to learn how to operate a firearm effectively.

With all that in mind, it would be easy for the DM to impose severe penalties to any die roll involving the volatile powder. While the explosive force may be impressive, if a character takes a −10 penalty to actually hit a target with it and each such weapon can only be fired once, you can bet he'll be swinging his sword instead. By giving Logan an incentive to avoid using gunpowder to break the game, the DM has enabled Logan to role-play his dwarf the way he wants and the DM is able to keep his game balanced and fun.

Narrative Game Mechanics

There are a number of ways you can use metagaming to help both the gameplay and the narrative of your role-playing game. Some game systems have tried to quantify the storytelling aspect of the hobby in order to work the narrative elements into the game system more explicitly, with varying degrees of success. Many role-playing games offer a "perks" and "flaws" system where the player may earn extra character points during character creation in exchange for taking personality flaws like being greedy or having a short temper. The Fourth Edition of D&D uses "action points" in a similar way, offering extra actions during combat or rerolling important checks, but the "hero point" system in Green Ronin's d20 superhero role-playing game *Mutants and Masterminds* is a more extreme example of what I'm talking about. In the *M&M* core rulebook, they write,

> Whether it's luck, talent, or sheer determination, heroes have something setting them apart from everyone else, allowing them to perform amazing deeds under the most difficult circumstances. In Mutants

and Masterminds that something is hero points. Spending a hero point can make the difference between success and failure. When you're entrusted with the safety of the world that means a lot! Hero points allow players to "edit" the plot of the adventure and the rules of the game to a degree. They give heroes the ability to do the amazing things heroes do in the comics, but with certain limits, and they encourage players to make the sort of choices heroes do in the comics, in order to get more hero points. (p. 121)

With a hero point, a character can "happen to have" just the gadget or gizmo the situation calls for, temporarily modify his or her powers to use them in an unorthodox way, or crawl away from what seemed to be certain death. The really interesting thing about hero points is the variety of ways players can earn them. A character can earn hero points by acting with a limiting sense of honor or time-consuming responsibilities. The player can allow the DM to have a villain figure out his or her character's secret identity, or find a way to strip him of his powers. All of these setbacks and complications allow the DM to construct stories and plot twists with a definite "comic book" feel whilst simultaneously encouraging players to role-play as heroically as they can. Similar systems crop up in various game systems, but they all share one trait—they try to work the storytelling aspect of the game into the ludology.

Hero points, action points, and their ilk are examples of "good" metagaming. They would not be possible without the combination of storytelling and gameplay found in role-playing games, and they utilize features from both sides to improve the overall gaming experience. Also notice that hero points and their ilk require a more sophisticated metagame, as characters' actions become more effective in the game due to factors of which only the players are aware. How does the character perceive his player spending a hero point? It will likely differ greatly depending on the context, both in- and out-of-game, but you can begin to see how ludology and story-telling can inform each other to help keep the game running smoothly.

Rolling Dice and Accountability

Perhaps the most recognizable metagaming tool is the venerable dice roll. The success or failure of any important action in

D&D is usually determined with a dice roll—having knowledge or expertise in the field simply grants the character a bonus to the roll, thus increasing his or her chances of success. Much gets lost in translation in the move from the real world to the game world. If a football player misses a catch, we usually don't think it was random or somehow out of the football player's control. *He* missed the catch—that's on *him* (and possibly the quarterback who threw the pass). With dice, it hardly makes sense to blame a role-player for a bad roll. It is out of his control—that is, in fact, the entire point of using dice to determine in-game success or failure.

So why do we use dice in role-playing games in the first place? Consider some children playing a game of make believe—cops and robbers, cowboys and Indians, whatever. Tommy points his finger gun at Billy and declares that he has "got" Billy—in his view, his imaginary attack hit its mark. Billy, not ready to quit playing, argues that Tommy's attack could not have hit him, as he was moving very fast and had a nearby tree for cover. The illusion of the game is broken as Tommy and Billy have to argue to work out what, precisely, happened.

Dice are used in role-playing games to help keep the ludology consistent and decisive. If Tommy rolls a seventeen to hit, and Billy's Armor Class is only fifteen, they can be little doubt that Tommy's attack found its mark and Billy was struck. Notice, however, that before the die was cast, neither Tommy nor Billy knew beforehand if the attack was going to succeed or not. Dice rolls provide an unbiased source of narrative tension—a "neutral ground" between the players and their Dungeon Master where the story can be told collectively and fairly. The excitement we feel when James Bond leaps from rooftop to rooftop is simulated in the rolling of dice, while keeping the gameplay objective.

The move from in-game to metagame can be described as a switching of the character's choices and chance events with the player's choices and chance events. This sounds complicated, but it really is not. Consider Logan and his character Jovan. For the in-game character, Jovan, attacking a goblin with his longsword is a matter of his own skill at sword-fighting, compared to the goblin's skill at not getting stabbed. But for the out-of-game player, Logan, the attack is a dice roll, modified by Jovan's Strength score, class features, and other circumstantial bonuses. Supposing Logan rolls a natural one, ensuring a miss, it would not make sense for another player to blame *him* for the failed attack.

Logan can't control what number he rolls—that's the point of using dice in the first place. At the same time, it would not make sense for in-game characters to dismiss all of Jovan's failed attacks as merely bad luck—instead, they would likely consider the failed attack as a reflection of a mistake Jovan made in his attempt to land a blow, perhaps allowing the goblin to read his movements and parry the attack just in time. Obviously, the details are extremely variable (especially the parts that are simply flavor-text provided by the DM or a player), but this example illustrates the way choice and chance are inverted in the move from in-game to metagame.

The swapping of choice and chance in the metagame works both ways. Consider character creation. As the player, Logan picks his character's race from the Player's Handbook and invents a backstory explaining how his character came to be who he is. Both of these factors are decidedly out of the character's control. No one gets to choose who their parents are or the kind of childhood they have. For the character those things are strictly matters of chance. So, while it is perfectly reasonable to hold the *player* responsible for his character's race and background, no sane character in-game will hold the character personally responsible for being a dwarf or an elf. To the characters, just as with people in real-life, those issues are matters of chance and folks can only make the most of the hand they are dealt. This choice-chance distinction is incredibly helpful in keeping the ludology distinct from the storytelling, especially when it comes to flavor text. For Dungeon Masters in particular, you must pick your wording carefully when describing the outcome of a dice roll. For example, let's say our player, Logan, and his character, Jovan, are fighting a troll. Logan's having a streak of bad luck with his rolls, and he rolls another miss. The Dungeon Master could describe the results in-game or out-of-game, and the other players (Thomas, in this example) could comment on the failed attack in-character or out-of-character.

An out-of-game exchange might look like this:

LOGAN: I attack the troll. (*rolls a miss*)

DM: You're going to have to roll higher than a four, man.

LOGAN: Oh, for goodness sake . . . I'm getting terrible rolls tonight . . .

THOMAS: I told you your Strength was too low for melee combat. You really should have put more points in it . . .

The same exchange held in-game could look like this:

LOGAN: I'll take this troll down. (*rolls a miss*)

DM: Haha, puny dwarf-thing! Your weapons do nothing!

LOGAN: Oh for Moradin's sake . . . the sun was in my eyes! I got this guy. He's mine.

THOMAS: Look, if angry gestures could kill trolls, there'd be a lot more adventures around. And fewer trolls, I guess . . . the point is, don't miss!

Both ways work, and different groups will prefer different styles of narration. The most important thing to remember is to keep it consistent. Characters are *accountable* for the results of players' dice rolls, just as players are *accountable* for their characters' background and details established during character creation. At the same time, characters are *unaccountable* for the choices the players make during character creation, just as players are *unaccountable* for the results on the dice they roll. Like action points or hero points, the important thing to remember is that dice are tools that are used to assist in good metagaming. Use them to keep the game running smoothly and never let them get in the way of your fun.

The Crisis Revisited

Let's look at our gunpowder crisis one more time. I've already illustrated three metagaming techniques that could have prevented the crisis without impeding on the fun of the game—one for the player, one for the DM, and one for the entire group. Now I want to look at how Logan and our DM should have handled the *aftermath* of their metagaming problem.

Logan felt the DM was being unfair to his character by refusing to allow him to experiment with gunpowder, but you can see now that he was holding the DM responsible in-game for a decision that was made out-of-game. Likewise, the DM should have come up with an in-game reason why the dwarf couldn't mix up some gunpowder so the character had something to role-play with. For example, the dwarf is allowed to make his concoction, but a stray spark from a torch ignites the mixture, causing a cave-in and nearly burning the dwarf's beard clean off! Since he now knows the danger of careless experimentation with black powder (dwarves are fiercely proud of their beards!), Logan's character has an in-game reason why he won't try to create explosive powder again . . . for a good long while, at least.

Thus, the crisis is resolved, Logan gets to role-play his character the way he wants, and the DM doesn't have to worry about game-breaking firearms in his campaign. While these may seem like small distinctions to make, they can help players role-play and help Dungeon Masters preserve the mystery and dramatic tension in *Dungeons and Dragons* games that keeps players engaged and immersed in the action.

21

To Know My Character Better than He Knows Himself

DAVID ALDRIDGE

The DM's guides for both version 3.5 and Fourth Edition D&D contain some brief guidance for Dungeon Masters on discouraging "metagame thinking." This is defined in Fourth Edition as "thinking about the game *as a game*" (p. 15) and in 3.5 we learn that "this behavior should always be discouraged, because it detracts from real role-playing and spoils the suspension of disbelief" (p. 11).

The term "metagaming" is used in RPG literature and discussion boards to refer to any time that "out-of-character knowledge" informs a player's decisions about their character's actions, and to moments when the discourse of a game session shifts focus on to the game itself rather than the actions or dialogue of the characters. A classic example might be when a player who has read the Monster Manual maneuvers to exploit a creature's weakness, even though her character has never encountered such a beast before.

Although the term isn't used in such a broad sense in the D&D rules, there are grounds for thinking from other advice given in core products over the years that it is considered good practice for players and DMs to limit the intrusion of out-of-character knowledge into the role-playing experience: DMG II for version 3.5, for example, contains guidance on regulating "information flow" that assumes that it is undesirable for players to act on information that their characters would not have, such as the activities of party members in other parts of the dungeon that might have been played out in front of them (pp. 22–25). The concern in Fourth Edition for a ruling on whether or not players make each other regularly aware of their Hit Point totals (p. 14) can surely only rest on the ambiguities of whether characters would have access to this information, and—if not—the extent to which players can be relied on not to act on this knowledge.

Different players and gaming groups have different levels of tolerance for the relative distribution of in-character and out–of–character speech within a game session, as well as the amount of self-conscious or reflexive discussion and commentary that goes on "around" their game. However most D&D players would suppose that characters should not act on knowledge that would be unavailable to them according to the usual causal laws (physical, magical, or otherwise) established within the particular setting.

There might be one or two newer indie RPGs out there that make a design feature of flouting this convention, but this only reinforces the claim that it is a pretty well-established custom in D&D and other similar games. This custom must rest on being able to make a reasonably clear distinction between in-character (IC) and out-of-character (OOC) knowledge, but I hold that behind the rule book's description of what's wrong with these events lurk some tricky questions about how we understand our characters and the events they participate in.

A Hermeneutics of Role-Playing

In his *Truth and Method*, Hans-Georg Gadamer claimed that he was attempting something that no-one had really tried before, namely to give an account of the "event of understanding" (p. 308). The name hermeneutics, incidentally, got attached to all of this early on because it is the ancient Greek word for understanding or interpreting. According to Gadamer, previous philosophers had been concerned with understanding only to the extent that they attempted to prescribe rules for how it should be done correctly. Literary theorists and philosophers of art, for example, offered a method for inferring the right meaning from a text or work of art, and theologians discussed how to properly understand the Bible, but none of them were concerned with giving an account of the nature of understnding or what it is that happens when somebody is said to understand.

What's the relevance of Gadamer's claim for role-playing? It is not clear that *role-play*ers have as their *aim* the understanding of their character, in the way that someone concerned with interpreting a text or a work of art is concerned primarily with understanding it. But you could admit that understanding your character to some extent must be a necessary condition for playing her, and (although this is a little more controversial) that coming to understand her better, even if it is not your primary aim in role-playing, it is something that we usually see happening during the course of the time we spend playing.

Gadamer offers an extended discussion of the nature of historical knowledge, or what it is that historians aim at in their understanding of historical events or characters, and the three models he proposes have direct bearing on the question of the admissibility of our-of-character knowledge in play. They can be developed into three alternative conceptions of the experience of role-playing.

To Know My Character as He Knows Himself

The first model Gadamer offers is closely associated with the historian and philosopher Robin George Collingwood, and it has come to be termed the "re-enactment thesis". It is simply explained in terms of the practice of history: historical understanding is concerned with acting out historical moments—not physically, of course, but in terms of re-thinking the thoughts and feelings of persons in history. To understand a historical text, says Collingwood, is to reconstruct or re-imagine the question that the author was intending to answer in that text. To understand a historical event is to see it from the point of view of a participant in that event, and to see the problems she faced as she saw them. This is the way that many people think of the way they relate to their character in a gaming session.

A similar idea to re-enactment is often invoked when a distinction is made between role-playing games and other kinds of games. Consider the reception by the RPG community of Fourth Edition D&D. Significant changes were made from previous editions: the role of miniatures and tabletop tactics became a more explicit and integrated feature of character creation and advancement; in addition, elements were imported from other successful fantasy gaming media, such as the character build options that resemble the "skill trees" common in PC and console role-playing, or the clearly defined party "roles" from co-operative online RPGs.

Most role-players agree that these changes represent a conscious decision to emphasize what might be called the "gamist" elements of previous editions. The direction of influence here is unimportant, and I don't doubt that the design of those other gaming media owe a debt to pen-and-paper RPGs that goes all the way back to Gary Gygax. What is significant is that the designers made a clear decision about the kind of game Fourth Edition was intended to be—I'm thinking here of the gamist-simulationist-narrativist distinction proposed by Ron Edwards—and rewrote the rules accordingly.

This decision, which emphasizes certain elements of the RPG experience and de-emphasizes others, has not appealed to everybody's style of play. There are those who feel that Fourth Edition is now too "gamey" (or war-gamey?) to suit their conception of a role-playing game—that something about these enhanced gamist elements is an impediment to achieving what makes table-top role-playing distinct from other gaming media.

It doesn't make sense to call this group the "role-players" (we're all role-playing, aren't we?), so let's maybe go for *immersionists*—those players and DMs who hold immersion in the fictional world of the game, or empathy with their characters and their own motivations and desires, to be the most important aspect of the RPG. On the other hand there are the *gamers*, who are happier to move miniatures around a tactical gaming surface or scrutinize power descriptions to optimize their characters' combat effectiveness. The immersion-gamer spectrum invoked here seems to correspond to how strongly you adhere to the re-enactment thesis.

Despite the strong "gamer" appeal of Fourth Edition, the guidance on metagaming in the DM's guide resonates strongly with a re-enactment model. In the discussion of "metagaming" in the Fourth Edition DM's guide, we're offered the example of a player wishing to search a door again on the grounds that the module writer would not have devoted such a long description to it in their flavor text unless it was a significant object. Then there's a player who presumably allows her character to attack a dragon of unknown power, knowing that, "The DM wouldn't throw such a tough monster at us" (p. 15). In version 3.5, a player claims that his character's looking for a hidden lever, since "the DM would never create a trap that we couldn't deactivate somehow" (p. 11).

In all of these examples the player is looking for some sort of advantage or benefit to their character: finding what's hidden, gaining XP from fighting rather than fleeing, beating the trap. However, the player is not being accused of "cheating." *Role-play*ers know that this is not really a concept that can apply to RPGs, however they might resemble other games we play.

Newcomers to the hobby often mistake the RPG situation for one of an adversarial relationship between players and DM, whereas what conflict exists in the game is more properly understood as being between characters and their in-game adversaries, the NPCs (and, yes—in some interesting situations—between characters). We're quick to explain to new players that the DM and group are collaborating in a shared story-telling experience; it's not really clear who *could* be cheated in this situation (only *yourself,* you might say . . .). The closest thing we get to cheating here is the advice given to DMs about how to curb metagaming practice: throwing in the odd overly powerful encounter, or asking for perception checks when there's nothing to be seen, effectively *tricking* the characters into thinking that they have OOC knowledge that they don't.

The language used to condemn metagaming (the reference to "real role-playing" marks this as *strong* condemnation) is not the language of games or gaming, but of another kind of playing, play-acting. The metaphors employed in this text are all drawn from the practice of drama: players are to be encouraged to "preserve the suspension of disbelief," and a comparison with characters in movies acting as if they know they're in a movie alludes to the concept of "breaking the fourth wall." The problem doesn't appear to be with characters gaining any sort of unfair advantage from metagaming (as if the concept of unfairness could apply here). It's that players break the spell of the shared fictional world. They interrupt the immersion in the role-playing experience by suddenly drawing attention to the fact that we players are not our characters, but are representing our characters in a game. These are moments of self-consciousness or reflexivity which it's held that good *role-play*ers, much like good actors, should avoid.

It might be all very desirable to achieve a total immersion in our character's thoughts and feelings, to see the fictional world of the game only through their eyes, but it certainly is not possible. Not in Fourth Edition in any case—it just doesn't play that way. Aside from the particularly jarring instances detailed above, you never get to go through a whole RPG session only thinking your character's thoughts and speaking in your character's voice. The third person will inevitably intrude, if not through a rules clarification or a question from the DM about what order your characters are marching in, then as soon as the miniatures come out.

That battle map is seen from a bird's eye, third person perspective, not through your character's eyes, and you invariably act on the knowledge you gain from it. Usually (unless you're using a sophisticated virtual table top on multiple screens) once someone else sees the Kobolds, you see them too, regardless of whether they're in your line of sight or not. Sometimes this seems to break the spell, and sometimes not. Often we just don't notice it.

Perhaps complete immersion in my character might be an ideal to which the best role-playing tends, even if it is not perfectly achievable. This is a view held by those players who tend to see contemporary D&D as a debased form of the medium— inferior to, say, a rules-lite narrativist game, or even live-action *role-play*. I'm not convinced, however, that the perfection of the process of immersion in one's character is even a desirable end.

I shudder to remember the various campaigns against D&D that I encountered as a young gamer in the 1980s that told of sensational events like players unwittingly enacting occult rituals, attempting to cast real spells, and committing suicide in the event of character death. These charges reveal misconceptions of the experience of role-playing, but they're hard to identify as such from the point of view of an immersion account of what's going on. Complete understanding of my character would, according to the re-enactment thesis, entail me having identical mental experiences to him, effectively becoming him.

Becoming my character in this way has never even seemed like the remotest possibility in my own experience of role-playing (or of acting either). My own preferred style has always been to hold a little distance between myself and my character. I'm not sure that this is really a philosophical decision. It's probably based on my feeling that some of my friends sound a bit silly when they're haranguing merchants in their best gruff dwarf voice, and I don't want them to laugh at me when I do the same! I tend to talk about what my character says and does in the third person. Now, I know this is largely a question of taste, and I'm not holding it up as a model for the best role-playing, but regardless of how I were to *speak* during a session of play, I believe I would always *think* of my character in this way.

It's agreed among all the members of my gaming group that if we are portraying a Tiefling who dislikes all Dragonborn—including, perhaps, one of the other characters in the party—we want our character to act on those prejudices, but we as players don't want to feel them too. We want to continue to know that certain antipathies are wrong even as we're playing our character; that means that there always needs to be a bit of us, and a bit of our knowledge, in there too. Role-playing is certainly an escape for us, but we don't want to *lose* our *selves* in the game in a literal sense.

To Know My Character Better than He Knows Himself

We ought to give Collingwood a little credit for realizing that something was not quite right with his re-enactment thesis. Although Gadamer does not dwell on this aspect of his work, Collingwood acknowledges that re-enactment cannot be the whole story of understanding. He wants to account for the kind of knowledge that we have of history, which must in some way exceed the knowledge that was available to participants in the events of the past, or it could not really have the character of *historical* knowledge. Collingwood held that historians learn from their study of history in a way that historical persons could not learn from their own direct participation in events. By relating the thoughts and feelings of historical persons to our own thoughts and feelings about our contemporary situation, he argued, we learn from the past about ourselves and shed light on our understanding of the present.

You could call what Collingwood developed a sort of "re-enactment plus" model. The practice of history does not consist only of re-enactment, but also something more, something else alongside. He writes that "the mere re-enactment of another's thought does not make historical knowledge; we must also know that we are enacting it" (p. 289). We don't become a historian simply by performing a thought that someone performed in the past—we must also know that *this is what we are doing*. To be a historian requires a certain self-consciousness. Relating this to an RPG, my understanding of my character would require a kind of dual awareness: on the one hand, the fullest awareness possible of what he's thinking or feeling, and on the other, the awareness that I'm a player representing that character. All sorts of things go along with that—the things that I know that my character does not, which range from the "off-screen" actions of other characters all the way to what I'm planning to have for dinner when the session is over. Having both perspectives on my character—the first and the third person, you might say—means that I know what he does *and more*. Gadamer reminds us of the theologian Schleiermacher's pronouncement that the aim of literary interpretation is to know the author "better than he understood himself."

The guidance on metagaming in Fourth Edition appears to assume this account of role-playing. The assumption is not that out-of-character knowledge does not or should not form part of our role-playing experience, but that, although it's there, we should aim to keep it distinct and separate from what only our character knows. OOC knowledge might in fact contribute to our enjoyment of a game session, but it impedes the authentic construing and representation of characters. The issue is not that players know the principles of dungeon design, or encounter balance, or the conventions of module authorship, but that they cause their characters to act on them. DMs are advised in these cases to direct players' attention back to their character's inner life—"But, what do your *characters* think?"

This advice resonates with a practice that Gadamer also discusses, which is that of "bracketing out" our own knowledge, assumptions and preconceptions in our attempts to understand the thoughts and feelings of others (p. 237). Gadamer's teacher Edmund Husserl argued that although we cannot rid ourselves of our own preoccupations and preconceptions, we can attempt to recognize them and hold them separate from our understanding of the phenomena we're trying to appreciate; this is what's often referred to in philosophy as "phenomenology."

In many anthropological disciplines (at least until the significance of Gadamer's thinking had been fully appreciated in the late twentieth century) field workers held that their aim as researchers was not to "go native" or become members of the foreign cultures that they studied (or they would cease to be anthropologists), but to bracket out their own cultural presuppositions so that they would not form a barrier to their understanding of their subjects.

Everyone acknowledges that identifying and holding apart one's own prejudices, or the things we know that our subjects do not, is *at least* difficult. We all have experience of being asked in high-school literature classes to try to appreciate a text as its readers would have, rather than according to our own sensitivities. Version 3.5's Dungeon Master's Guide II acknowledges this difficulty. In the guidance on information flow, for example, the range of options offered seems dependent on how much players can be trusted to "bracket out" information about other characters that is gained through watching their scenes being played out. You can either do this in front of them (allowing spectators to offer advice, but strictly along lines that would be available to the particular character's consciousness!) or take players off into other rooms when their characters are split from the main party. This latter even seems to be the preferred option, at least in terms of a roleplaying ideal, although it is acknowledged that it may have the side effect of other players getting bored while it's going on.

In a table-top RPG session, the boundaries between acting on what we know and what our characters know can blur in some interesting ways. One example is the tactical combat discussions that go on in a typical Fourth Edition game. These conversations can be longer or shorter depending on the tolerance of the group and the style of the DM, but there's no doubt that they contribute a distinctive part of the Fourth Edition experience.

The encouragement in the Players' Guide to carefully design parties so that they cover all possible combat bases suggests that a certain kind of discussion between players is the default setting for Fourth Edition. It's assumed in the core rules that clever tactical play and attention to the features of the combat map will enable players to beat foes that are often significantly more powerful than their players, but less tactically aware.

We make a case for the cleric to heal or buff us before another member of the party, we discuss with our defender whether they might block off that corridor so that we can move safely into position to cast a particular spell. What's going on here? Are our characters loudly shouting these discussions as free actions for the benefit of any of their foes that happen to speak Common? Do we explain this by claiming that our party members are so highly attuned to each other's fighting styles that they naturally select the combat options that will maximize the team's co-operative performance, and can assume that others are doing the same (almost, but not quite, a form of telepathy or group mind . . .)? Or are we in fact "metagaming," performing some sort of technically illegitimate role-playing practice?

To further muddy the waters here, and looking on the other hand at the "OOC thread," I would question whether the proposition that a player rolled a certain number, which constitutes a hit, for a certain number of HP damage, really constitutes solely "out of character" knowledge. The character knows that her shot connected, and that it drew blood, and she felt it hit with a certain amount of force. She doesn't know the numbers, but she knows *something*. It might be more accurate to say that this is something a character knows, but knows *differently*. My character knows, I think, that he can't shoot an arrow at someone who's standing round a corner, even though he has no inkling of the "line of sight" rules. In addition, he has certain expectations about the metaphysical nature of the world he lives in, although he could never—even if he was philosophically inclined—come to express them in terms similar to the "core assumptions" laid out in the Dungeon Master's Guide.

To Know My Character *Differently*

Although he acknowledges a significant debt to Collingwood's thought, Gadamer instigates a significant shift from his attempt to describe the phenomenon of understanding. We do not re-enact the thoughts of the person we seek to understand, or do this *and something else as well*, but something different altogether. In a great play on words, Gadamer criticises a prevailing "prejudice against prejudice" that he traces back to the philosophical thought of the enlightenment period (2004, p. 271-2). He does not question that our own knowledge and preconceptions can often prove a hindrance to understanding the unfamiliar or the alien, but argues however that the bracketing out of all prejudice is neither desirable nor achievable. Prejudice must instead be respected as an essential and facilitating aspect of understanding. Following another of his teachers and another pupil of Husserl, Martin Heidegger, Gadamer argues that there can be no understanding without a pre-understanding (p. 369).

To return to the RPG: I don't know of any system in which GMs, DMs, storytellers or whatever are not urged to make their characters aware of the unfamiliar in terms of the familiar. Whatever it might be—props, setting music, information that appeals to the senses, vivid similes—a good DM in their descriptions paints a picture of a game world that's not present in terms of the world that is.

It wouldn't make sense to describe an encounter solely in terms of alien sights, sounds and concepts, however well known these are supposed to be to characters. Players would not have access to this experience, would not be able to grasp it, so it must be related to their own experience, which requires the activation of OOC knowledge. However, the familiar can be a barrier to understanding the unfamiliar, as if our understanding of this experience is too "familiar," it's not an understanding of a new or alien experience at all, but of one we have already had.

Plato famously describes this problem as it applies to learning: if we come to know the unknown in terms of what is already known, either the unknown must already be known, or there cannot be a possibility of coming to know anything new. For many philosophers, this is a logical paradox, but for Gadamer it constitutes the essence of understanding, where the familiar and the unfamiliar are preserved together, but not as two distinct elements. Understanding my character does not consist of objectively seeing his thoughts from some external or dispassionate perspective, but is a single moment which combines his prejudices, preoccupations and awareness, and my own.

This is an act of transposition that Gadamer describes as the "fusion of horizons" (p. 305). I must put myself in the shoes of my character, but the possibility of my own understanding requires that I am not lost in this situation—that it is I who stands in those shoes; I both venture forth into unfamiliar territory and return home, all at once.

We come to any situation, any event of understanding, armed with a host of preset frames of reference, expectations, and questions to ask of it. In scientific terms, this would be the "method" that prescribes the possibility of correct understanding. The system of *Dungeons and Dragons* could be thought of as a method: detailed lists of powers, statistics and spells prescribe what my character can achieve, his capacities and abilities. A whole host of genre expectations and game world details prescribe the kinds of desires and dispositions available to him.

*Role-play*ers are well aware that a character sheet is reductive, that it doesn't capture our character in his or her entirety, but merely some selected aspects that are significant for the kinds of activities covered by the rules. But we can't specify before play the entirety of the ways in which these descriptions will be found wanting; we often encounter in play unexpected shortcomings in our numerical descriptions of our characters. This illustrates Gadamer's argument that we cannot separate out our prejudices or preconceptions in advance: rather, it's through and within the event of understanding that we can come to be aware of many of our prejudices, through seeing that they are insufficient to the task of making sense of the phenomenon at hand. This is an experience that Gadamer calls being "brought up short" by the text (p. 270). It's an uncomfortable or negative experience, but one which is vital to the achievement of real understanding, as opposed to finding in the text exactly what we expected to find.

Running the Risk?

In the 3.5 DMG, the player who gives an alternative explanation for looking for a lever—one which evokes the "verisimilitude" of the fictional world, rather than the constraints on the DM—is commended (p. 12). We might be tempted, then, to make a distinction between *having* out of character knowledge (legitimate) and *acting* on it (illegitimate). This is not a distinction which holds up if we accept Gadamer's account, because any understanding we might act on will necessarily be imbued with OOC knowledge.

I might not act on my knowledge that those Kobolds are lurking round the corner, but I inevitably perceive my character in relation to their position. I can't completely separate my character's metaphysical understanding of magic, of how and why his spells work, from the spell description offered in the Player's Handbook. This is something we both know "differently," but I have no access to a pre-set formula that might elucidate this difference, and allow me to identify in advance a "metagame" use of this power.

We might also try to make a distinction between uttering the OOC reason for looking for that lever, and keeping it to ourselves and giving an "in character" reason to other players. Uttered or not, though, this knowledge informs our decision. We cannot prescribe the kinds of unsettling situations in which we will be "brought up short" by the distance between our character's knowledge and our own. The medium of the RPG entails that we will run the risk of being presented with an awareness of ourselves and our own situation precisely as we grasp our characters in their fantastical aspect in these unfamiliar situations.

One of the prejudices we bring to our understanding of our characters is our knowledge that they are taking part in a shared narrative in which their success or failure has a particular significance to us and other members of our group. This is an essential element of why we play role-playing games, but it further highlights how we will never be able completely to share our characters' perspectives on the world. Too much emphasis on the verisimilitude of the fictional world neglects the creative role we play in maintaining this world, and the fact that we are both active and passive in its unfolding.

Although it might seem counter-intuitive, it's also the fact that we are the continuous creators of our characters that makes possible our discovering something about them. We constantly make new decisions about our characters' priorities, history and motivations, and consequently interpret their previous actions in light of them, sometimes coming to see them in a new way. But our characters already perceived those previous actions in that way, because they already had access to those motivations, that backstory. It is precisely because my character is completely the product of my own imagination that *I cannot hope to know everything he knows at any given time.*

One important aspect of Gamader's hermeneutics is that in understanding, and thus becoming aware of a prejudice I hold that I had not previously perceived, I am edified or morally improved. Thus any event of understanding is necessarily transformational, and leaves my perspective changed forever. It is by this aspect of Gadamer's thought that I am encouraged to continue to hold the highest hope that anyone has for our hobby, that in playing D&D we might learn about ourselves from our characters.

Player Characters

DAVID ALDRIDGE lectures in education and the philosophy of education at Oxford Brookes University, UK. He has convinced himself that he is the only Chaotic Good adventurer in a world of Lawful Neutrals, but possibly this is to compensate for the academic reality that he is a low-level, hard-toiling Wizard in a kingdom of effortless Sorcerers. In any case, he's beginning to see an end to the capricious early career onslaughts of guard dogs, Kobolds, and rat swarms, and looks forward to slaying some of the nastier Gnolls of English curriculum theory with a +1 sword of phenomenology.

CHRIS BATEMAN is a Chaotic Good, level-twenty-three dual-class Philosopher-Game Designer, with a Ring of Protection Against Rules Updates that renders him immune to all versions of the *Dungeons and Dragons* rules published after 1985. He has worked on more than forty different videogames, and designed five of the world's most obscure tabletop role-playing games. His latest book is *Imaginary Games*, which uses Kendall Walton's make-believe theory of representation to show that all games are art. He lives with his wife, child and dog in a portable hole that can be found sometimes in Tennessee and sometimes in Manchester, UK.

ADAM BRACKIN is a neutral-good level-thirty-six half-orc barbarian with a penchant for large axes and poetry—whichever is likely to cause more permanent damage. He sometimes likes to role-play that he is a Texas-certified English and Art teacher with a Master's in Gifted Education and even claims to be the co-owner and Executive Director of a local private school. Internet goblins also report that he was the director of game development at Fundi Interactive Games from 2006 to 2008, during which time he was the head writer and Creator of various works of Collaborative Online Fiction, such as the 2006–2007 "Deus City" ARG, and the 2008 "Conspiracy Asylum"

Online Interactive Fiction spin-off. Brackin apparently created the "Circular Model of ARG Development" which allows for new ways of ARG diagramming such as the "Adjacent ARG," "Inclusive ARG" and "ARG Cluster" models. He earned his PhD focusing on Arts and Technology at UTD, where he now teaches storytelling for new media forms including video game design, with an emphasis on online interactive and collaborative storytelling, and special topics courses like "The History and Development of RPGs" as often as he can get away with assigning character creation as "homework."

LEVI R. BRYANT is a Professor of Philosophy at Collin College in Frisco. In a previous incarnation he was a lawful neutral dark elf magician, struggling to appear lawful evil among his fellow drow. He is the author of *The Democracy of Objects* (2011) and *Difference and Givenness: Deleuze's Transcendental Empiricism and the Ontology of Immanence* (2008), and co-editor of *The Speculative Turn: Continental Materialism/Realism* (2011) with Nick Srnicek and Graham Harman.

TIMOTHY CHRISTOPHER is a neutral good human adventurer gaining levels in the prestige class "Visiting Assistant Professor." Most of his quests center upon teaching and research in the areas of traditional game design, educational game design, and simulation design. He toils in the realm of the University of Texas at Dallas, Arts and Technology Department. There he continues to swear by the *Dungeons and Dragons* 3.5 alignment system, and is charged with protecting the Eye of Vecna.

JON COGBURN is in actuality the half-orc cleric Severin, just on the cusp of avenging a wretched childhood through crazed liberation theological evangelism, converting Zoebeck's downtrodden kobolds into an army of fanatical lizard men, delivering the city to the tender ministrations of the God who Dies. He is also Mikhail, a stumbling, drug-addled rogue with none of the charm of Keith Richards, but who can nonetheless wield a sword-cane like bards play lutes. In this plane of existence Cogburn is an Associate Professor of Philosophy at the Louisiana State University. He is co-author (with Mark Silcox) of *Philosophy Through Video Games* (2009) as well as several academic articles that fair minded judges find weirder than anything Severin and Mikhail manage to get up to.

BRANDON COOKE is an Associate Professor of Philosophy at Minnesota State University Mankato, a poorly defended frontier outpost ripe for pillaging. He received his PhD in 2003 from the University of St. Andrews, Scotland, and it has been said that he went there in the belief that drinking sufficient quantities of whisky while wearing a kilt might enable him to locate ancient druidic circles and secretive faerie folk. Indeed, he found that there is a level of whisky intake which, if properly maintained, guarantees success at these very quests, and raises charisma and strength with an acceptable dexterity penalty.

JONATHAN COX grew up Fairbanks, Alaska, not far from Icewind Dale. In Second Grade he was introduced by several friends and a couple of older brothers to *Dungeons and Dragons*. After that first session, Jonathan critically failed his save vs charms and was caught by a great love for the game and its possibilities. After heading south and crossing over the Spine of the World, he now studies Philosophy under a council of epic-level monks at the University of Central Oklahoma, in addition to dabbling with game design and Historical European Martial Arts, and (of course) running a weekly D&D Fourth Edition game that has been ongoing since 2007.

EVA M. DADLEZ is a Professor of Philosophy at the University of Central Oklahoma. She received her Ph.D. from Syracuse University. She writes on issues at the intersection (often at the collision) of aesthetics, ethics and epistemology. She has written two books on the preceding: *What's Hecuba to Him? Fictional Events and Actual Emotions* (1997) and *Mirrors to One Another: Emotion and Value in Jane Austen and David Hume* (2009). She is also a feminist ethics dilettante. She has recently written a mean-spirited academic satire (*The Sleep of Reason*) that lampoons higher education in America. Dadlez's most typical RPG persona, at least when she's not selling her services to the forces of darkness at reasonable rates (call today to find out about our bulk assassination package), is Euryidice Rosebloom, Rogue Jungian Psychologist. This, she feels, quite effectively speaks for itself.

CARL EHRETT's new theory of vagueness continues to defeat all opponents in single combat. It can be found at <http://furman.academia.edu/CarlEhrett>. Challengers welcome.

MONICA EVANS is an assistant professor of computer game design at the University of Texas at Dallas. Her current research focuses on educational game design and development, narrative for interactive systems, digital ethics, and critical game studies. She can still calculate THAC0 in her head, explain the grappling rules on command, and interpret the original "true neutral" alignment in at least seven different ways. She may or may not have the Hand of Vecna in a box in her office.

TIMOTHY FRANKLIN. Frequency: Rare. Treasure Type: Nerd loot. Intelligence: Animal. Alignment: Reverse Nihilism. Special Attacks: Blogging. Size: That's a very personal question. This grotesque aberration feeds on internet memes, podcasts and Xbox games and can be found lurking on forums, surfacing occasionally to post rudimentary questions and videos of kittens. This creature spends most of its time mimicking an adult human and can be found among packs of literary professionals in or near to book festivals, but it is actually a philosophy graduate from the University of Warwick, and there is a five percent chance it will be able to participate lucidly in philosophical debate. Currently it resides in the West Midlands. Its attempts at communication can be studied at @tjohnfranklin or <www.unsuitableforadults.wordpress.com>.

NEAL HEBERT is a level-thirteen hybrid PhD Candidate in Theatre History and Historiography | Spiral Tactician Warlord. Although he was originally a student at Faerun's Neverwinter College, he transferred to Louisiana State University's MA program in Philosophy in 1385 DR (2003 in Earth reckoning) to escape the effects of the Spellplague. Hebert wields a +6 longsword of directing for the stage, and has never in his life slapped a player while Dungeon Mastering (not even when it was warranted). He has been known to invoke his Spiral of Fey Death teaching Introduction to Theatre and Introduction to Philosophy. Hebert's research interests include professional wrestling as performance art, role-playing games as personal performance, queer Mardi Gras practices in Baton Rouge, historical iterations of thwarted masculinities, and the proper care and breeding of pseudodragons.

GREG LITTMANN is a half-horse, half-cow creature that can fly at thirty feet per second and shoots lightning bolts out of its nose. It is immune to psionic attack, has a PhD in Philosophy from the University of North Carolina at Chapel Hill, and can cast *Otto's Irresistible Dance* at will. Greg Littmann can usually be found asleep in its lair atop a pile of its publications. Its hoard includes papers in metaphysics and the philosophy of logic and seventeen chapters for books relating philosophy to popular culture, including volumes on *Breaking Bad, Doctor Who, Dune, Final Fantasy*, Neil Gaiman, Sherlock Holmes, and *The Walking Dead*. The pile will also contain a small quantity of silver and copper earned by working as an Associate Professor at Southern Illinois University Edwardsville and a ring that allows a Dwarf to walk on water.

DAVID MERLI is a third-level associate professor of philosophy at Franklin and Marshall College in Lancaster, Pennsylvania; this is much like the Keep on the Borderlands except with Amish instead of kobolds. His research interests are in meta-ethics and, more recently, medical ethics. Most of his scholarly work is what you would expect of a cleric: nothing sharp, only bludgeoning.

TIMOTHY MORTON is Professor of English (Literature and the Environment) at the University of California, Davis. Prior to this he was a Druid, a Neutral Evil Magic User, an Illusionist-Cleric (his favorite) and a character he made up called a Taoist (details on request). He is the author of *Realist Magic* (forthcoming), *The Ecological Thought* (2010), *Ecology without Nature* (2007), seven other books and over seventy essays on philosophy, ecology, literature, food, and music. He still has uneasy memories about his DM transporting him to a world that turned out to be inhabited by beings from the Cthulhu mythos. He is currently finishing *Hyperobjects*. And he blogs regularly at <www.ecologywithoutnature.blogspot.com>.

HEIDI OLSON holds a bachelor's degree from the Ohio State University, a law degree from the University of Akron School of Law, and a master's degree from the University of Central Oklahoma. She's currently working toward a PhD on the topic of literary aesthetics and earning her keep as a GTA in the English department at the University of Oklahoma. On Wednesday nights, however, she takes on the persona of a male human mage in order to decimate tar devils. She is eagerly seeking lawful good life forms, of any race and gender, to join her party.

MONA ROCHA, secretly an eladrin, and JAMES ROCHA, secretly a drow, fell in forbidden love. Forced to live a lie to be together, James became a Kantian ethicist—the one profession that no one would expect from a drow—at Louisiana State University, while Mona studies militant feminists of the 1960s as a history graduate student, also at Louisiana State University, to conceal her moon elf identity. Together, they've written on race and feminism in popular culture—and, when this eladrin and drow are together, they cannot be defeated.

JASON ROSE started playing *Dungeons and Dragons* 2e at the age of ten with his first character, a half-elf rouge named Razon. The game's blend of gameplay and story-telling drew him in to the hobby, and since then, he has run and played in every sort of role-playing game he could find. From pen-and-paper games to single-player and massively-multiplayer computer games, from superheroes to zombies to gangs roaming the post-apocalyptic wasteland, Jason has spent a lot of time thinking about RPGs. His love of role-playing games drove him to study how stories are made, how stories are understood, and what stories can do for those who hear them (and write them). Jason eventually earned his Master of Arts degree in Philosophy at Louisiana State University. Needless to say, he was excited and thrilled when the opportunity came to type out what he'd already spent countless hours pondering. Vindication is sweet!

MARK SILCOX was born and raised in Toronto, received his PhD from The Ohio State University and is presently an Associate Professor of Philosophy at the University of Central Oklahoma. His book *Philosophy through Video Games* (co-written with Jon Cogburn) was released to the sound of trumpets from many parapets in December of 2008. He lives beneath a creaky drawbridge in Edmond, Oklahoma, with his Mage wife, two canine Paladins, and a friendly Gelatinous Cube.

PETE WOLFENDALE is a twelfth-level Kantian, and he wields a +3 transcendental saber on his many adventures through the planes of contemporary philosophy. The brave and the bold may find the tales of these adventures hidden in the archives of his blogosphere fortress <http://deontologistics.wordpress.com>, or floating in the turbulent streams of the twitterverse <@deontologistics>. In his spare time, Pete plays, runs, and even designs a variety of interesting role-playing games. He has mastered the delicate art of playing a chaotic neutral cleric, shocked (and appalled) his players with the secrets of the Unknown Armies universe, and is currently writing a weird fiction RPG called Zone with the eldritch Tim Franklin.

SARAH WORTH is a professor of philosophy at Furman University where she teaches classes, mostly in Aesthetics and Ancient Philosophy. She likes writing articles about fictional worlds, and occasionally likes *being in* fictional worlds too . . . hence the fascination with D&D.

References

Abercrombie, Joe. 2007. *The Blade Itself: The First Law, Book One*. Amherst: Pyr.

————. 2008. *Before They Are Hanged: The First Law, Book Two*. Amherst: Pyr.

————. 2009. *The Last Argument of Kings: The First Law, Book Three*. Amherst: Pyr.

Agamben, Giorgio. 2004. *The Open: Man and Animal*. Translated by Kevin Attell. Stanford: Stanford University Press.

Anderson, Poul. 1961. *Three Hearts and Three Lions*, New York: Doubleday.

Appiah, Kwame. 1990. Racisms. In *Anatomy of Racism*, edited by David Goldberg. Minneapolis: University of Minnesota Press.

Arendt, Hannah. 2006. *Eichman in Jerusalem*. New York: Penguin.

Aristotle. 1984. Categories. In *The Complete Works of Aristotle: Volume One*, edited by Jonathan Barnes. Princeton: Princeton University Press.

————. 1987. *Poetics*. Indianapolis: Hackett.

————. 1998. *Politics*. Indianapolis: Hackett.

————. 1999. *Nicomachean Ethics*. Second Edition. Translated by Terence Irwin. Indianapolis: Hackett.

Badiou, Alain. 2000. *Ethics: An Essay on the Understanding of Evil*. Translated by Peter Hallward. New York: Verso.

Baker, Keith. 2004. *Eberron Campaign Setting*. Renton: Wizards of the Coast.

Bakker, R. Scott. 2005. *The Darkness that Comes Before*. New York: Overlook.

————. 2008a. *The Warrior Prophet*. New York: Overlook.

————. 2008b. *The Thousandthfold Thought*. New York: Overlook.

Banks, Jessica. 2010. My Big Fat Geek Wedding. *RP Girl Zine*. August.

Barker, Clive. 1980. *The Great and Secret Show*. New York: HarperCollins.

Barker, M.A.R. 1975. *Empire of the Petal Throne*, Lake Geneva: TSR.

Bartle, Richard. 2004. *Designing Virtual Worlds*. Indianapolis: New Riders.

Barton, Matt. 2008. *Dungeons and Desktops: The History of Computer Role-Playing Games*. Wellesley: A.K Peters.

Bentham, Jeremy. 1789. *An Introduction to the Principles of Morals and Legislation*.

Bogost, Ian. 2008. *Unit Operations: An Approach to Videogame Criticism*. Cambridge: MIT Press.

Bonner, Logan, Eytan Bernstein, and Chris Sims. 2008. *Adventurer's Vault: Arms and Equipment for All Character Classes*. Renton: Wizards of the Coast.

Braver, L. 2007. *A Thing of This World: A History of Continental Anti-Realism*. Chicago: Northwestern University Press.

Brin, David. 2008. The Lord of the Rings: J.R. Tolkien vs. the Modern Age. In *Through Stranger Eyes*. New York: Nimble.

Brown, James Robert. 1991. *The Laboratory of the Mind*. New York: Routledge.

Bryant, Levi R. 2011. *The Democracy of Objects*. Ann Arbor: Open Humanities.

Caillois, Roger. 1958. *Man, Play, and Games*. Paris: Gallimard.

Carey, Jacqueline. 2006a. *Banewreaker: Volume One of the Sundering*. New York: Tor Fantasy.

———. 2006b. *Godslayer: Volume Two of the Sundering*. New York: Tor Fantasy.

Carroll, Bart, and Steve Winter. 2009. Open Grave. *D&D Alumni*. Last Modified January 23. http://www.wizards.com/DnD/Article.aspx?x=dnd/4alum/20090121.

Carroll, Noël. 1990. *The Philosophy of Horror: Or Paradoxes of the Heart*. New York: Routledge.

———. 1996. Moderate Moralism. *British Journal of Aesthetics* 36.

———. 2002. The Wheel of Virtue: Art, Literature, and Moral Knowledge. *Journal of Aesthetics and Art Criticism* 60.

Chen, Jenova. 2011. Flow in Games. Accessed September 16th. http://www.jenovachen.com/flowingames/flowtheory.htm.

Chordelos de Laclos, Pierre. 2006. *Dangerous Liaisons*. Translated by Helen Constantine. New York: Penguin.

Clark, Andy. 2011. *Supersizing the Mind: Embodiment, Action, and Cognitive Extension*. New York: Oxford University Press.

Clark, Andy, and David Chalmers. 1998. The Extended Mind. *Analysis* 58.

Cogburn, Jon, and Mark Silcox. 2009. *Philosophy through Video Games*. New York: Routledge.

Collingwood, Robin George. 1956. *The Idea of History*. New York: Oxford University Press.

Companion, Michèle, and Roger Sambrook. 2008 Rapid Communication: The Influence of Sex on Character Attribute Preferences. *CyberPsychology and Behavior* 11.

Cook, Monte, Jonathan Tweet, and Skip Williams. 2000. *Dungeons and Dragons Player's Handbook: Core Rulebook I*. Renton: Wizards of the Coast.

Crawford, Jeremy, Mike Mearls, and James Wyatt. 2009. *Dungeons and Dragons Player's Handbook 2: Primal, Arcane, and Divine Heroes*. Renton: Wizards of the Coast.

Decker, Jesse, David Noonan, Chris Thomasson, James Jacobs, and Robin D. Laws. 2005. *Dungeons and Dragons: Dungeon Master's Guide II*. Edition 3.5. Renton: Wizards of the Coast.

Deleuze, Gilles. 1980. *Spinoza: Practical Philosophy*. Translated by Robert Hurley. San Francisco: City Lights.

Deleuze, Gilles, and Claire Parnet. 1987. *Dialogues*. Translated by Hugh Tomlinson and Barbara Habberjam. New York: Columbia University Press.

Derrida, Jacques. 1991. *Of Spirit: Heidegger and the Question*. Translated by Geoffrey Bennington and Rachel Bowlby. Chicago: University of Chicago Press.

Descartes, René. 1974. Meditations on First Philosophy. Translated by John Veitch. In *The Rationalists*. New York: Doubleday.

Dillon, Samuel. 2011. Running a Story Driven Game. Last modified July 18th. 1http://www.rpDMusings.com/2010/07/running-a-story-driven-game/.

Douglas, Mary. 1996. *Purity and Danger*. London: Routledge.

Dowsett, Jeni Sands. 2009. I'm Your Man. *RPG=Role-playing Girl*. August.

Du Bois, W.E.B. 1897. Conservation of the Races. In *American Negro Academy Occasional Papers*. Washington, DC: American Negro Academy.

Edwards, Ron. 2001. *Sorcerer: An Intense Role-playing Game*. Chicago: Adept.

Erikson, Steven. 2002. *House of Chains*. New York: Tor.

Feuerstein, Georg. 1989. *The Yoga Sutras of Patanjali: A New Translation and Commentary*. Rochester: Inner Traditions.

Fine, Gary A. 2002. *Shared Fantasy*. Chicago: University of Chicago Press.

Forgotten Realms. 2011. Forgotten Realms Wiki: Main Page. Accessed July 17th. http://forgottenrealms.wikia.com/wiki/main_page.

Frasca, Gonzalo. 2011. Digital Games Research Conference 2003 Proceedings. Accessed December 22nd. http://www.digra.org/dl/order_by_author?publication=Level%20U p%20Conference%20Proceedings

Freud, Sigmund. 2005. *Civilization and Its Discontents*. New York: Norton.

Friedman, Marilyn, and Angela Bolte. 2007. Ethics and Feminism. In *The Blackwell Guide to Feminist Philosophy.* Malden: Wiley-Blackwell.

Gadamer, Hans-Georg. 2004. *Truth and Method.* Second, revised edition. London: Continuum.

Gaut, Berys. 1998. The Ethical Criticism of Art. In *Aesthetics and Ethics: Essays at the Intersection,* edited by Jerrold Levinson. Cambridge: Cambridge University Press.

Gee, James Paul. 2003. *What Video Games Have to Teach Us about Learning and Literacy.* New York: Palgrave Macmillan.

Gendler, Tamar Szabó. 2000. The Puzzle of Imaginative Resistance. *Journal of Philosophy* 97.

———. 2010. Imaginative Resistance Revisited. In *Intuition, Imagination, and Philosophical Methodology.* Oxford: Oxford University Press.

Graves, Joseph L. 2005. *The Race Myth: Why We Pretend Race Exists in America.* New York: Plume.

Gygax, Gary. 1978. *Monster Manual: An Illustrated Compendium of Monsters, Aerial Servant to Zombie.* Lake Geneva: TSR.

———. 1979. *Dungeon Master's Guide.* Lake Geneva: TSR.

———. 1980. *Advanced Dungeons and Dragons Players' Handbook: Compiled Information for Players and Dungeon Masters.* Lake Geneva: TSR.

———. 1982a. *The Lost Caverns of Tsojcanth.* Lake Geneva: TSR.

———. 1982b. Loyal Readers: A Beautiful Idea. *Dragon* 67.

———. 1985. *Unearthed Arcana.* Lake Geneva: TSR.

———. 2001. Jack Vance and the D&D Game. Accessed August 16th. http://www.dyingearth.com/files/GARY%20GYGAX%20JACK%20VANCE.pdf.

Gygax, Gary, and Dave Arneson. 1974. *Dungeons and Dragons.* Lake Geneva: TSR.

Gygax, Gary, and Rob Kuntz. 1975. *Greyhawk.* Lake Geneva: TSR.

Harlan, Thomas. 2000. *The Shadow of Ararat.* New York: Doherty.

———. 2001a. *The Gate of Fire.* New York: Doherty.

———. 2001b. *The Storm of Heaven.* New York: Doherty.

———. 2003. *The Dark Lord.* New York: Doherty.

Harman, Graham. 2002. *Tool-Being: Heidegger and the Metaphysics of Objects.* Chicago: Open Court.

———. 2005. *Guerrilla Metaphysics: Phenomenology and the Carpentry of Things.* Chicago: Open Court.

Havelock, Eric A. 1963. *Preface to Plato (History of the Greek Mind).* Cambridge: Harvard University Press.

Heidegger, Martin. 1971. The Origin of the Work of Art. In *Poetry, Language, Thought,* translated by Albert Hofstadter. New York: Harper and Row.

———. 1993. On the Origin of the Work of Art. In *Basic Writings,* edited by David Farrell Krell. San Francisco: Harper.

―――. 1996. *Being and Time*. Translated by Joan Stambaugh. Albany: State University of New York Press.

Heinsoo, Rob, Andy Collins, and James Wyatt. 2008. *Dungeons and Dragons Player's Handbook*. Fourth Edition. Renton: Wizards of the Coast.

Herrigel, Eugen. 1999. *Zen in the Art of Archery*. Translated by R.F.C. Hull. New York: Vintage.

Hobb, Robin. 2006. *Shaman's Crossing*. Seattle: Eos.

―――. 2007. *Forest Mage*. Seattle: Eos.

―――. 2009. *Renegade's Magic*. Seattle: Eos.

Howard, Jeff. 2008. *Quests*. Wellesley: Peters.

Huizinga, Johan. 1950. *Homo Ludens*. Boston: Beacon.

Hume, David. 1987. Of the Standard of Taste. In *Essays: Moral, Political, and Literary*, edited by Eugene Miller. Indianapolis: Liberty.

Hursthouse, Rosalind. 1999. *On Virtue Ethics*. Oxford: Oxford University Press.

Jacobson, Daniel. 2005. Seeing by Feeling. *Ethical Theory and Moral Practice* 8.

Jeffery, Renée. 2007. *Evil and International Relations: Human Suffering in an Age of Terror*. New York: Palgrave Macmillan.

Johnson, Robert. 2003. Virtue and Right. *Ethics* 113.

Jones, Kat. 2010. Possibilities Are Endless: Creating New Worlds in an All-Woman Game. *RP Girl Zine*. August.

Joravsky, David. 1986. *The Lysenko Affair*. Chicago: University of Chicago Press.

Kant, Immanuel. 1995. *Foundations of the Metaphysics of Morals*. Translated by Lewis White Beck. Upper Saddle River: Library of Liberal Arts.

―――. 2000. *Critique of the Power of Judgment*. Translated by Paul Guyer and Eric Matthews. New York: Cambridge University Press.

Kehoe, Alice. 2000. *Shamans and Religion: An Anthropological Exploration in Critical Thinking*. Long Grove: Waveland.

Kelly, Kevin. 2010. *What Technology Wants*. New York: Viking.

Kenson, Steve. 2005. *Mutants and Masterminds*. Second Edition. Seattle: Green Ronin.

King, Stephen. 2002. *From a Buick 8*. New York: Scribner's.

Krawczyk, Marianne, and Jeannie Novak. 2006. *Game Development Essentials: Game Story and Character Development*. Clifton Park: Thompson Delmar.

Lacan, Jacques. 1977. *Ecrits: A Selection*. Translated by Alan Sheridan. London: Tavistock.

―――. 1981. *Le Seminaire, Livre III: Les Psychoses*. Paris: Editions de Seuil.

Latour, Bruno. 1999. A Collective of Humans and Nonhumans: Following Daedalus's Labyrinth. In *Pandora's Hope: Essays on the Reality of Science Studies.* Cambridge: Harvard University Press.

———. Latour, Bruno. 2005. *Reassembling the Social: An Introduction to Actor-Network-Theory.* New York: Oxford University Press.

Law, Charlotte. 2009. Making It as a Woman in the Gaming Industry. *RPG=Role-playing Girl.* August.

Leiber, Fritz. 1970. Ill Met in Lankhmar. *Magazine of Fantasy and Science Fiction* 38.

Levinas, Emmanuel. 1969. *Totality and Infinity: An Essay on Exteriority.* Translated by Alphonso Lingis. Pittsburgh: Duquesne University Press.

———. Levinas, Emmanuel. 1988. *Existence and Existents.* Translated by Alphonso Lingis. Pittsburgh: Dusquesne University Press.

Liambic. 2008. DMs Corner—Min/Maxers and Powergamers. *The Geek Emporium,* October 20th. http://thegeekemporium.com/index/?p=508.

Lingis, Alfonso. 1998. *The Imperative.* Bloomington: Indiana University Press.

Linklater, Richard, director. 1991. *Slacker* (movie). Los Angeles: Orion Classics.

Lodge, David. 2001. *Thinks . . .* New York: Penguin.

Lovecraft, H.P. 2008a. The Dunwich Horror. In *Necronomicon,* edited by Stephen Jones. London: Orion. Originally published in *Weird Tales,* April 1929.

———. 2008b. The Outsider. In *Necronomicon,* edited by Stephen Jones. London: Orion. Originally published in *Weird Tales,* April 1926.

MacIntyre, Alasdair. 2001. *Dependent Rational Animals: Why Human Beings Need the Virtues.* Chicago: Open Court.

Marmell, Ari, and Scott Fitzgerald Gray. 2010. *Tomb of Horrors: Dungeons and Dragons Super Adventure.* Renton: Wizards of the Coast.

Mazis, Glen. 2008. *Humans, Animals, Machines: Blurring Boundaries.* Albany: SUNY Press.

Mazzanoble, Shelly. 2007. *Confessions of a Part-Time Sorceress.* Renton: Wizards of the Coast.

McDowell, John. 1998. Virtue and Reason. In *Mind, Value, and Reality.* Cambridge: Harvard University Press.

McGinley, Meghan. 2010. You Play Like a Girl. *RP Girl Zine.* August.

McGonigal, Jane. 2010. Gaming Can Make a Better World. TED Conference, Long Beach, March 17th, 2010.

McLuhan, Marshall. 1994. *Understanding Media: The Extensions of Man.* Cambridge: MIT Press.

McLuhan, Marshall, and Eric McLuhan. 1992. *Laws of Media: The New Science.* Toronto: University of Toronto Press.

Mearls, Mike, Robin Laws, and Greg Gordon. 2009. *Dungeon Master's Guide 2*. Renton: Wizards of the Coast.

Mieville, China. 2000. *Perdido Street Station*. London: Macmillan.

———. 2000. *The Iron Council*. London: Macmillan.

———. 2002. *The Scar*. London: Macmillan.

Mill, John Stuart. 1863. *Utilitarianism*. London: Parker, Son, and Bourn.

———. 2001. *Utilitarianism*. Indianapolis: Hackett.

Miller, Marc W. 1977. *Traveller*. Normal: Game Designers Workshop.

Molnar, George. 2006. *Powers: A Study in Metaphysics*. Oxford: Oxford University Press.

Mondschein, Ken. 2010. Michael Moorcock on Politics, Punk, Tolkien, and Everything Else. http://corporatemofo.com/politics_and_other_bullshit/michael_mo orcock_on_politics_p.html.

Montefiore, Simon. 2005. *Stalin: Court of the Red Tsar*. New York: Vintage.

Moorcock, Michael. 1961. The Dreaming City. *Science Fantasy* 47.

———. 1965. *Stormbringer*. London: Herbert Jenkins.

———. 1987. *Elric of Melniboné*. New York: Ace.

Moorcock, Michael, and Colin Greenland. 1992. *Death Is No Obstacle*. Manchester: Savoy.

Morton, Timothy, 2008. Ecologocentrism: Unworking Animals. *SubStance* 37.

Nagel, Thomas. 1974. What Is It Like to Be a Bat? *Philosophical Review*. Reprinted in many, many places.

———. 1979. Death. In *Mortal Questions*. New York: Cambridge University Press.

Nietzsche, Friedrich. 1883. *Thus Spoke Zarathustra*. Chemnitz: Ernst Schmeitzner.

Ortega y Gasset, José. 1975. *Phenomenology and Art*. Translated by Philip W. Silver. New York: Norton.

Outlaw, Lucius. 1996. *On Race and Philosophy*. London: Routledge.

Parfit, Derek. 1987. Divided Minds and the Nature of Persons. In *Mindwaves: Thoughts on Intelligence, Identity and Consciousness*, edited by Colin Blakemore and Susan Greenfield. Oxford: Blackwell.

Perrin, Steve, Ray Turney, Steve Henderson, Warren James, and Greg Stafford. 1978. *RuneQuest*. Haywood: Chaosium.

Peterson, Sandy. 1981. *Call of Cthulhu*. Haywood: Chaosium.

Plato, 1956. *Plato: Protagoras and Meno:* Translated by W.K.C. Guthrie. London: Penguin.

———. 1992. *Republic*. Translated by G.M.A. Grube. Indianapolis: Hackett.

———. 2011. *Theaetetus*. Translated by Benjamin Jowett. Seattle: Pacific.

Plutarch. 1975. *Theseus.* Translated by John Dryden. Cambridge: The Internet Classics Archive. http://classics.mit.edu/Plutarch/theseus.html.

Pratt, Anthony E. 1949. *Cluedo* (board game). Leeds: Waddingtons.

Priest, Graham. 2003. *Beyond the Limits of Thought.* Oxford: Oxford University Press.

Rachels, James. 2009. *The Elements of Moral Philosophy.* Fifth Edition. New York: McGraw Hill.

Radford, Colin. 1975. How Can We Be Moved by the Fate of Anna Karenina? *Proceedings of the Aristotelian Society,* Supplemental Volume 49.

Randall, Vernellia. 2006. *Dying While Black.* Dayton: Seven Principles.

Rein-Hagen, Mark. 1991. *Vampire: The Masquerade.* Stone Mountain: White Wolf.

Richter, W.D, director. 1984. *The Adventures of Buckaroo Banzai across the Eighth Dimension* (movie). 20th Century Fox.

Roberts, Charles S. 1954. *Tactics* (wargame). Renton: Avalon Hill.

Rose, Frank. 2011. *The Art of Immersion.* New York: Norton.

Rouse, Richard R., III. 2005. *Game Design: Theory and Practice.* Plano: Wordware.

Rowling, J.K. 2006. *Harry Potter Paperback Box Set: Books 1–6.* New York: Scholastic.

St. Andre, Ken. 1975. *Tunnels and Trolls.* Scottsdale: Flying Buffalo.

Salen, Katie, and Eric Zimmerman. 2004. *Rules of Play: Game Design Fundamentals.* Cambridge: MIT Press.

Salvatore, R.A. *Canticle.* 2000. Renton: Wizards of the Coast.

———. 2005. *Homeland: The Dark Elf Trilogy, Part 1(Forgotten Realms: The Legend of Drizzt, Book 1).* Renton: Wizards of the Coast.

Sartre, Jean-Paul. 1963. *Nausea.* Translated by Lloyd Alexander. New York: New Directions.

Schell, Jesse. 2010. *Design Outside the Box.* DICE Summit presentation, Las Vegas, Nevada February 18th.

Schick, Lawrence. 1991. *Heroic Worlds.* Amherst: Prometheus.

ScienceDaily. 2007. New Research Proves Single Origin of Humans in Africa. Last modified July 19th.
http://www.sciencedaily.com/releases/2007/07/070718140829.htm.

———. 2009. African Genetics Study Revealing Origins, Migrations and 'Startling Diversity' of African Peoples. Last modified May 2nd.
http://www.sciencedaily.com/releases/2009/04/090430144524.htm.

Schoonover, Jen Seiden. 2009. Designing Women. *RPG=Role-playing Girl.* August.

Sicart, Miguel. 2009. *The Ethics of Computer Games.* Cambridge: MIT Press.

Siembieda, Kevin. 1990. *Rifts*, Westland: Palladium.

Siembieda, Kevin, and Erick Wujcik. 1983. *Palladium Role-playing Game*. Westland: Palladium.

Singer, Dorothy G., and Jerome L. Singer. 1990. *The House of Make-Believe*. Cambridge: Harvard University Press.

Sirridge, Mary. 1975. Truth from Fiction? *Philosophy and Phenomenological Research* 35.

Sofge, Eric. 2008. Orc Holocaust: The Reprehensible Moral Universe of Gary Gygax's *Dungeons and Dragons*. *Slate*. Last Modified March 10th.
http://www.slate.com/articles/news_and_politics/hey_wait_a_minute/2008/03/orc_holocaust.html.

Spielberg, Steven, director. 1982. *E.T. The Extra-Terrestrial* (movie). Universal City: Amblin.

Spinoza, Benedict de. 2002. *Ethics*. In *Spinoza: Complete Works*, edited by Michael L. Morgan. Indianapolis: Hackett.

Stock, Kathleen. 2005. Resisting Imaginative Resistance. *Philosophical Quarterly* 5.

Stoltze, Greg and John Tynes. 2002. *Unknown Armies: Second Edition*. Atlas Games.

Stone, Rob, and Sean Tisdale. 1999. *Agent X*. Mind Interactive LLC.

Szulborski, Dave. 2005. *This Is Not a Game*. Raleigh: Lulu.com.

Taylor, Charles. 1989. *Sources of The Self: The Making of Modern Identity*. Cambridge: Harvard University Press.

Tittle, Peg. 2005. *What if . . .?: Collected Thought Experiments in Philosophy*. New York: Pearson-Education.

Tolkien, J.R.R. 1991. *The Lord of the Rings*. Boston: Houghton Mifflin.

———. 2005. *The Lord of the Rings*. New York: Mariner.

Tosca, Susan. 2009. More than a Private Joke: Cross-Media Parody in Role-playing Games. *Cinema Journal* 48.

Treadwell, James. 2003. *Interpreting Wagner*. New Haven: Yale University Press.

Turing, A.M. 1950. Computing Machinery and Intelligence. *Mind* 59.

Turner, Victor. 1969. *The Ritual Process*. Ithaca: Cornell University Press.

TVTropes, 2011. Dork Age: Television Tropes and Idioms. Accessed August 15th,
http://tvtropes.org/pmwiki/pmwiki.php/Main/DorkAge.

Tweet, Jonathan, Monte Cook, and Skip Williams. 2003. *Dungeons and Dragons: Dungeon Master's Guide*. Core Rulebook II. v.3.5. Renton: Wizards of the Coast.

Uexküll, Jakob von. 2010. *A Foray into the Worlds of Animals and Humans; with a Theory of Meaning*. Translated by Joseph D. O'Neil. Minneapolis: University of Minnesota Press.

Vice, Samantha. 2003. Literature and the Narrative Self. *Philosophy* 73.

Walton, Kendall L. 1978. Fearing Fictions. *Journal of Philosophy* 75.

———. 1990. *Mimesis as Make-believe: On the Foundations of the Representational Arts*. Cambridge: Harvard University Press.

———. 1994. Morals in Fiction and Fictional Morality (I). *Proceedings of the Aristotelian Society* Supplement 68.

Warren, Mary Anne. 1973. On the Moral and Legal Status of Abortion. *The Monist* 57:1.

Waters, Darren. 2010. What Happened to *Dungeons and Dragons*? Accessed January 16th. http://news.bbc.co.uk/2/hi/uk_news/magazine/3655627.stm.

Wheaton, Wil. 2009. I'm Saying This for the Last Time: HIS. NAME. IS. AEOFEL! *WWdN: In Exile*, October 16th. http://wilwheaton.typepad.com/wwdnbackup/2009/10/im-saying-this-for-the-last-time-his-name-is-aeofel.html.

Wick, John. 2009. *Houses of the Blooded*. Oxford: Cubicle 7 Entertainment.

Wittgenstein, Ludwig. 1999. *Philosophical Investigations*. New York: Prentice Hall.

———. 2001. *Philosophical Investigations*. Third Edition. Translated by G.E.M. Anscombe. Oxford: Blackwell.

Wizards of the Coast. 2006. A Look Back at Player's Handbooks. Last modified June 2nd. http://www.wizards.com/default.asp?x=dnd/aumni/20060602a.

———. 2009. Roll-playing for Role-playing Last modified April 1st. http://www.wizards.com/dnd/Article.aspx?x=dnd/4news/20100401b.

Wood, Allen. 2002. What Is Kantian Ethics? In *Groundwork for the Metaphysics of Morals*. Binghamton: Yale University Press.

———. 2011. Humanity as an End in Itself. In *On What Matters, Volume 2*. Edited by Derek Parfit. Oxford: Oxford University Press.

Worch, Matthias. 2011. The Identity Bubble: A Design Approach to Character and Story Creation. Presented at the 25th Annual Game Developers Conference, San Francisco, February 28th–March 4th.

Wordsworth, William. 2008. *The Major Works: Including The Prelude*. Oxford: Oxford University Press.

Wujcik, Erick. 1991. *Amber Diceless Role-playing Game*. Detroit: Phage.

Wyatt, J. 2008. *Dungeon Master's Guide*. Fourth Edition. Renton: Wizards of the Coast.

Zack, Naomi, 1998. Mixed Black and White Race and Public Policy. In *Race, Class, Gender, and Sexuality: The Big Questions*, edited by Naomi Zack, Lauri Shrage, and Crispin Sartwell. New York: Blackwell.

Žižek, Slavoj. 2006. *The Parallax View*. Cambridge: MIT Press.

Index

Abercrombie, Joe: *The First Law* trilogy, 41

act utilitarianism, 52

Aeofel, 181, 183–84

aesthetic experience, 212–16; building worlds in, 215; as disinterested, 214; free play in, 214–15

affects, of substances, 165, 173

Agent X (game), vii

Alien (movie), 73

Anderson, Craig, 110

Anderson, Poul, 50; *Three Hearts and Three Lions*, 49

anti-race philosophers, 94, 101

Appiah, Kwame Anthony: "Racisms," 101

archetypes, in stories, 33

Arendt, Hannah: *Eichmann in Jerusalem*, 41

Aristotle, 79; on art, 8, 14; — moral virtue in, 12–13; on catharsis, 8; on comedy, 1–3; critique of, 21, 24, 26; on internal sense of plot, 10–12; on natural function, 4–5; *Nicomachean Ethics*, 5; on pleasure, 4; *Poetics*, 8–9; *Politics*, 4, 5; on tragedy, 10, 12–13; on virtue, 21, 24

Arneson, Dave, vii, x, 4, 207, 224, 233; innovations of, 208–09

Arthur, King, 38

Asimov, Isaac: *Foundation*, 216

Augustine, St., 122

Austen, Jane, 8, 26, 162

bad behavior, purported causes of, 85–86

Badiou, Alain, 53

Bakker, R. Scott: *The Prince of Nothing* trilogy, 138

Baldur's Gate (game), 266

"banality of evil," 41

Banks, Jessica, 113–14

Banzai, Buckaroo, 156

Barker, Clive, 149; *The Great and Secret Show*, 45

The Barrier Peaks (game), 161

Bartle, Richard, 256; on player types, 184, 185

Bay, Michael, 213

Beckett, Samuel: *Waiting for Godot*, 58

Beethoven, Ludwig van, 222

Bentham, Jeremy: "felicific calculus," 52

Bill and Ted's Bogus Journey (movie), 195

Priest, Graham: *Beyond the
  Limits of Thought*, 134
projective identity, 181, 183
propaganda, 78
pro-race philosophers, 94,
  100–01, 103
psionics, 158

quest, components of, 250

race, 93; critique of, 101–03;
  lack of, in humans, 93; and
  racism, 102–03
Radford, Colin, 202
Randall, Vernellia: *Dying While
  Black*, 99
Rausch, Jim, vii
realism, 162
"re-enactment thesis," 281,
  284–86
regime of attraction, 175
Reign (game), 223
Riefenstahl, Leni, 71
Rilke, Rainer Maria, 217
Rimbaud, Arthur, 217
ritual purity codes, 140–41
Robert, Charles S., 230
roleplay, duality of, 239
role-playing games (RPGs), 207,
  239, 269; abstraction in, 233;
  aesthetic experience of,
  217–19, 221–22, 224; and
  anti-social behavior, 113; as
  artform, 238; campaign
  setting in, 208; character
  generation systems in,
  232–33; character sheet in,
  233; choice-chance distinction
  in, 276; class systems in,
  231–33; as collaborative, 219;
  conceptions of, 281–82; critical
  hit in, 231; depth in, 219,
  221–22; dice in, 229–231,
  275–77; as dynamic, 222;

experience points in, 236;
  game-story distinction,
  240–43, 269, 270–72, 274–75;
  imagination in, 231–32; and
  immersion, 282, 284–85; as
  interactive, 217–18; and life,
  differences between, 61–63;
  moral dilemmas in, 17;
  numeric representation in,
  235; value of, 27
roll-play, 244
Roll-Playing for Roleplaying,
  243
Romantic narrative, 159–160
Roosevelt, Franklin Delano, 38
Rose, Frank, 250
Rowling, J. K., 135
rpDMusings.com, 247
RP Girl (magazine), 113, 114
Rules of Play (book), 240

Salvatore, R.A., 63; *Canticle*,
  135; *Wubba Wubba*, 210
Sambrook, Roger, 112
Santeria, 136
Sartre, Jean-Paul: *Nausea*,
  138–39
Schell, Jesse, 251
Schick, Lawrence: *Heroic
  Worlds*, 238
Schleiermacher, Friedrich, 286
Schoonover, Jen Seiden, 114,
  115, 118
Schwarzenegger, Arnold, 45
self, as metanarrative, 63
Shakespeare, William, 211;
  Hamlet, 8
Ship of Theseus paradox, 180
Shoemaker, Elizabeth: *It's
  Complicated*, 60
Sicart, Miguel, 150
Siembieda, Kevin, 226
Silcox, Mark, 109, 110;
  *Philosophy through
  Videogames*, 108